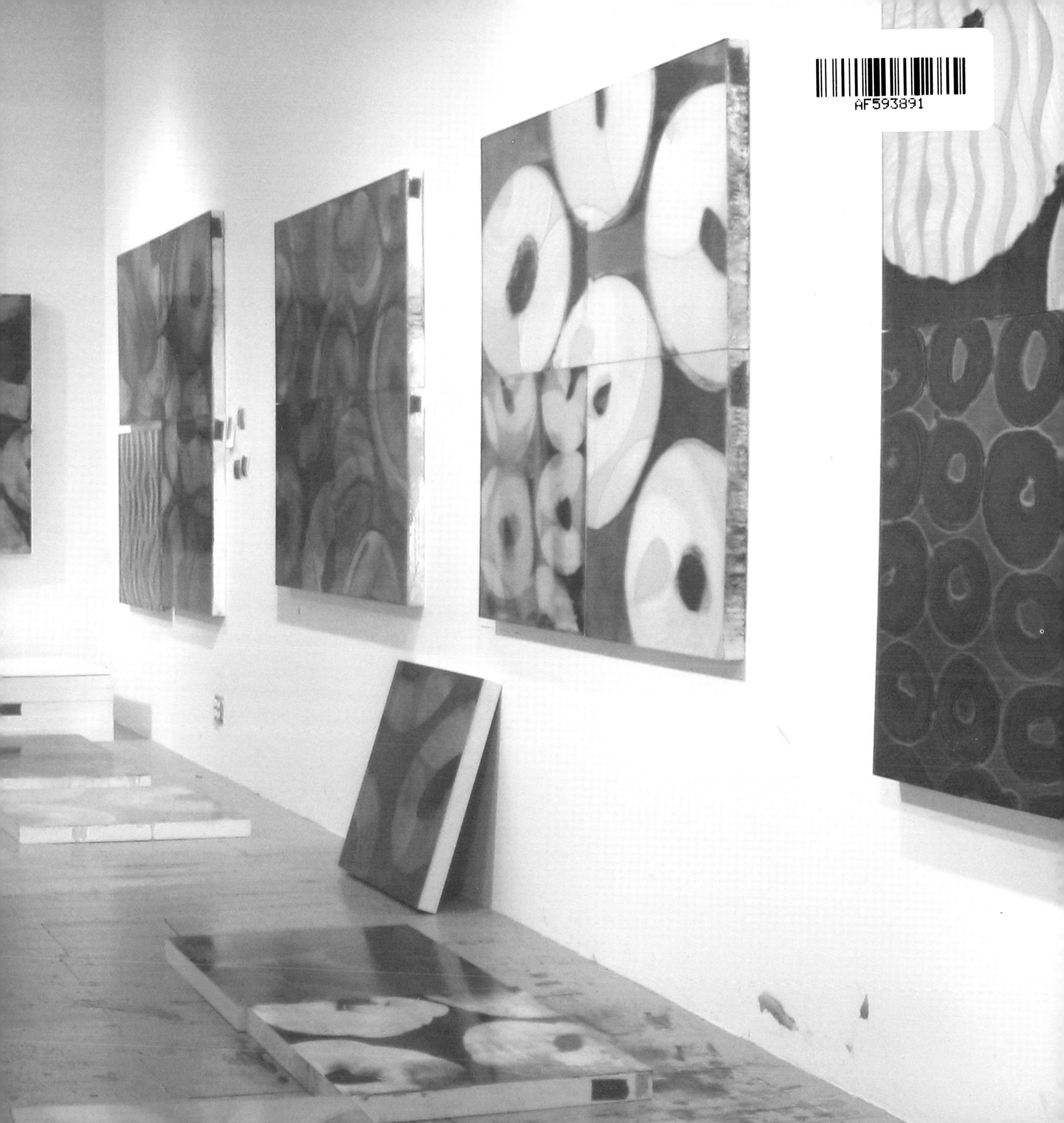

MARYLYN DINTENFASS
PAINTINGS

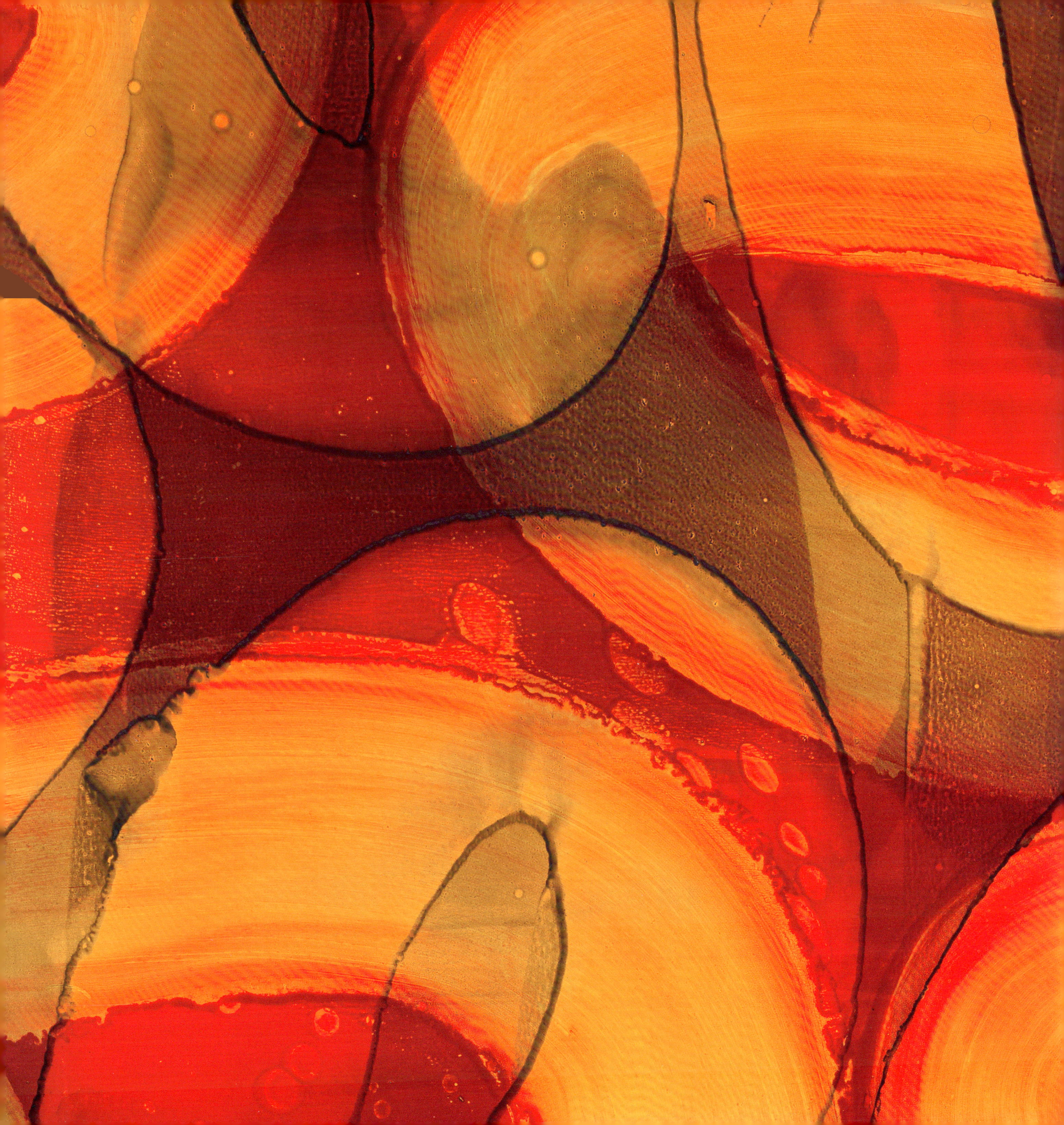

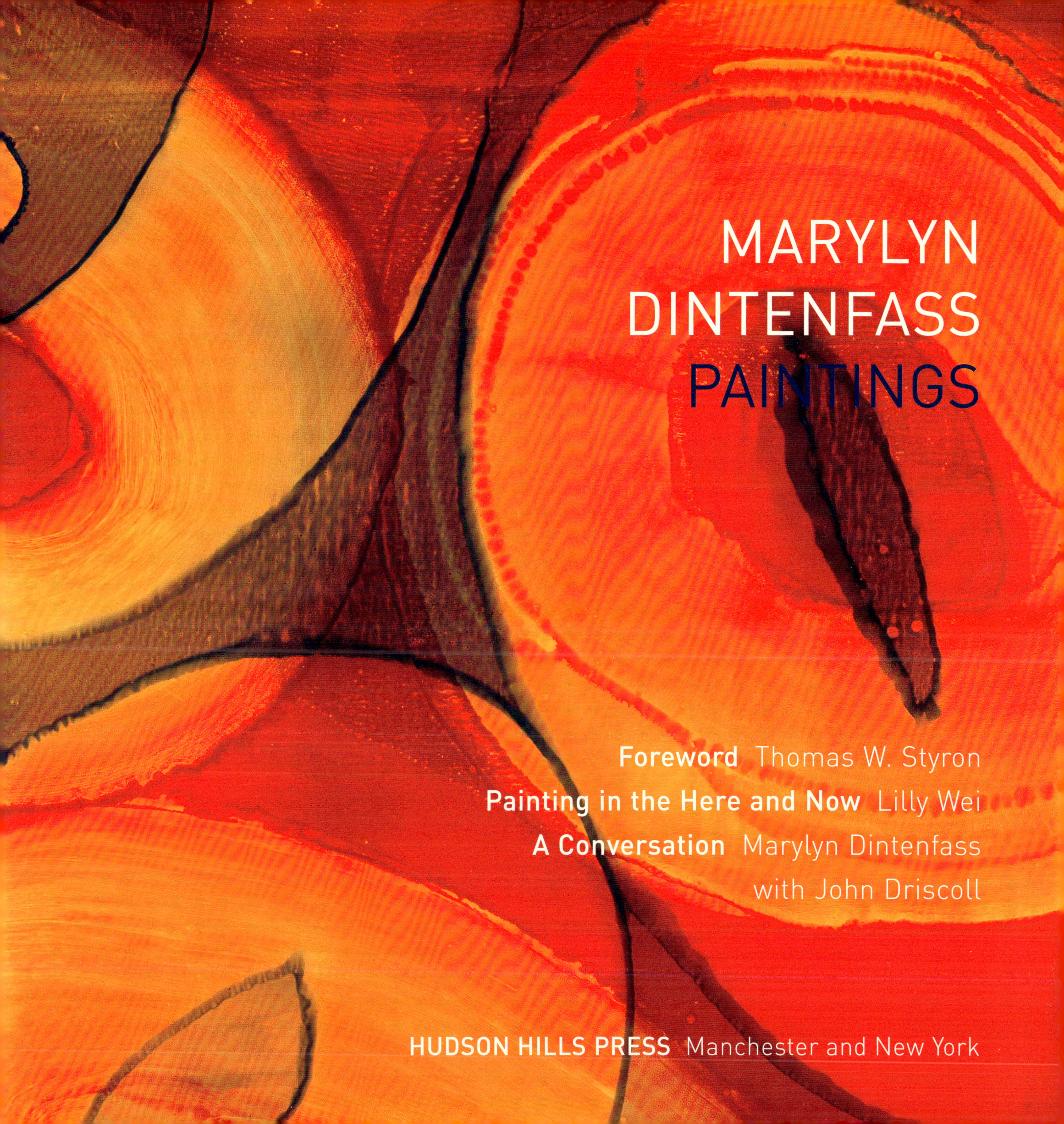

MARYLYN DINTENFASS PAINTINGS

Foreword Thomas W. Styron

Painting in the Here and Now Lilly Wei

A Conversation Marylyn Dintenfass with John Driscoll

HUDSON HILLS PRESS Manchester and New York

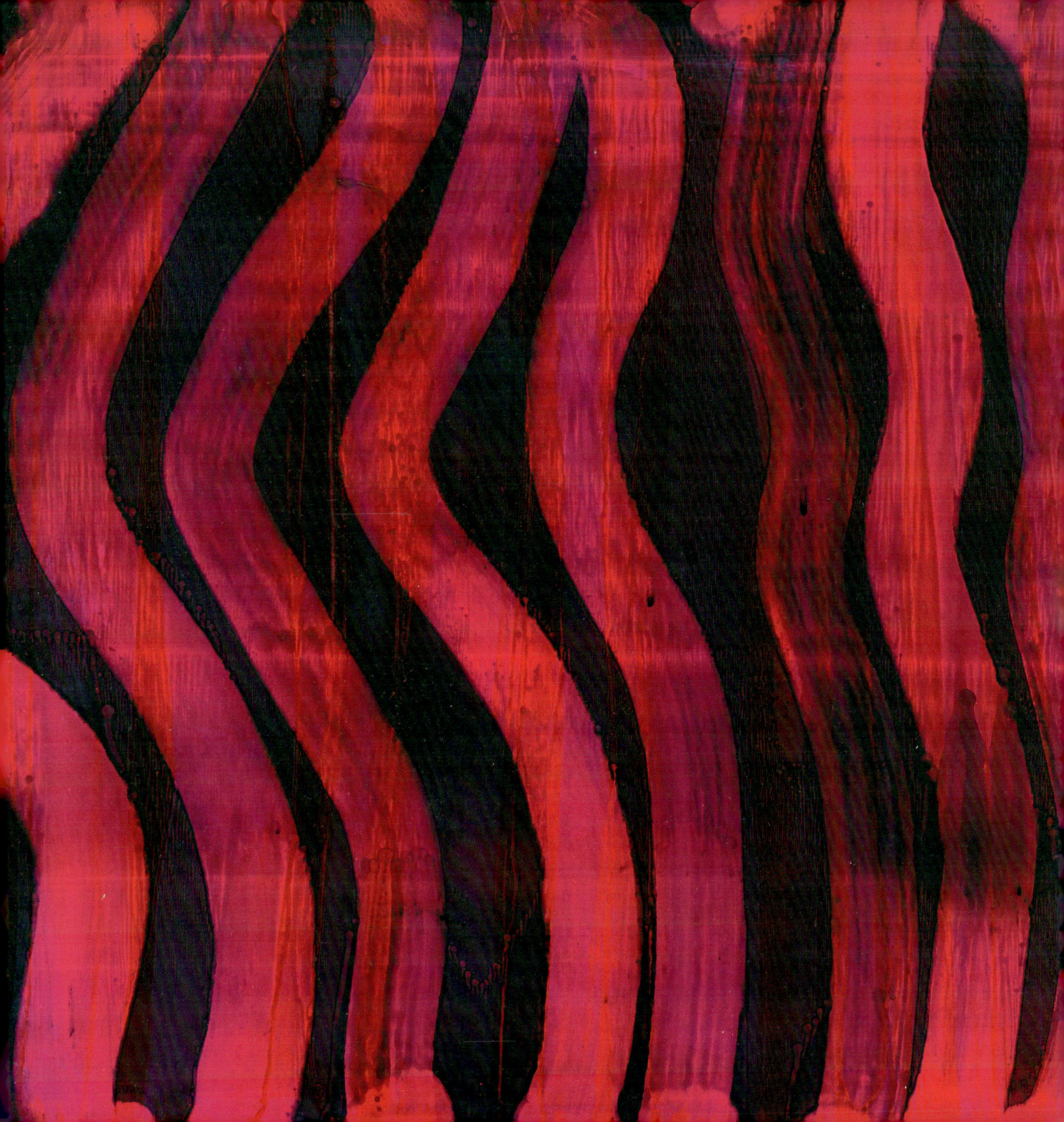

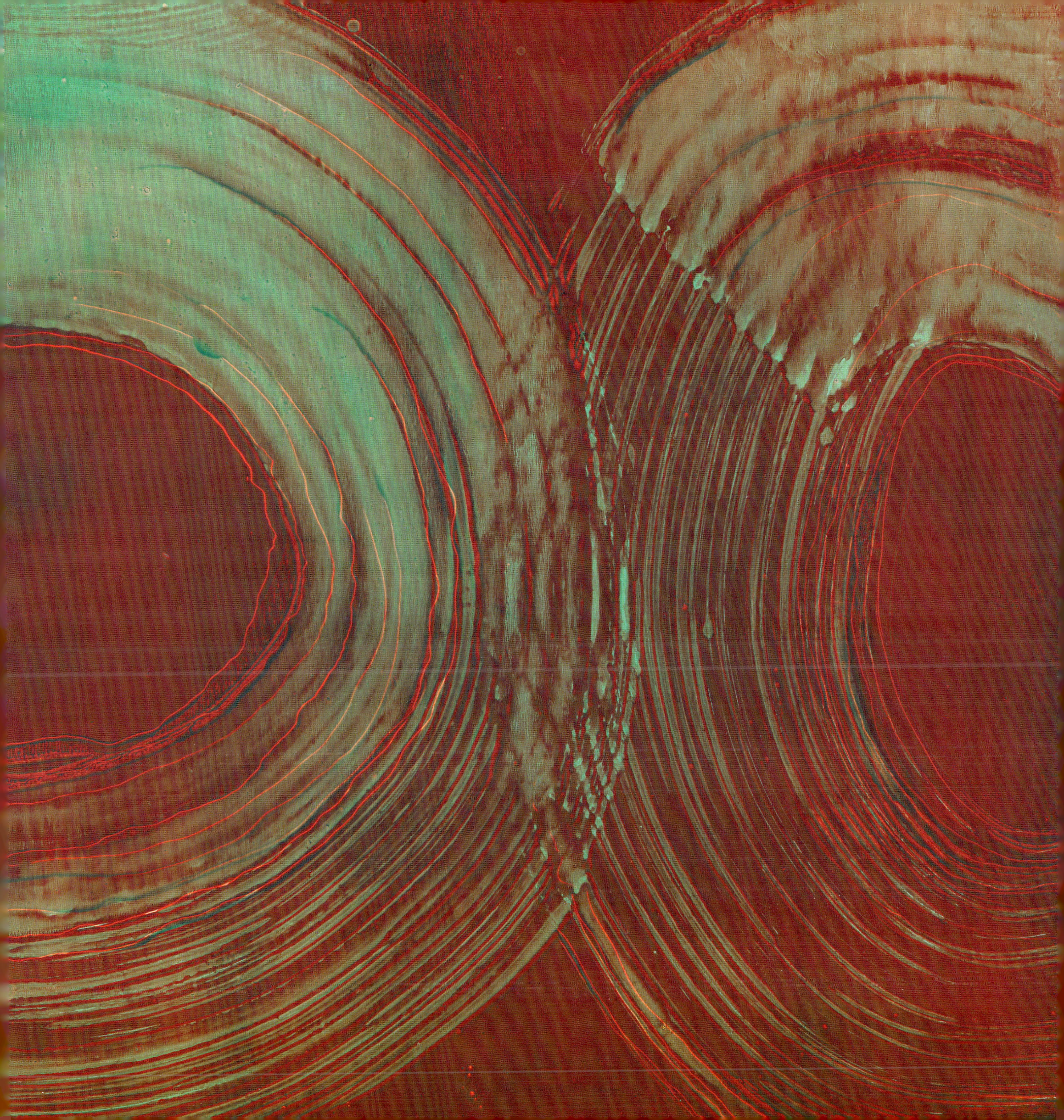

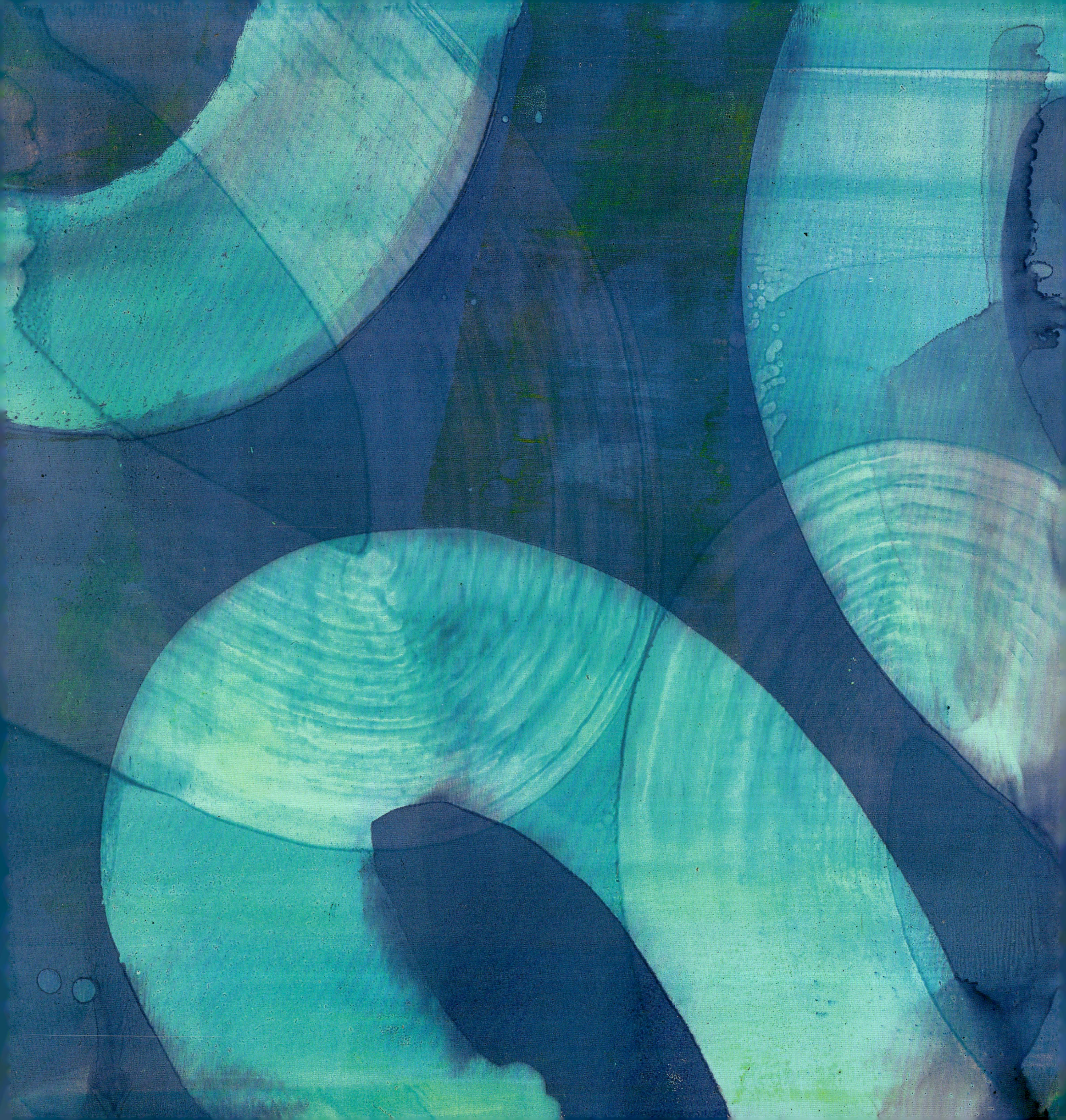

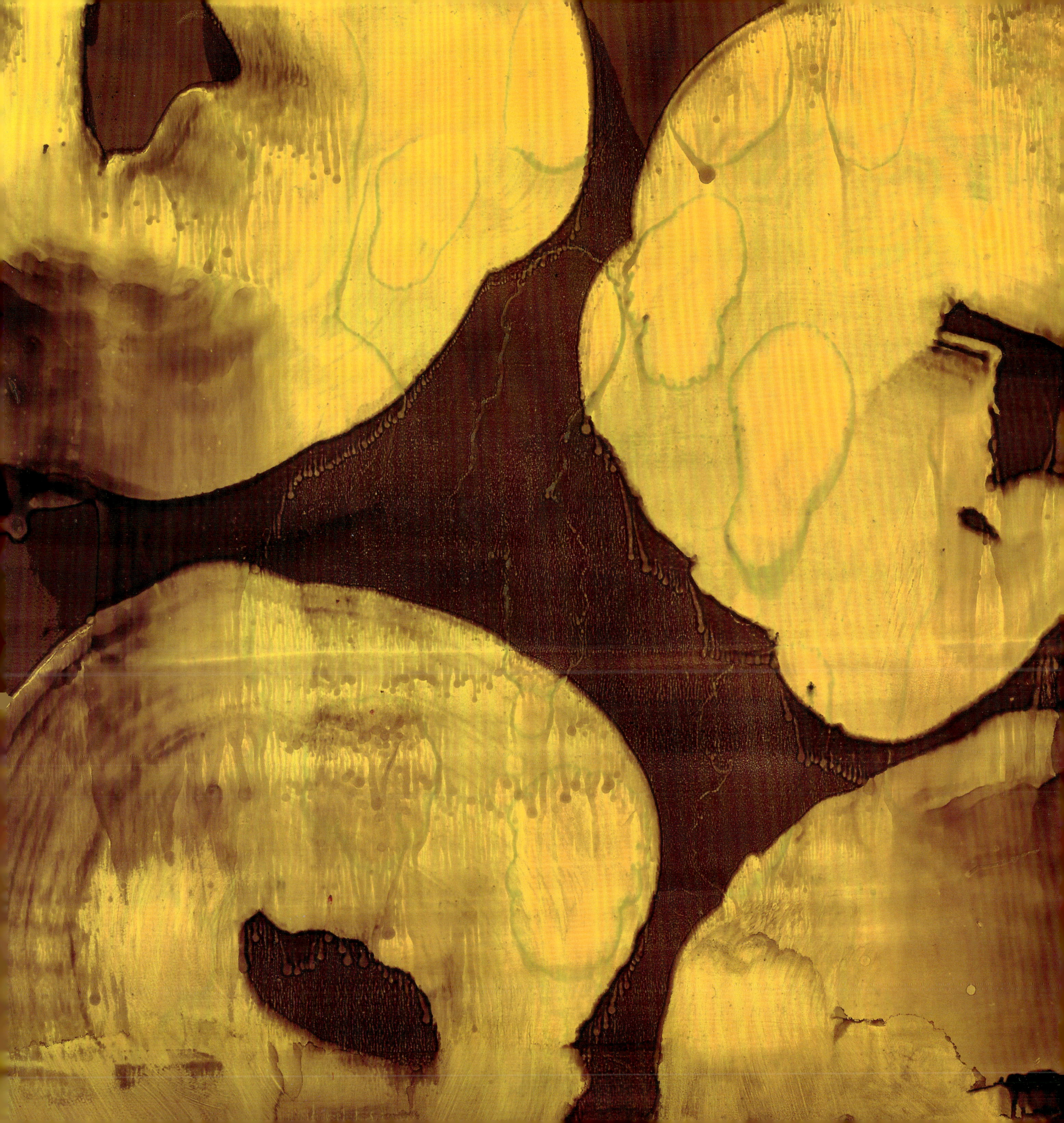

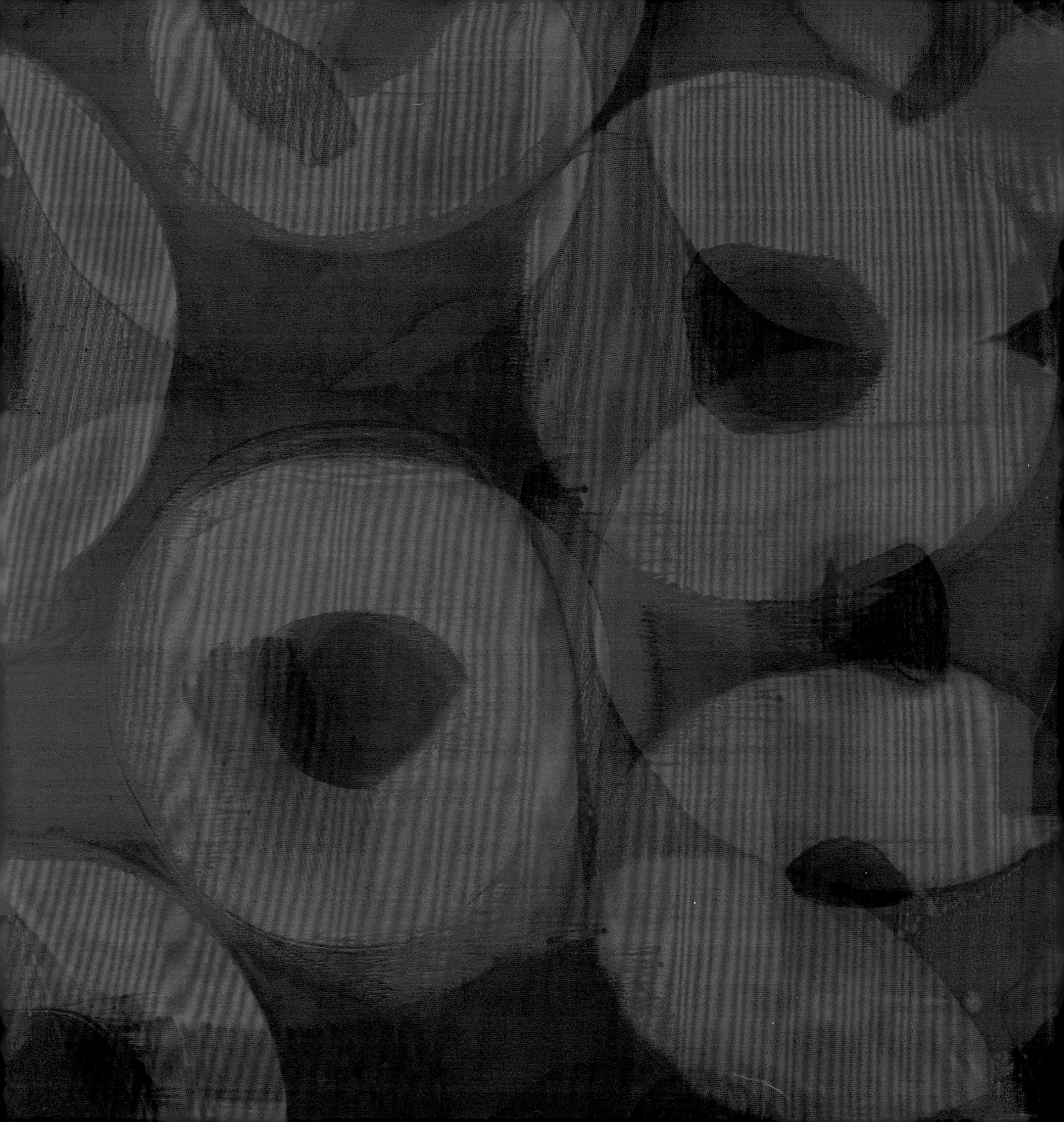

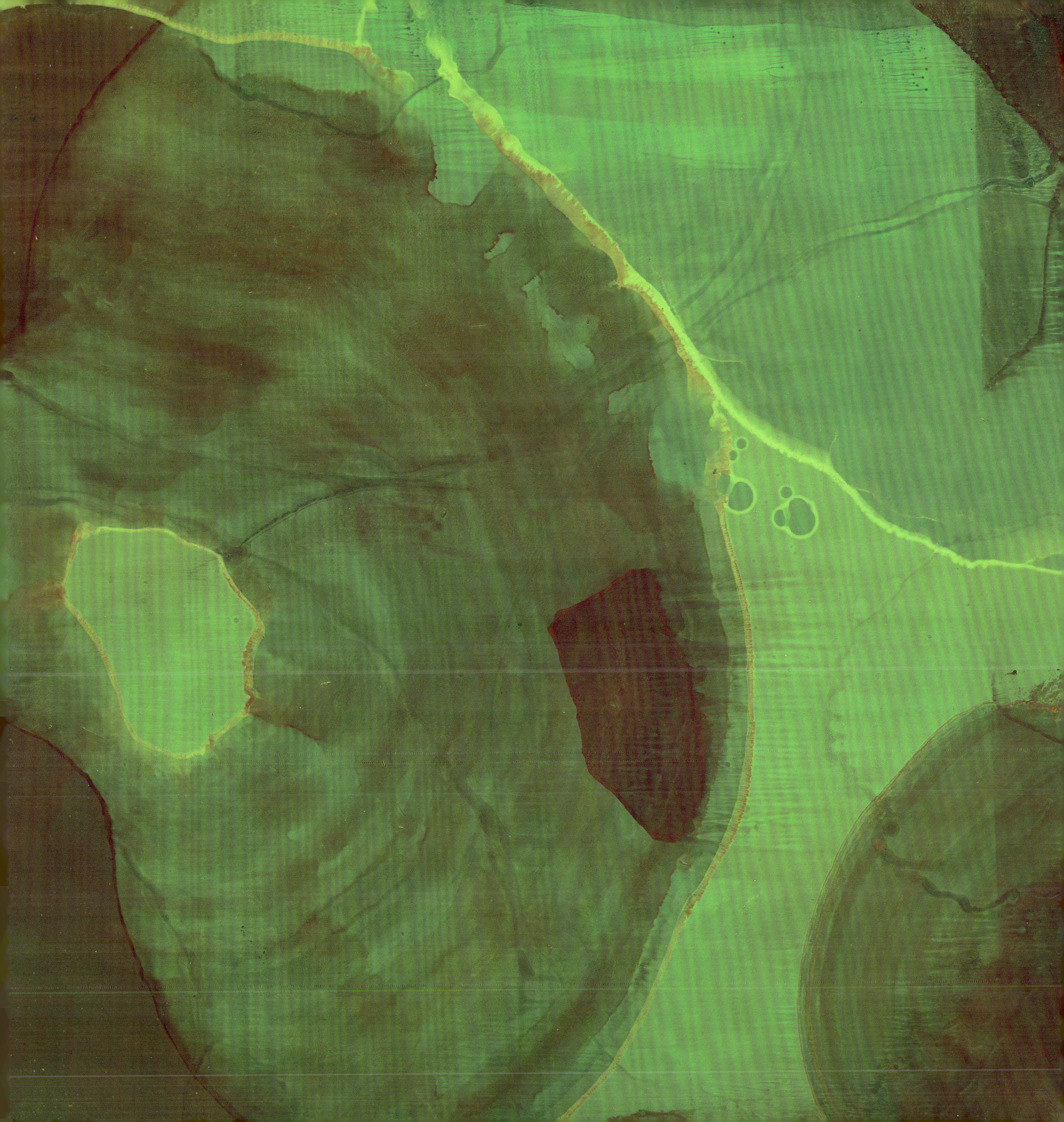

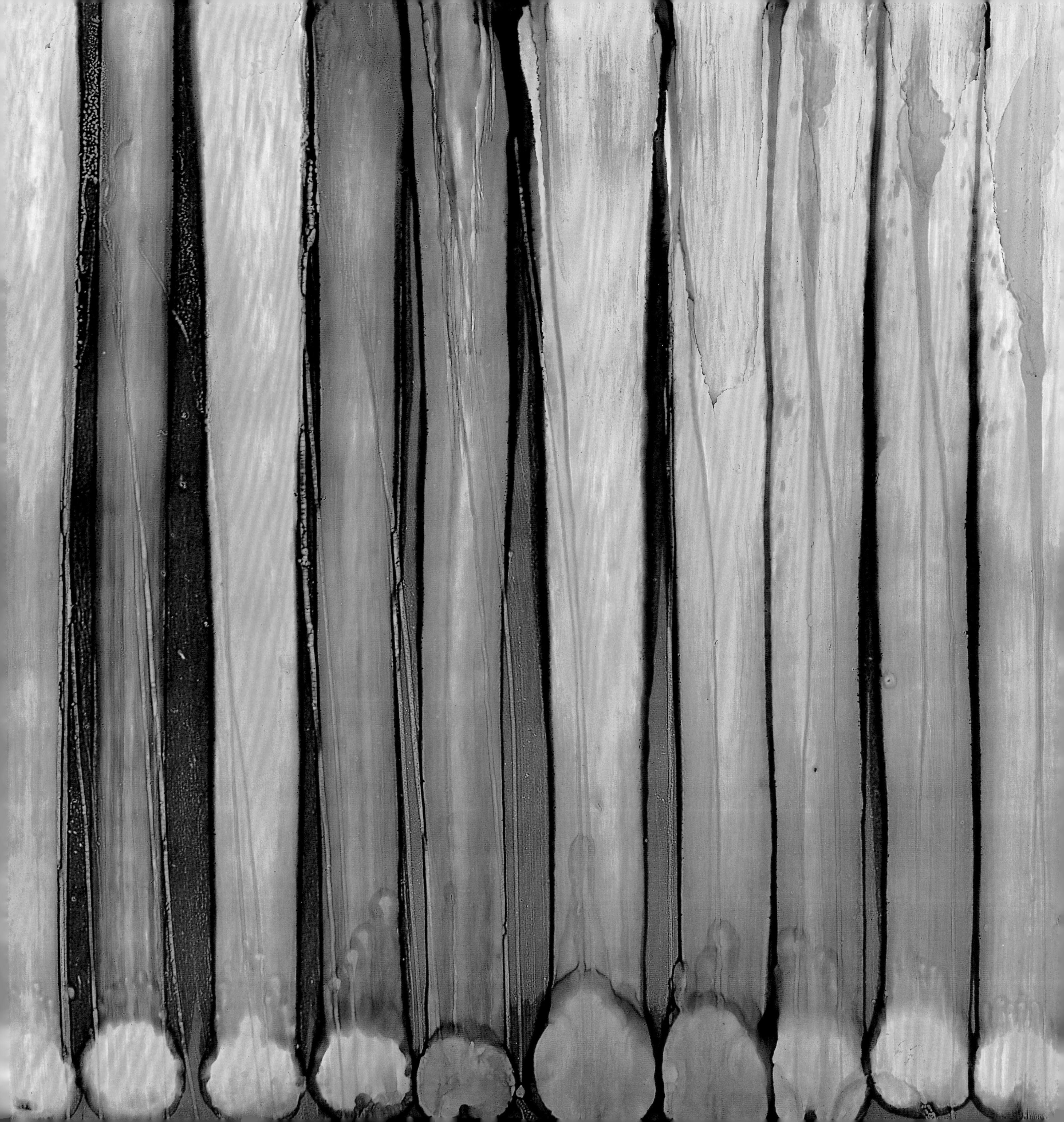

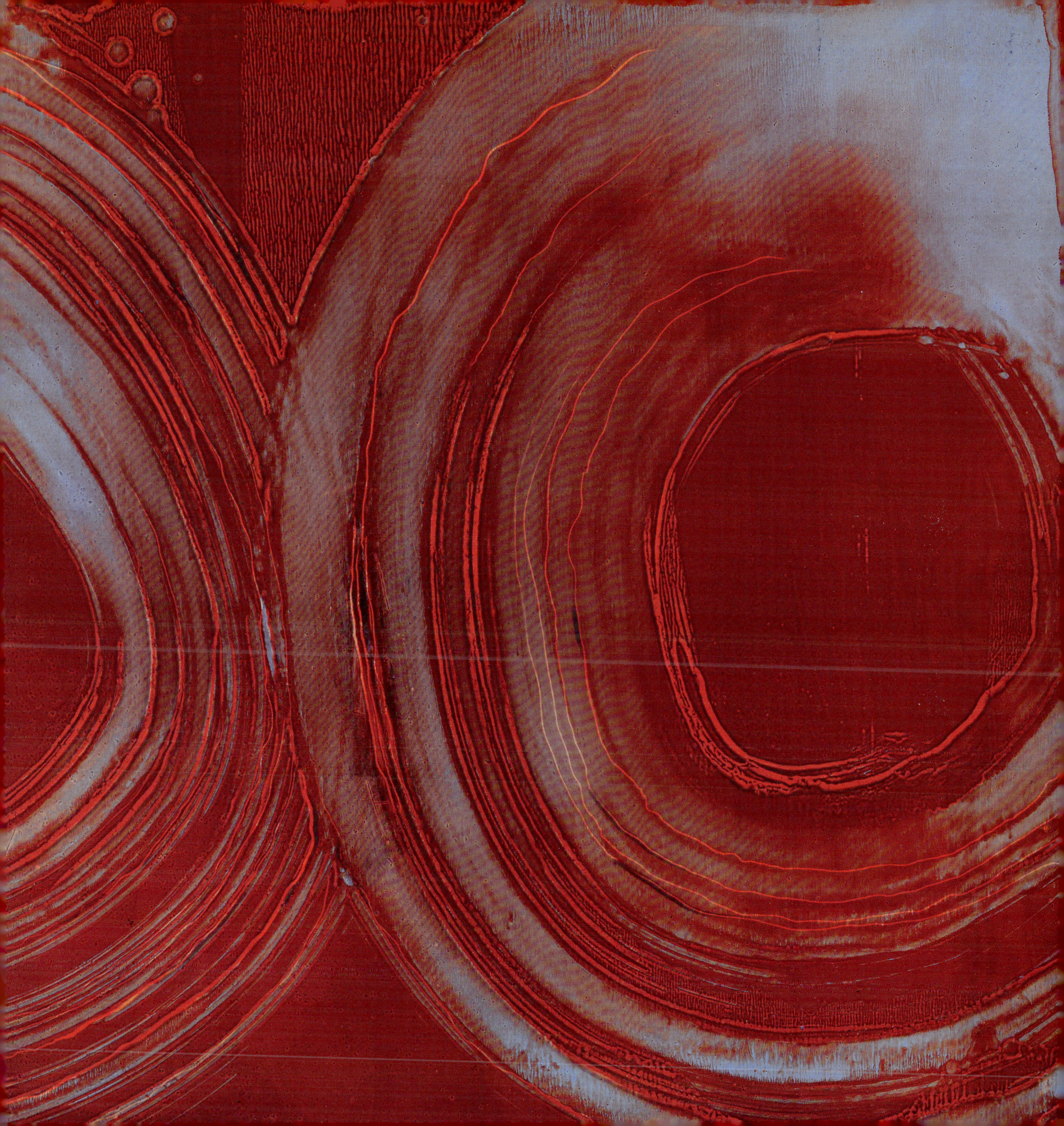

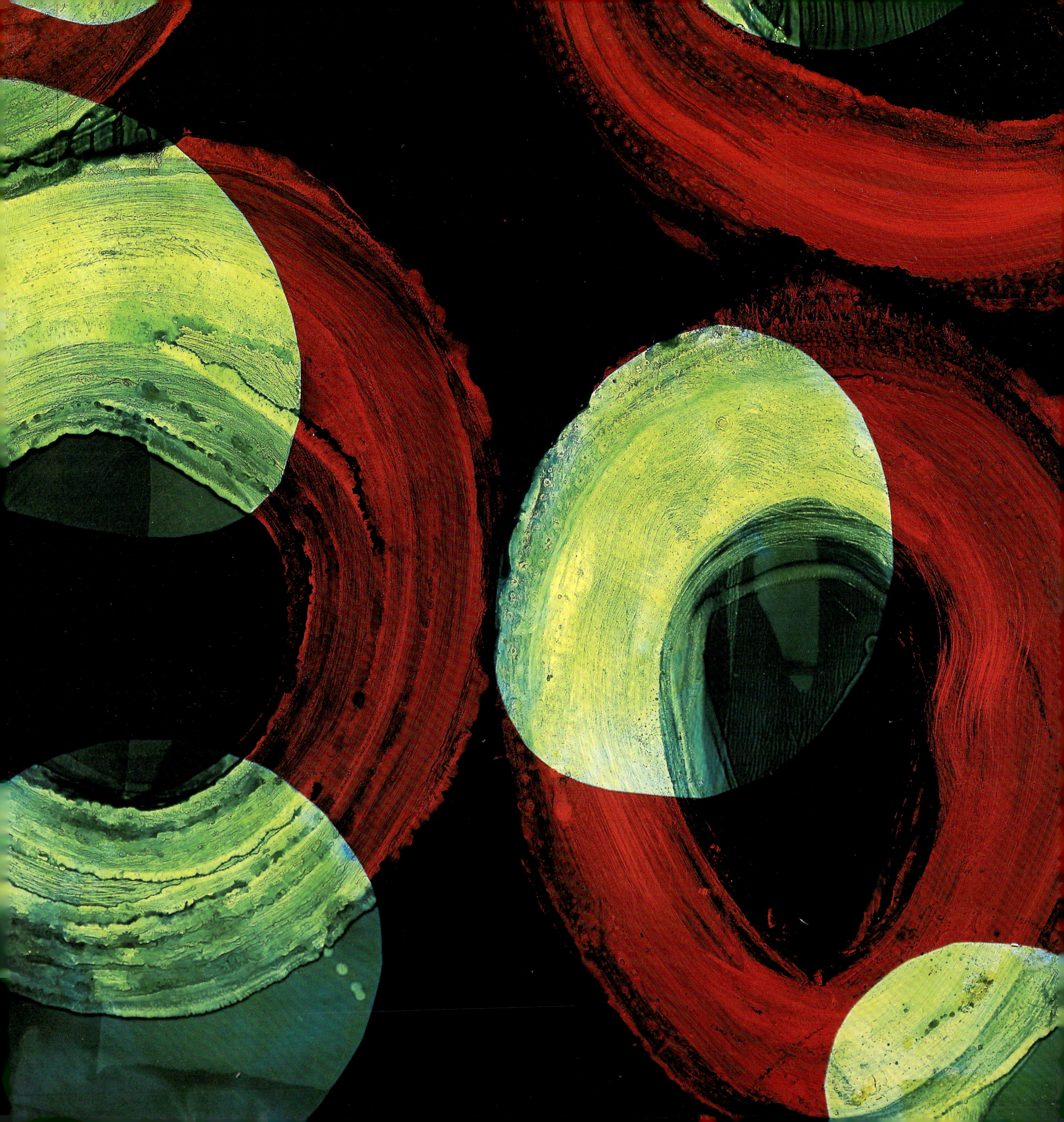

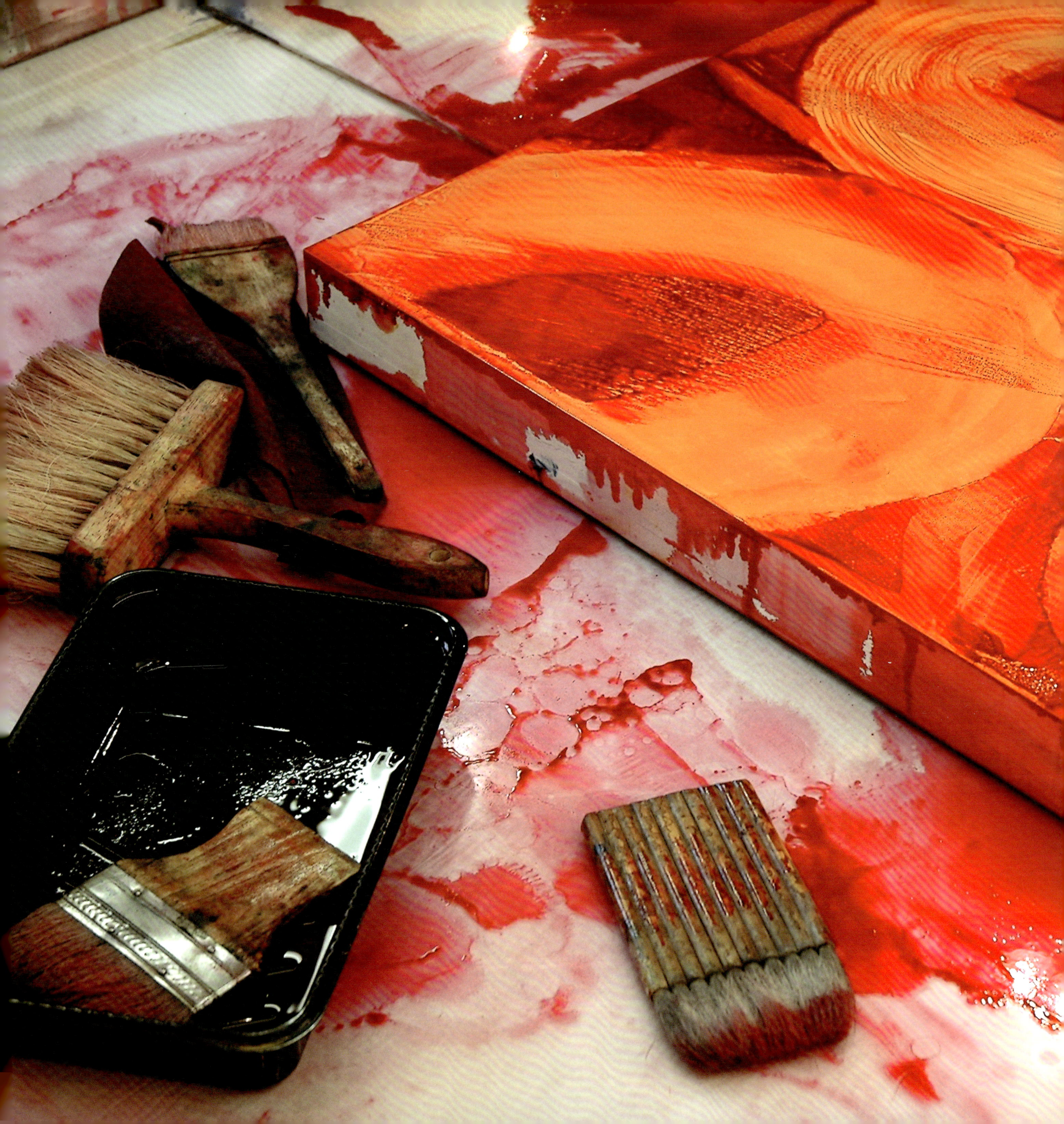

FOREWORD

This publication is the first monograph on the art of Marylyn Dintenfass, although her mature work as a painter, printmaker, and sculptor extends back thirty years. *Marylyn Dintenfass Paintings*, which we at the Greenville County Museum of Art are proud to present, is the artist's seventh one-person museum exhibition in a distinguished career. My involvement with this project—the studio visits, planning sessions, discussions with Marylyn about process and inspiration—had been most pleasant and rewarding . . . until I was asked to write this. To paraphrase a president, it's hard work writing about painting; or it *should* be. And it's especially difficult laboring under the hope of adding anything valuable to your experience of seeing the paintings themselves. But, as the New Pornographers have assured us, hope grows greener than grass stains.

A friend advised me to use simple declarative sentences and to avoid multisyllabic (oops) words. Another friend once cautioned against throwing a dictionary out the window of a moving vehicle: it might be a provocative performance, but it ain't writing. So, chastened but undaunted, I would posit that as a symbolic abstract colorist . . . or a colorful symbolic abstractionist . . . er, an abstract color symbolist . . . oh, never mind.

Like Georgia O'Keeffe, who denied it, or Judy Chicago, who served it up on a platter, or Gustave Courbet and Joan Semmel, both of whom put it in our faces, Marylyn Dintenfass paints orifices—holes. Of course, you can see that they are much more than that, but painters don't want to communicate so directly that you don't consider the options. Otherwise, they'd just haul off and knock you out; and this painter floats like a butterfly.

Exactly how many does it take to fill the Albert Hall? It's a thick bubbling environment in there; it may be hard and glossy on the outside, but there's heat under the ice. Sensual? This stuff is carnal. Striped skirt pulled away to reveal . . .

Then there's the odd corner counterweight that flips everything spinning around again. Poetry in motion. Perpetual emotion.

Did an abstract expressionist ever perk you up like this? Did they ever paint about anything but themselves? Yes, Marylyn Dintenfass embodies herself in her art, embeds herself deeply; yet there is also a place inside for you. Welcome! Feel free to luxuriate, to move around. Shall we dance? The greatest compliment between actors: she is generous. I feel love.

Thomas W. Styron
Director, Greenville County Museum of Art

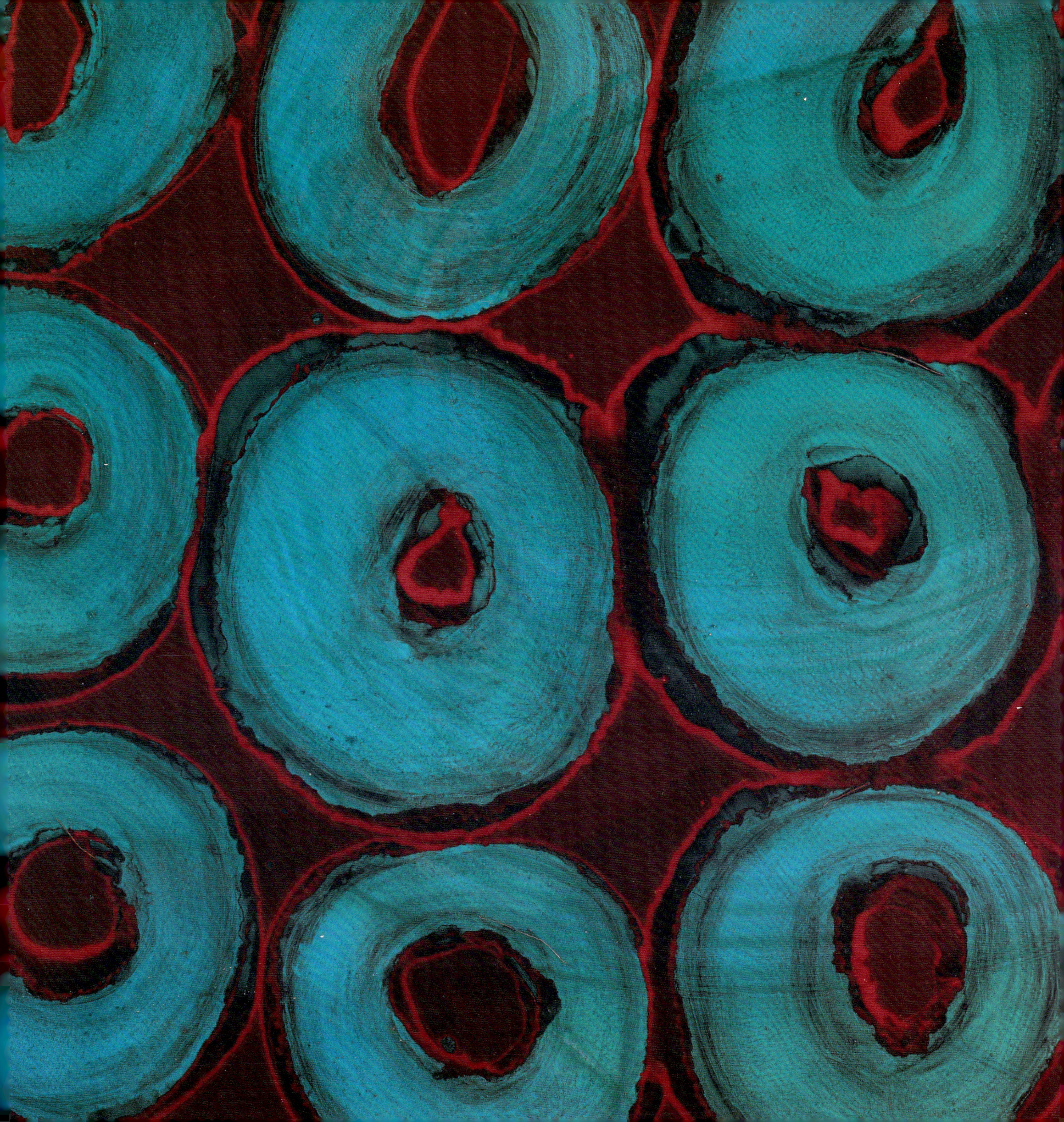

PAINTING IN THE HERE AND NOW LILLY WEI

FOR MORE THAN A CENTURY AND A HALF, as painting's mimetic function became less and less essential, at first usurped—or liberated, depending on your point of view—by photography and then edged out by ever more ingenious technologies of visual reproduction, the medium underwent a series of examinations, its nature deconstructed and revised. Theorists of the modernist, postmodernist, and contemporary formulated new conceptual models for painting in an attempt to reconcile the oldest medium with present culture. By the 1960s, after decades of triumph, a besieged modernism was declared bankrupt, and painting—its anointed medium—was pronounced dead. Painting, however, proved to be more resilient and more necessary than originally suspected, and reports of its death were not only greatly exaggerated but also completely untrue. Painting had not died; it had merely gone into retreat.

When it returned in the 1980s, it returned in a more expansive mode, one that reprised modernist tropes on the one hand, and was more conceptualized on the other. Painting, like other mediums, was also no longer autonomous. Crossing disciplines, it matter-of-factly incorporated performance, installation, film, video, and electronic and other media into its repertoire—or was incorporated itself. But that's an old story. At the moment, painting is flourishing once again, more complicated than it once was, reflecting its adaptability and our more complex, heterogeneous worldview. Painting today is less innocent, less metaphysical, less heroic and immediate than it was in the glory days of the Abstract Expressionists, but it is also not cynical, not emptied-out simulacra, not mere commodity—and certainly not dead. Whatever else it has become in its search for alternative resolutions and identities, painting, for the moment, is much less narrow, much less dogmatic in the way it regards itself and its current possibilities.

Marylyn Dintenfass, who made her artistic debut in the 1970s, was inevitably shaped by those heady, groundbreaking years as well as by the ideological and aesthetic shifts that followed. A practitioner in this expanded field, Dintenfass's paintings—as well as her ceramics, prints, and drawings—touch on a wide range of sources, merging modernist precepts with current tendencies. They are frequently modular in format or installed systematically, devices based on modernism's iconic image, the grid, and the serial formulations of minimalists like Sol LeWitt, who was an early influence. In her recent oil paintings—so luminous at times that they approximate the miracles of stained-glass windows flooded by light—Dintenfass uses square or rectangular, moderate-sized wood panels as the support, although the rectangles are often formed from squares that have been doubled. The panels are then assembled to make a multipart, puzzle-like construct, usually consisting of two, three, or four sections. Dintenfass, although trained as a painter and printmaker, has had many architectural commissions and has long worked with modular systems. The modules serve as the scaffold—the painting's architecture and underlying geometry—but one that recognizes fragmentation, that the whole is the sum of many parts. It is a serial kind of order that is underlined by the discontinuity of the surface images of the pictorial composition.

DETAIL PAGE 91

After completing a painting, Dintenfass literally takes it apart, treating each panel as a discrete entity, exchanging panels between works in an aesthetic mix and match as she searches for interactions and relationships of color and form that satisfy her sense of visual excitement, sparked by the frisson of the dissonant. In this gambit—which is partly controlled, partly by chance—Dintenfass subtracts one or more panels from the original picture and adds one or more—usually placing a panel in the lower left quadrant if it is a single alteration. This process of exchange—hands-on, very physical, and dependent on the accumulated experience and sensibility of the artist—is critical to her enterprise, a process spurred on by a spirit of adventure and a desire to surprise and be surprised, to embrace both the carefully calculated and the fortuitous. The substitution demonstrates her dialectical leanings and her canny orchestration of disparate elements to maximize visual synergy and achieve a skewed, more dynamic, and precarious balance.

Dintenfass admits that she has always been interested in finding unrelated things and making them fit together in ways that jostle and tantalize the eye. These paintings, like much current art, are invested in the representation of an idea about painting and a language of painting. The painted panels, reshuffled, act as a syntactical structure that creates the image rather than being merely dictated by it. This premise is one of the reasons that the antagonism between abstract and representational artists, once so bitterly vehement, no longer seems to matter. Ideas about painting have changed; painting is now recognized as being about more than one thing, presented in more than one guise. Consequently, there is a sense of play, of the open-ended and experimental, in Dintenfass's productions that mirrors contemporary theories of contingency and incompleteness, an acknowledgment that in reality there is no possibility of an omniscient eye that sees all or of an object that includes all; in essence, we are all unreliable narrators.

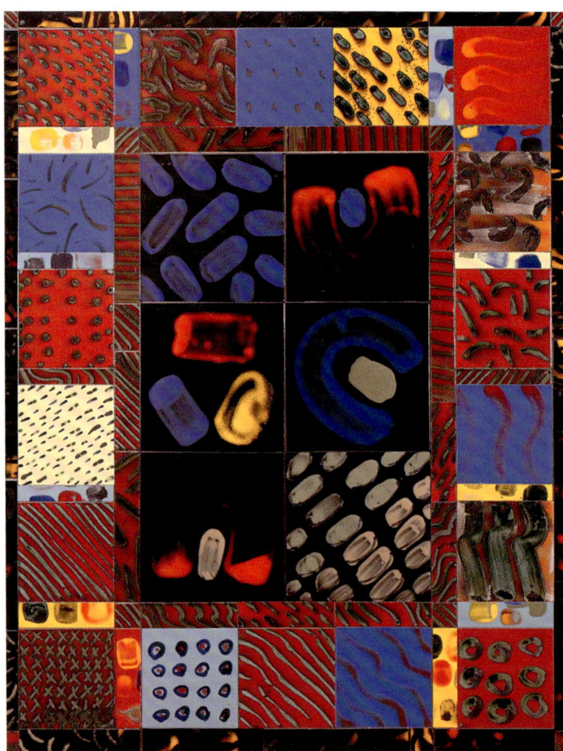

NEGEV IMPRINT 1995
CERAMIC TILE 60" X 48"
BOSTON CONSULTING GROUP, NEW YORK

Ultimately, however, Dintenfass is more sensualist than theorist, and her paintings owe much of their allure to their materiality and the dazzle of color. Her array of ripe, radiant, saturated hues—a palette of gorgeous diversity—can be silkily smooth and nuanced; boldly exuberant; or edgily, feverishly discordant. Her oranges, yellows, reds, greens, turquoises, and purples reach back to the Fauves and forward to the sleek, synthetically enhanced, cinematic colors of today, recalling Matisse's proto-postmodernist claim that his greens were greener than nature, his oranges more orange. Dintenfass explains that she has always seen a preternaturally vivid world, and it is this subjective world that she is attempting to reproduce. As a child, she thought everyone saw colors the way she did, but she eventually realized that they did not—at least not with the same impact and startling, searing immediacy.

Two unmistakable motifs—a stripe and a circle and variations thereof—appear throughout this body of work, as they have throughout her entire oeuvre. Dintenfass confesses that she is amazed at how consistent her visual language has been over the years, a consistency that has nonetheless resulted in a wide range of effects, as she adapts her vocabulary to suit whatever medium she is working in. Like many contemporary artists, Dintenfass is proficient in several, including ceramics—a discipline she took up later in her career. In her ceramic projects, the stripe has been modified into a flat, sometimes undulating band, which she installs in great numbers on a wall and layers to create a rippled, façade-like construction. Transferred to the paintings, the stripe becomes more rod-like, sometimes emphatically straight and placed in a row next to other stripes, each ending in a round knob where the brushstroke stops, like the cut ends of stems. Other times the stripe is drawn as a squiggled, squirming line, on a diagonal or straight up—a mildly phallic figure that also suggests more organic entities such as worms, branches, and roots: a jungle in neon colors.

In opposition to the stripes are the circular forms—flat or inflated, female in principal and vaguely suggestive of breasts and vaginal openings. They also could be foliated botanical shapes, depictions of

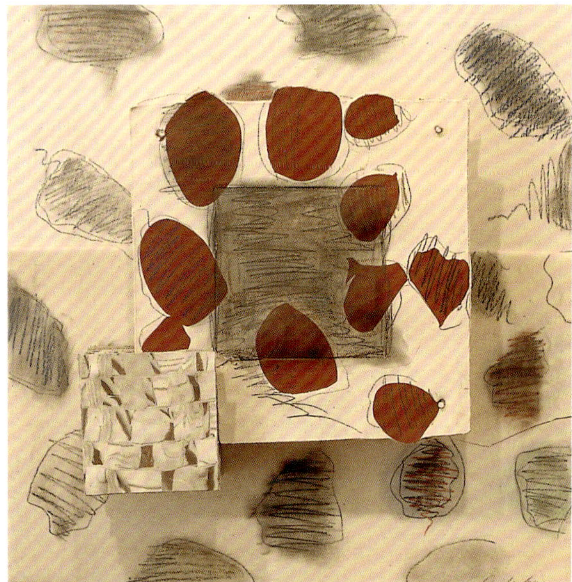

PARADIGM SERIES: RED POTATO 1990
CERAMIC, GRAPHITE, STEEL 24" X 24" X 6"
PRIVATE COLLECTION

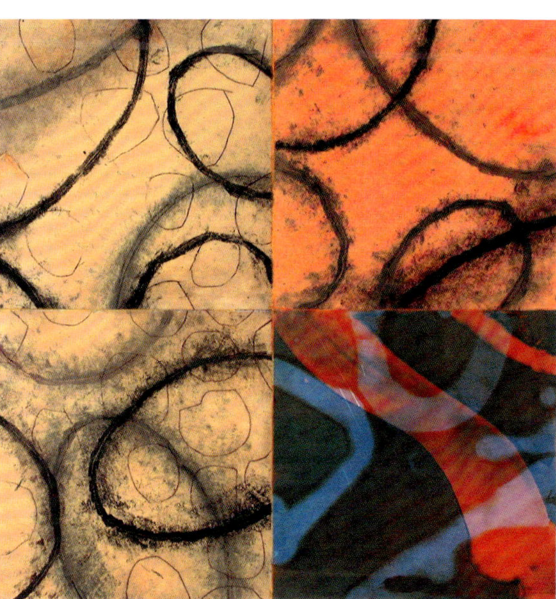

ACANTHUS QUATTRO XVIII 2002
OIL ON PAPER MONOTYPE 32" X 32"
THE METROPOLITAN MUSEUM OF ART, NEW YORK

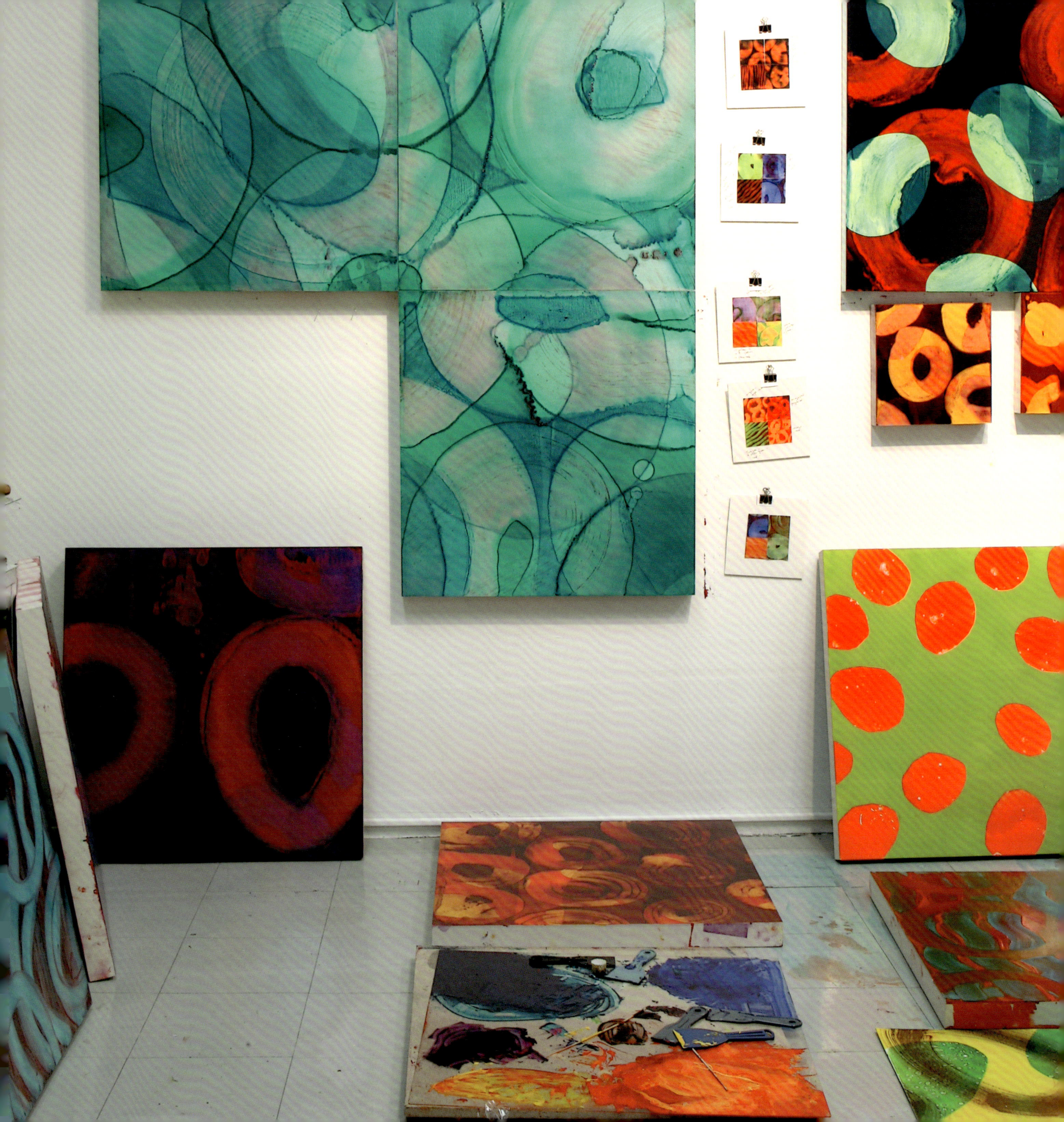

things seen under a microscope, like protozoa, or through a telescope, like distant cosmic phenomena. The discs are sometimes compressed, translucent, and grooved, as in *Covert Hues* (p. 99), with its supple, sensitive circular bands in shades of acid green or violet edged by red, or incandescent orange traced by red. They might be brushy and swollen, as in the ghostly blue rings rising to the surface in *Bombay Sapphire, Night* (p. 119), veiled by twisting, celebratory ribbons of wine red dropped from top to bottom like a curtain. One of its panels is characteristically anomalous and consists of green circles streaked with wriggles of yellow swimming through a field of diagonal orange waves. Other buoyant, cushiony rings dappled in iridescent tints glow like strange flowers or haloed sunbursts in such paintings as *Good & Plenty: Ultra Blue* (p. 93) and *Amber Sky & Tangerine Moon* (p. 117). Both stripe and circle also suggest kaleidoscopically spun close-ups of particles, waves, and atoms, the magnified, colorized, deconstructed constituents of matter, filtered—through Warhol, Pop, David Lynch's *Blue Velvet* (the exemplary postmodern film with its brilliant opening sequence), graphic design, comics and anime—into anti-matter, the anti-natural.

What is impossible to see except in the presence of the paintings themselves, however, is the pattern of high gloss and matte that maps the surface of each. In essence, it is the record of the construction of the painting in which each layer is visible. The shiny areas are those with the most layers of color, a color that becomes dimensional, revealed from the first layer put down to its topmost application. The matte areas, in contrast, are not as dense, not as built up. These paintings, while they may be read many ways, most closely conjure up a garden, one constituted out of an assemblage of signs; a contemporary still life or landscape, teetering on the cusp of the abstract and the representational—a narrative of the unreal. Looking into the paintings as through a looking glass, through the streaming forms—some hidden behind others, barely perceptible—the viewer encounters a more mysterious, less benign realm, an alternative location, as if this imagined Eden of bold and resplendent colors held darker intimations within its indeterminate fictive spaces, as Eden itself is forever—and ironically—a fiction beyond reach; an intimation of loss and mortality.

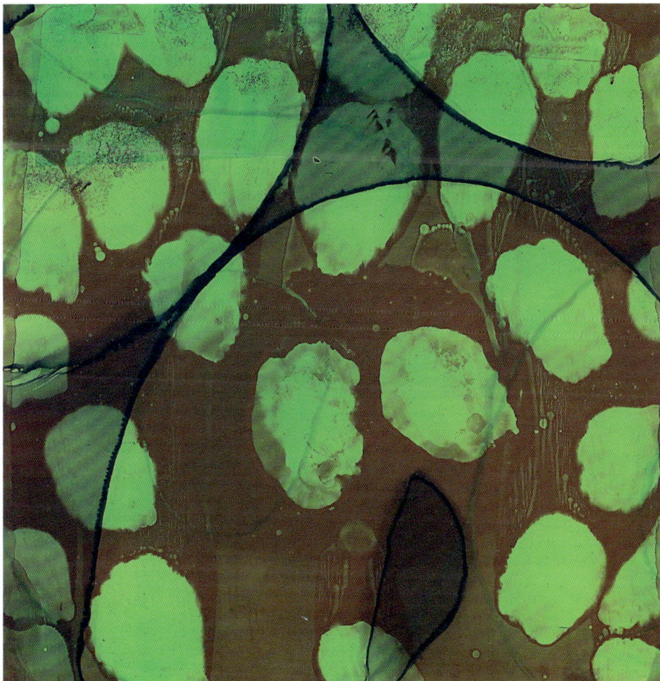

DETAIL PAGE 79

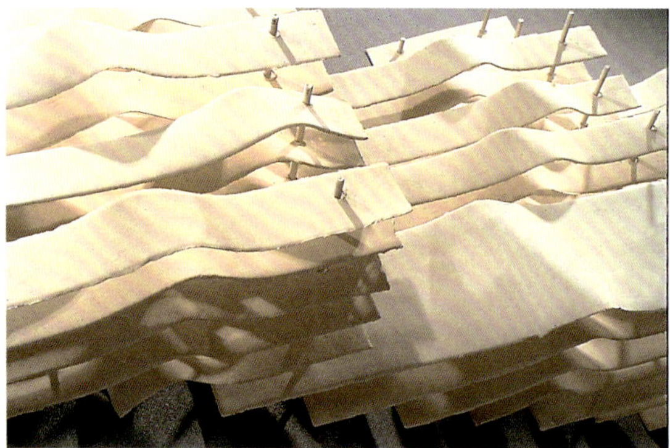

Dintenfass considers her work to be autobiographical, the references embedded in the paintings. These coded, hermetic associations—alluded to in her titles—blend life and art, the abstract and the representational, as they both conceal and confess. They are also an artistic autobiography, a record of her visual dialogue—however oblique, subsumed, and transformed—with artists who have intrigued her, such as Marsden Hartley, Mark Rothko, Paul Klee, Joan Mitchell, Elizabeth Murray, Jennifer Bartlett, Mary Heilmann, Matthew Ritchie, and Karin Davie. Dintenfass might also be grouped with such painters as David Row, David Reed, and Stephen Ellis, who use abstract images as syntax, with narrative as well as formal implications. Like her, they are almost all colorists and tend toward the phenomenological rather than the ideological. They are almost all abstract narrators and fabulists, inventors of specific worlds and specific spaces. In this context, it is also difficult not to think of Howard Hodgkin and, of course, Matisse.

The master of joyous, sun-drenched paintings, Matisse was an artist who served visual pleasure, substituting a keen eye, intuitive intelligence, boundless drive, and a seemingly blissful ease of production for theoretical concerns; an artist who gave color new expressiveness and independence, and made of his vision a new model for beauty. Matisse's reputation, however, had suffered in the more conceptual bastions of the art world, where retinal art and beauty are dismissed as inconsequential, as mandarin pastimes for the privileged, although both retinal art—if any art can be purely retinal—and beauty have been rehabilitated of late. As claimed by various critics of the opposing faction—including Dave Hickey, who played an essential role in the restoration of beauty to the discourse—any theory of images that is not grounded in the pleasure of the beholder and the language of visual affect is insufficient. As Agnes Martin, another artist Dintenfass greatly admires, once stated with exemplary succinctness and simplicity, "When I think of art, I think of beauty. Beauty is the mystery of life." Dintenfass, as is obvious from her paintings, is also on the side of visual pleasure, a believer in contemporary beauty. Lush but also astringent, with a glittered coolness and reserve that offsets its heat, her work offers a bracing example of an experiential painting for the present. ⊞

DETAIL, DIAGONAL FRIEZE 1986 PAGE 39

DETAIL PAGE 67

(OVERLEAF) **DETAIL** PAGE 111

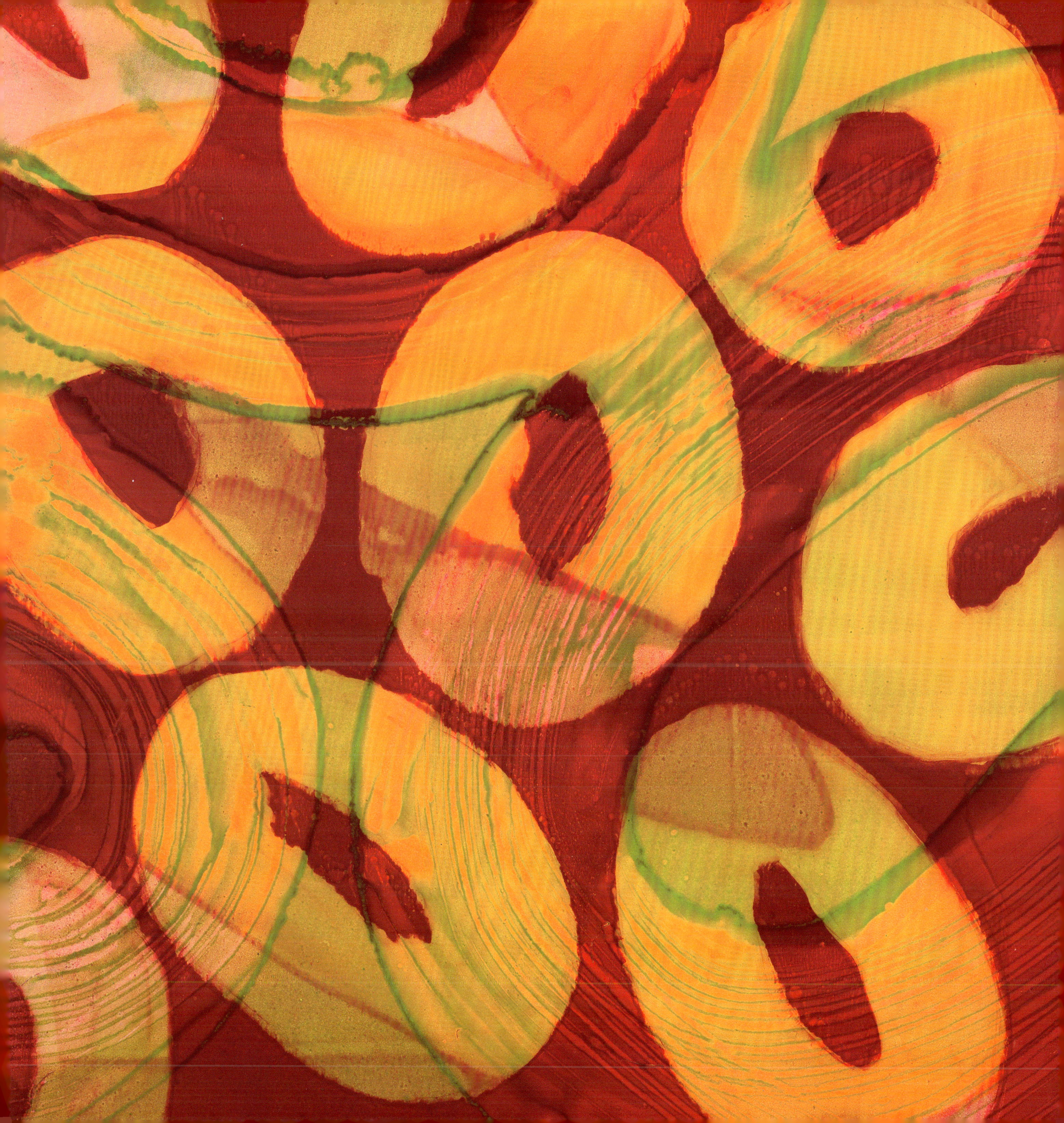

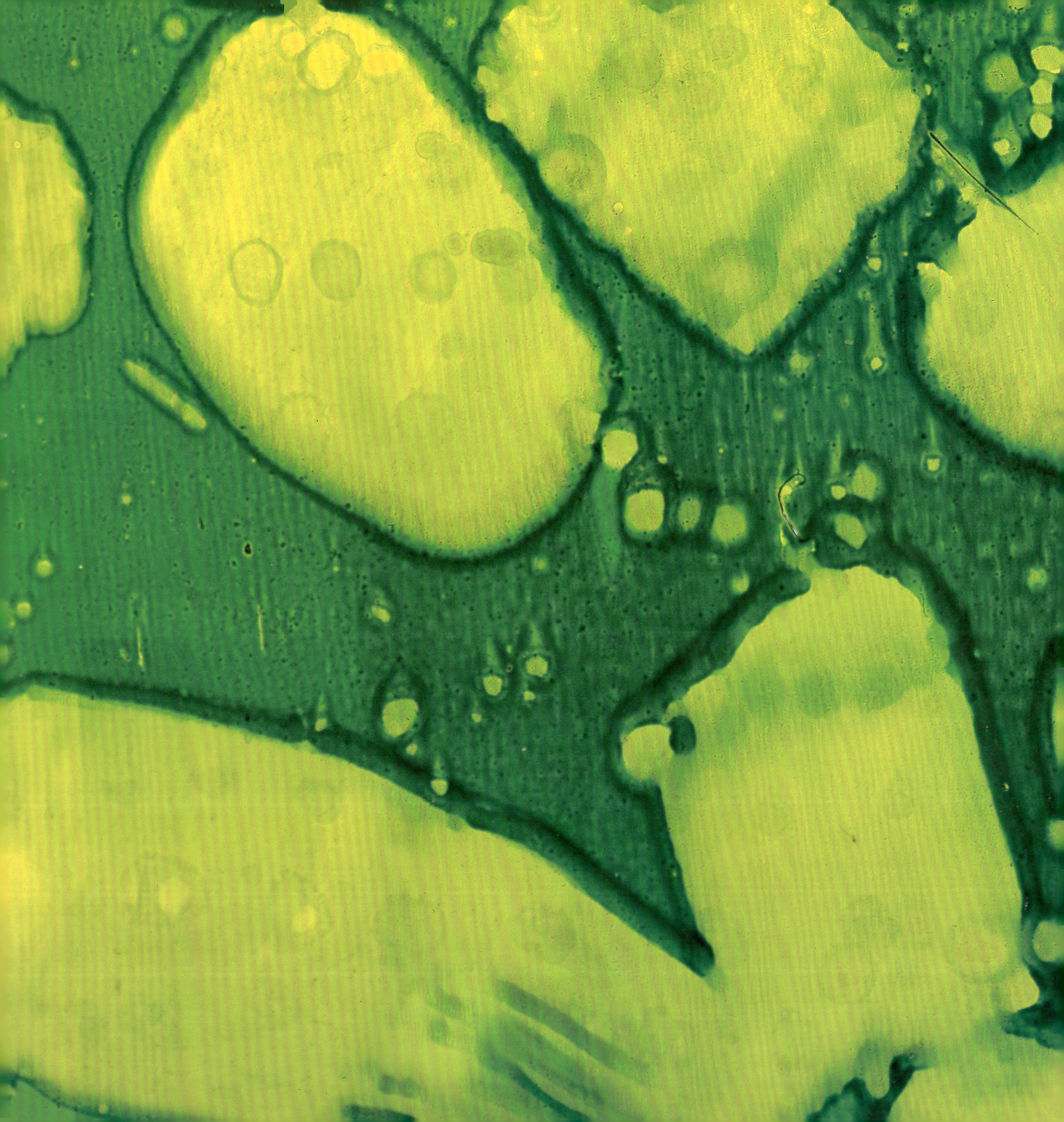

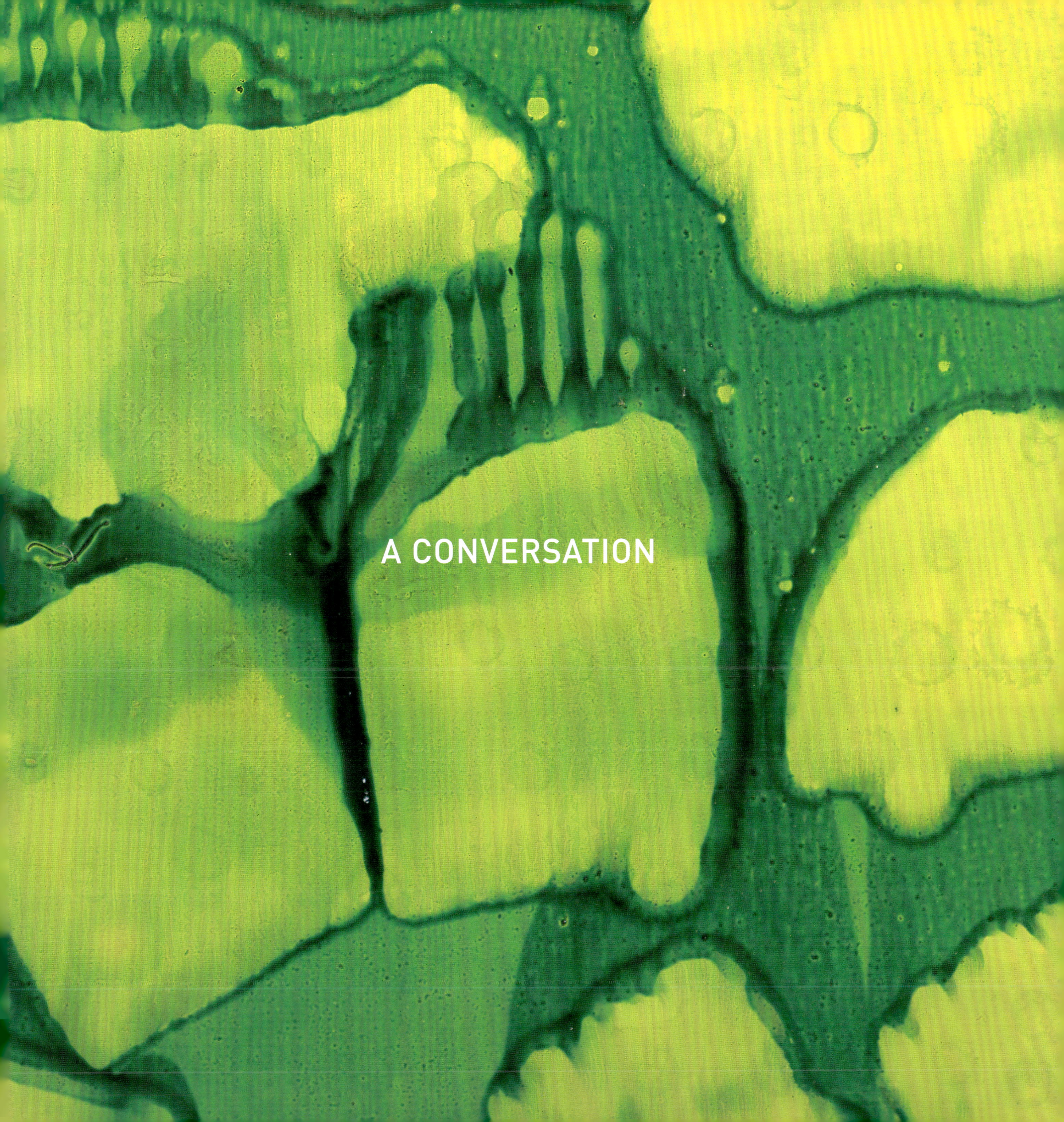

A CONVERSATION

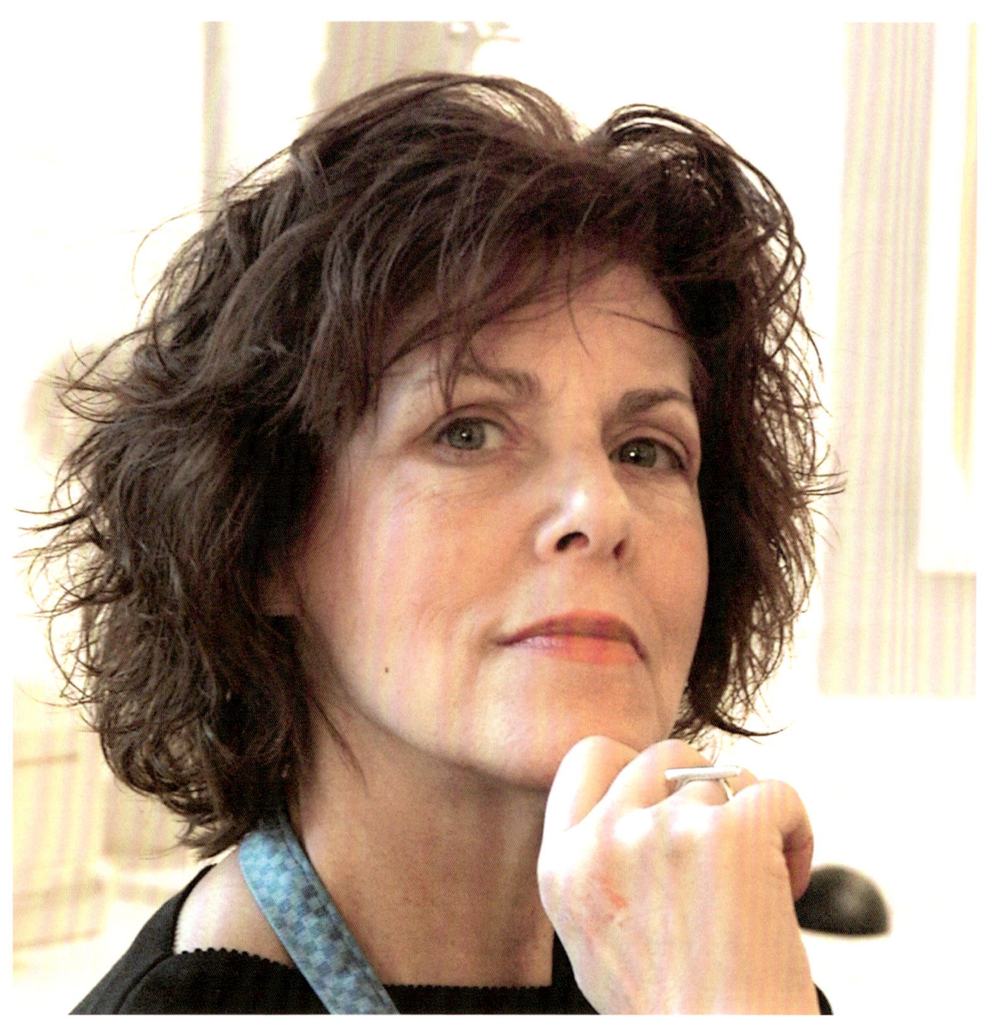

A CONVERSATION MARYLYN DINTENFASS WITH JOHN DRISCOLL

Where does your imagery come from?

It's an interesting question. I have been amazed, as I've gone through stacks and stacks of old drawings, sketches, and photos of my work, to realize how consistent I've been through the years in referencing the same lexicon of personal markings. It is a scripted language that feels like it has always been there. I am usually infusing some earthy expressive emotional symbols within an organized construct of some kind, ordering rich unrestrained characters within some grid-like "scrim," which are the components I am using for whatever I am working on.

There are times when the markings in my work are like representations of a cosmic scene: the planets, the sky, space. At other times, the marks are reminiscent of organisms viewed under a microscope. I am fascinated by how similar the micro and macro worlds are, and it is exciting to hold these views simultaneously. In fact, that's one of the things the multiple-panel pieces offer—the ability to see disparate things at the same time.

The desire to order comes both from wanting to impose a bit of restraint on the ardent symbolism and from the strong affinity I feel for the power of architecture and spatial design. The imagery is, in many cases, a personal, contemporary response to ornamented classical architecture. Throughout history, stories were told through wall drawings and symbols, in caves, tombs, huts, homes, and public buildings; painting and architecture have always been potently paired; and in a way I am building an ornamented structure.

Some years ago, the wonderful critic and writer Ted Castle, who sadly just recently passed away, posed the question, "Why does a painter turn to clay?" I responded then that the dialogue with the material was extremely intense and mutable, and that I was stimulated by the mental gymnastics of alchemy and aesthetics and the intellectual rigor of mentally holding an image of a desired final result through all the stages of fabrication.

What is so interesting about my new paintings is that all the intrigue, all the challenge, all the possibilities, and all the elements of creating lush, sensual pictoral constructions are here. When I was younger, I think I needed more elements to work with to be able to produce the complex integration of image and form that interested me. Today, I am more in control and satisfied with fewer components; I can say more with less. I am energized, infused with vigor and inspiration to do this work; in a way I feel as if I am a prose writer who's become a poet.

You began as a representational painter of still life, human figures, and landscape. You say your work is layered with personal meanings, which suggests representation, and yet the role of abstraction—of abstract if not non-objective imagery—from very early in your career, has been profound.

I had a traditional fine arts education: life drawing, 2-D design, 3-D design, painting all the classical elements. It's like learning to write music and then becoming a composer: you order the notes to compose your unique vision.

My vision has been to create work that satisfies visually like painting but has a powerful sense of place like architecture; painting that defines and holds its space.

With that in mind, the storytelling aspect of my work has evolved, and the narrative has become abstract elements that absorb and project meaning. Before there was the written word, ideas were communicated through symbols and marks. Now communication is overwhelmingly diverse and ubiquitous; my work refers to communication through the visceral channel.

What are the underlying themes of your work?

Things are not what they seem. There is a duality to human experience, which completely intrigues me.

People are in the same place and time and yet are focusing on different things. People's particular histories cause them to see things that others miss entirely. We have an inside/outside experience; we are in a place but it's as if we are also outside, observing the situation and ourselves in it. This ability to be and feel, to see and observe, or to have simultaneous parallel knowledge and instinct that are out of synch—that is what my work is about.

I am engaged in my art as in life, through my emotions, my intellect, my visual awareness, and my intuition. I am observing and collecting these intriguing and remarkable disparities in life's experiences. A celebration of some sort is attended, but only some participants know the pathos that is unspoken. We are standing in a place, conjuring up ancient or recent histories that impact on the here and now.

I am engaged in the process of taking in observed or intuited inconsistencies and coalescing them into a meaningful if sometimes unexpected aesthetic whole.

What are your thoughts about color?

Color considerations are always primary. I think about concepts, and I think about colors. It is a chicken and egg dilemma about which comes first, and ultimately they are so intertwined that I cannot always separate them, or even wish to separate them. I begin painting by thinking about what color I am interested in working with and then deciding, do I want to work with it or against it, do I want to enhance it with close relative hues, or do I want to go against the pulse of the color? Hue refers to what color some-

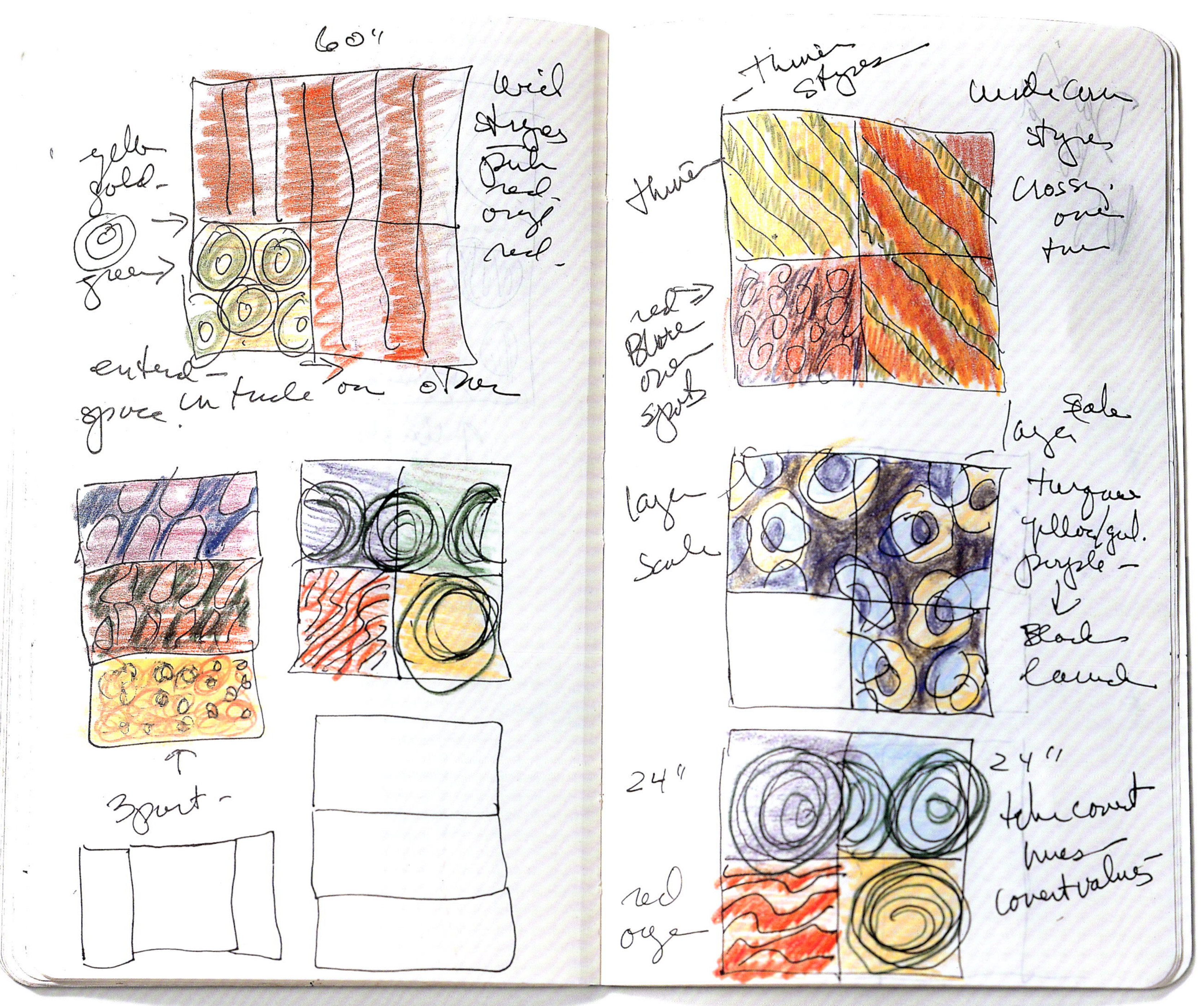

60"
green
3 part -
layer
scale
24"
24"
red

thing is—is it red moving toward orange or red sliding into blue? Value is how light or dark something is. Saturation refers to how intense a color is. All these variations are crucial, subtle, and highly variable.

This thinking is for me a very intense experience—mental, visual, and visceral. Although the range of the internal discourse is quite narrow (should I use acid green, yellow-orange green, or a blue-green?), it feels enormously vast. The decisions about shifting hues even slightly can totally amend my attitude toward other colors I may be using and even change the way I perceive the work or how I think it will be experienced by others. The exercise is real; it is challenging and tactile for me, and the subtle decisions about hue, saturation, and value are monumental in my thinking about each painting.

As I think about color, or the colors I need to use to convey an idea, I devise a plan of how I need to map the colors to create dominate and subordinate hues and values. Sometimes I am in the mood to work with a certain color or color family, and a concept emerges from that color. Then I plot out the components of this family. Remember, color families are usually just as dysfunctional as any other families, and my compositions create dynamics that often require serious intervention to make them work.

Color is concrete to me. It has body and substance; it's tactile; and, in certain important ways, it has life. I think about colors and hold them in my mind the way I believe a composer thinks about notes and can hear them in his or her head without access to an instrument. A composer selects notes and composes before setting anything down on paper. Then he may notate or record. That's how my paintings develop. I think about a specific color nuance and how it can be made to affect and influence other colors. I sketch the map and begin laying down thin coats of color, adding and subtracting to create translucent layers and a sense of the painting's visual and technical history of the process. The representation of concept and process as layers of color and tangible discrete steps is exciting.

I am also inspired by experiences—particularly travel. It is the visceral aspect of travel that I commemorate. Certain places have a huge presence in my work; Turkey, Italy, Argentina, Japan, Israel, and New York, where I live, have all been rich sources of composition and chromatic influences. My son and his family live in Colorado, and during a visit there, an entire flood of color associations filled my head and led to the Boulder Series. An afternoon in the Baptistery in Florence, with all those magnificent mosaic, marble floors, led to another series of images. And Turkey. . . Well, the colors of Turkey are always in my mind. Some locations map color associations and color palettes as clearly as their rainfall and temperature statistics. These are the ones that keep reoccurring as subjects for paintings, and the experiences and associations are varied and memorable.

My relationship to color is intimate and precise. I sit quietly and think about different colors and compositional variations. I do this endlessly. I constantly make sketches and works on paper, or photographs that capture the essence of what I need to do to progress to the next iteration, to help capture variations to refresh later contemplation or work.

What about surfaces of your work?

One of the things I appreciated about creating paintings with ceramic media was the ability to control the surface—the texture—and thereby the reflection of light. The nature of the surface determines the way that light will hit it, interact with it, and play off it. This is a significant aesthetic consideration. The surface of the ceramic paintings was very similar to the creamy, dry surface of the works on paper. I had expected that my interest in light reflection could not be replicated in another medium.

With the current oil paintings, however, I've learned to create a lush reflective surface and control tactile surface decisions from the get-go. I work on gessoed Masonite panels with oil-based pigment. I use various additives, oils, and dryers to build a reflective surface up to where I want it while simultaneously contrasting certain layers with a more matte finish. The paintings are created through a protracted process of layering and building paint areas. The paintings look spontaneous and fluent, and in many respects they are, but the process is methodical and takes a long time. Things are not what they seem. I like that.

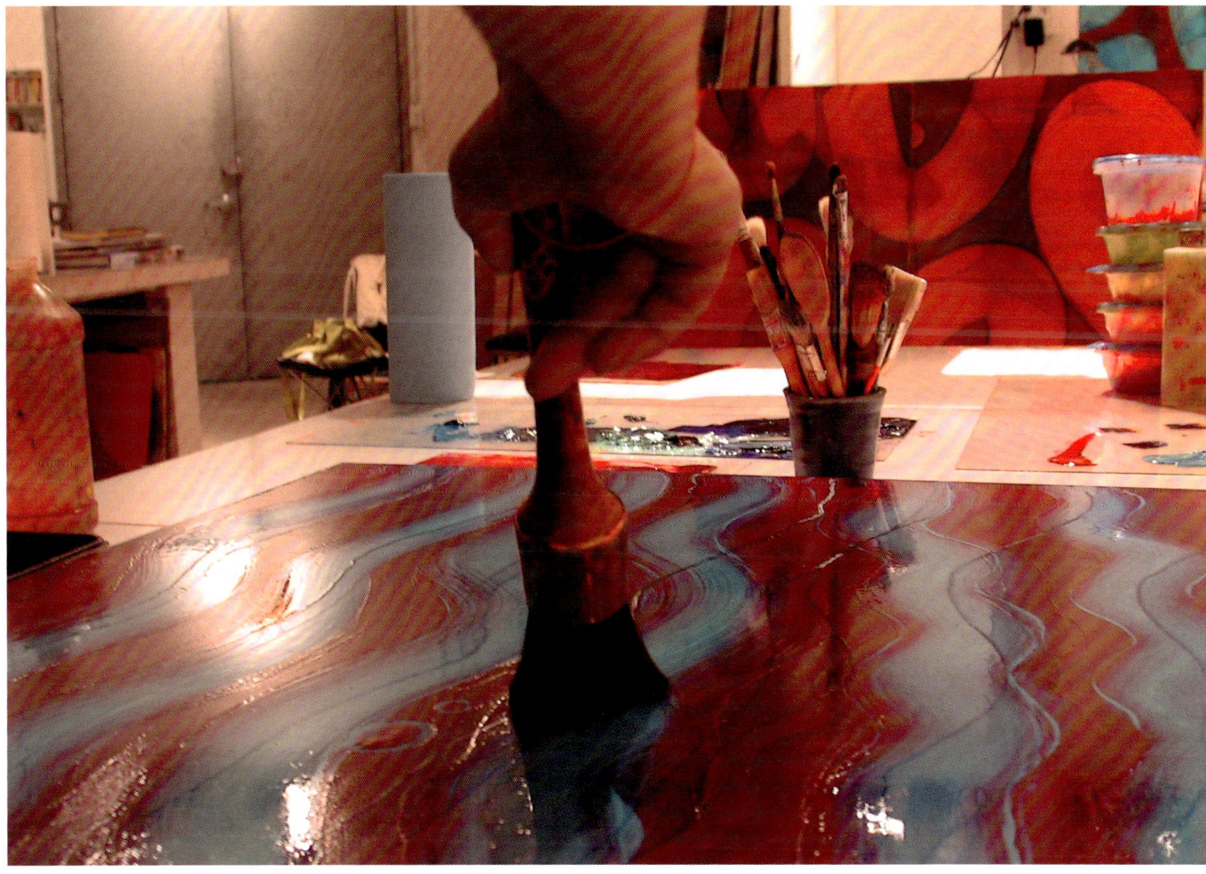

What would you say about the grid, about working with modular component pieces that combine to construct a whole?

One of my favorite classes in art school was color theory. This class was with John Ferren and I was especially fascinated by the assignments in which we were to change perception through modifying a color selection or alignment. It was very impressive to be able to change the way a color looked merely by changing what was next to it, and to discover how a small move could make an enormous change. These exercises, à la Josef Albers, were done in series and viewed as component elements on the crit wall. I was struck by the power and interest these multiple iterations commanded.

Early on I was interested in the analogous aspects of the individual steps inherent in the process of working—how movement or action could be broken down, and how each step could be observed and evaluated. I was fascinated by the photo images of Eadweard Muybridge and began a group of works called *Progressions*. This became a series of many pieces that examined an action or process. What I learned, which later became essential for working on a large scale, was that no matter how many modules it took to complete a particular action, each element had to stand on its own as a complete piece. And this held true for even the mammoth pieces where elements were exceedingly small.

These iterations become narratives, and the power of a small component telling a story and making a large visual impact became an essential element of much of my work, including *Tetrahedron, Diagonal Curve, Autumn Palette, Aerialscape,* and *Quadrille*.

What about scale?

Scale is everything. Scale is human; it is a measure and a pace of life. Scale is crucial to how I think about my work. Scale is a universal unit of response. I think everyone responds automatically and intuitively to elements of scale. In architecture, sculpture, painting, and drawing, scale determines response, reaction, and life.

Every piece is felt and conceived in relation to scale. The increments are human and therefore universal: relation of hand to arm and face, span of outstretched arms to height of body, and so on. The permutations in the human body are limitless, and in nature, the same.

The reaction to scale is in direct proportion to how powerful a person feels, how significant. The great Gothic cathedrals of Europe were designed to enshrine the glory of God; even today, hundreds of years after they were built, their effect on people—making the flock feel small, insignificant, humble—is still profound. And in political buildings, scale is used to bolster the sense of the state's power, a kind of deification of political leaders. Scale is a powerful and meaningful tool.

I'm very sensitive to the aspects of scale and think about it for every piece. I also enjoy working in the extremes of scale at different times. I like the change between the intimacy of small scale in a drawing or painting and the exponentially different experience of working with large, modular grid-oriented pieces. Of course, scale is the inherent measure of the grid, the module whether it is in the human body, in architecture, or in visual expression. There is a different kind of excitement that is generated by extreme changes in scale, even more than changes in medium. I like the challenge of some of the huge pieces I've done. There is excitement in the tactical process of fabrication, of installation, and there is a tremendous rush when it finally comes together and is completed. After working large, whether on an installation or on a large painting, it is exceedingly pleasurable to focus on a small-scale, intimate piece.

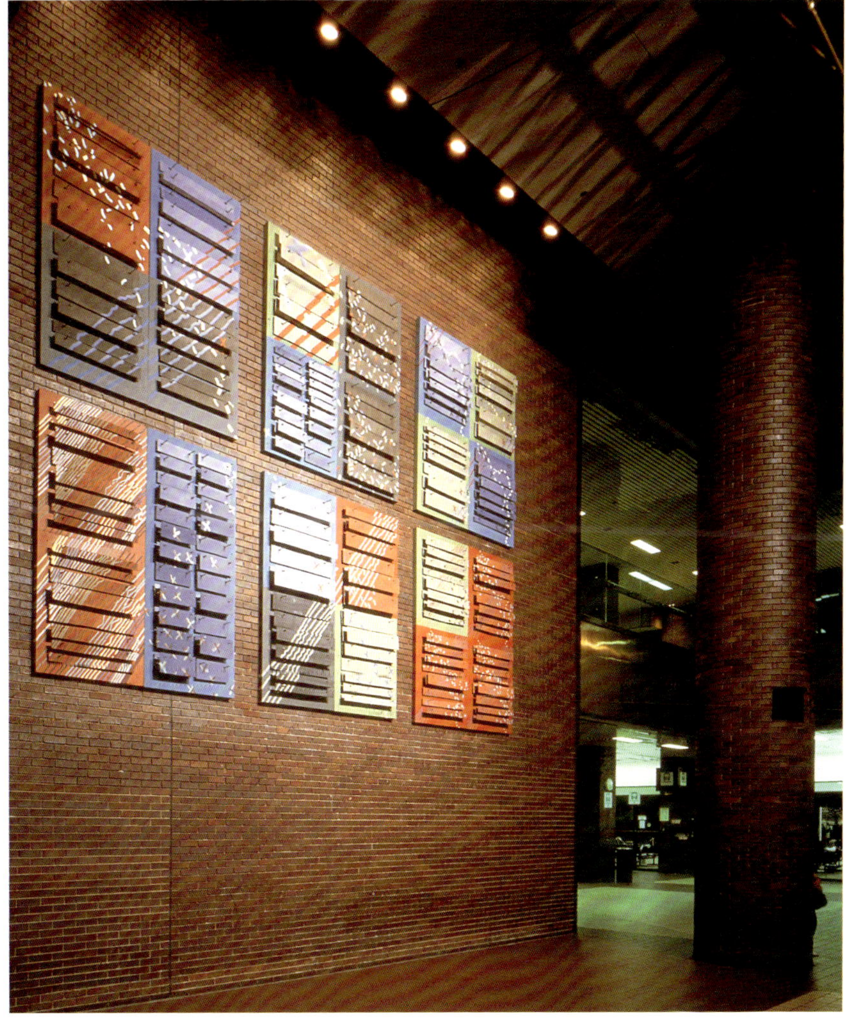

IMPRINT FRESCO 1985
CERAMIC, METALLIC OXIDES, POLYCHROME ON PANEL 192" X 336" X 9"
INSTALLATION, PORT AUTHORITY OF NY/NJ, 42ND STREET TERMINAL, NEW YORK

Your paintings are often composed of four separate pieces, one of which is different from the others. What are your thoughts about the fourth piece? Is it simply an aesthetic issue?

I did a series of constructed pieces called *Annotated Fresco* (1987), and I had the idea of doing a painting and then creating a section of the painting where there was "commentary," the painting disclosing information about itself in a kind of sidebar. I liked this idea of disclosure, or expansion of information about the painting in its own terms. I continued with this thought with the constructed *Paradigm Series,* the *Monadnock Series* of wall sculptures, and large-scale drawings. These and other works had distinct areas within that were designated as commentators on the other sections. Later, with a group of monotypes called *Mara's Series,* I really began to place disparate elements into a dialogue.

I soon realized that in addition to a dialogue being established, unexpected affinities between pieces developed. I was often completely surprised by the connections made, by the tensions established by the work itself. The concept developed further, and this "other piece" adds to the painting in a variety of ways.

Sometimes this other piece:

- is a hidden element or layer that I get to reveal
- is a commentary on the dominant image
- deepens the visual experience by representing an element not seen in the other image
- has an intense attraction to the dominant image and they come together, seemingly without my intervention
- has only a minimum connection, and they're "just out for a ride"
- creates a powerful dynamic, which changes the dominant image completely
- has an unexplained affinity, quite odd yet compatible
- brings decorum to the dominant image
- adds an element of danger, tension, naughtiness
- brings exuberance, spontaneity, comic relief
- is a mitigating force
- is a welcome relief
- annotates the other image with visual "historical" references
- is an example of a time continuum showing what the dominant image was in the past or what it will/might be in the future

It is always an aesthetic issue, but never just an aesthetic issue.

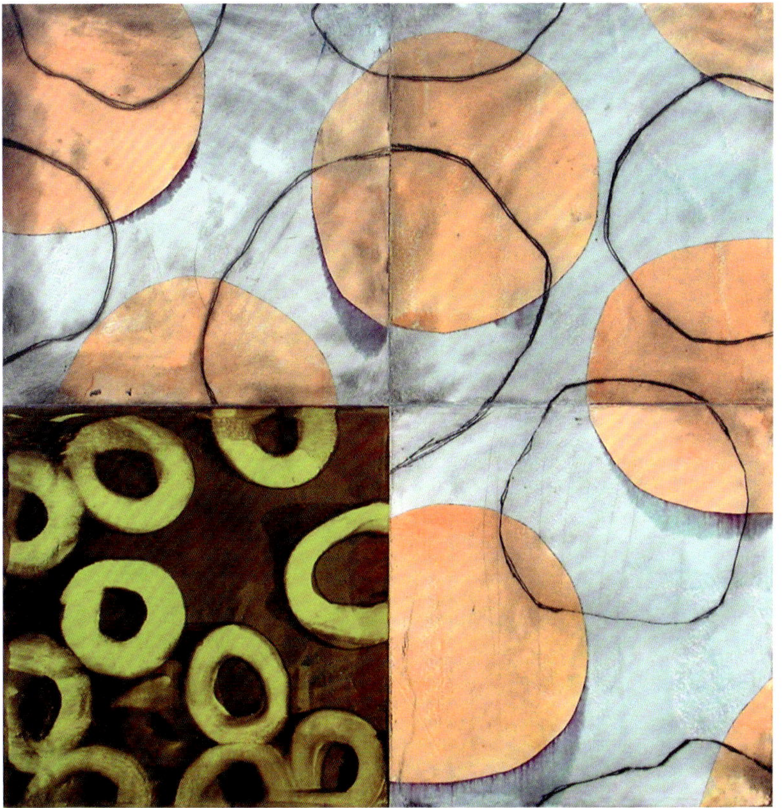

What about when you do a single panel, one that stands alone?

What intrigues me when I am working with the grid is following the tenet I developed about my work, which is that all elements in a component piece must work in concert with each other but must also be able to stand aesthetically and visually on their own. Conversely, when I work on a single piece (like the *Solo Series* or the *Uno Series*), it is on its own but also part of a continuum, of an uber-grid series, which is an invisible grid that exists around each piece but has yet to be defined or filled in. In other words, the grid is there; I have just made a single element of it and the rest may or may not come into being later. So the single pieces—no matter their scale—hold their own as individual works and, potentially, as part of a component series or grid. The nature of creativity has a way of taking care of this on its own.

What is the best thing about working, about painting?

I revel in the act of painting. The juice in the gestural marking is hypnotic and addictive. The works are an integration of the visceral and the intellectual, a ledge I like to occupy. The excitement is to decide on a theme, a color association, and then visualize some graphic biomorphic symbols from a family of narrative markings that I have composed over the years. I set them in a color-field environment, which suits

GOOD & PLENTY QUATTRO VI 2002
OIL ON PAPER MONOTYPE 32" X 32"
THE NEW ORLEANS MUSEUM OF ART, NEW ORLEANS, LA

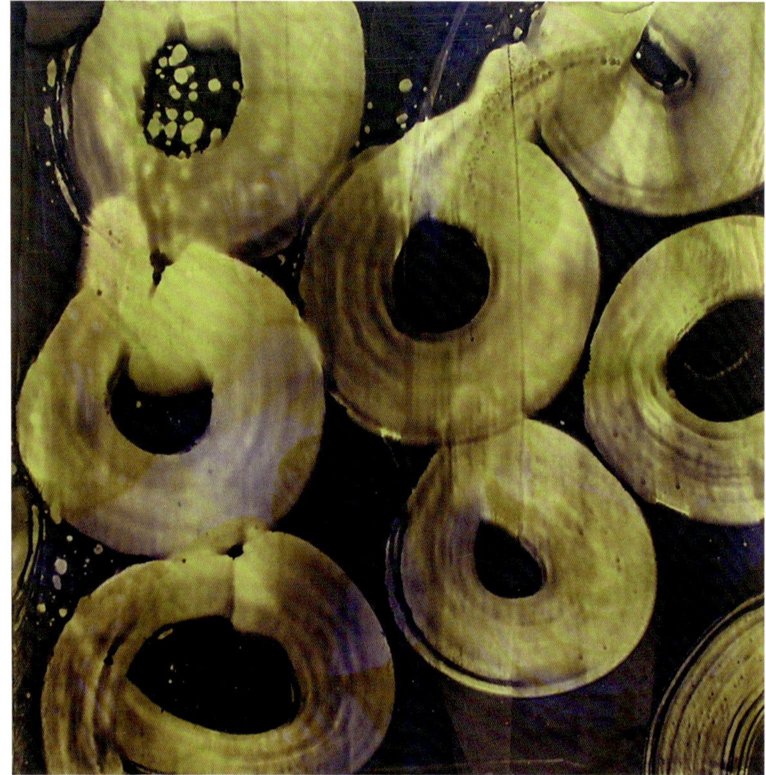

the intent of the piece. Then I plan the attack. Since I build color through a system of layering transparent pigments, I must carefully plot the order of the placement, intuitively choosing the proper value and hue of each layer to obtain the results I want. While this orderly mental mapping is taking place, I am also considering the gesture, which will ultimately carry the impact of the piece. These activities are simultaneous yet opposing. The inconsistency of the gestural, emotional, and spontaneous coexisting with preconceived, orderly, science-based thought creates a good deal of tension. I live and breathe for that tension.

The hook for continuing to work is what I refer to as getting to the payoff. The payoff is seeing the results of an internal vision, like the composer hearing a symphony finally being played. No matter how long he has heard it in his head, it's a thrill to hear it played by an orchestra. For me, seeing the painting finished with all the planned layers of color, the unexpected detours, the spontaneous brushstrokes, the reality of the color vibration, the internal torsion and tension in place, is a thrilling experience. That's the payoff.

You have done many commissions over the years. Do you see a difference between doing work on commissions and working on your own concepts?

I really enjoy doing commission work, but the process is totally different from the act of producing my own work. For me, commissions are a lot about problem solving. When I come into a commission situ-

GOOD & PLENTY #2 2002
OIL ON PAPER MONOTYPE 32" X 32"
THE CLEVELAND MUSEUM OF ART, CLEVELAND, OH

ation, no matter how early in the process, there is already a series of set premises or parameters. Major aesthetic decisions have already been made, and I need to find a way to insert my work within boundaries that already exist. I find that intriguing, stimulating, and often creatively demanding. Commissions are not as intimate or emotionally charged as the private act of creating imagery fueled by personal instincts and unknown ramifications.

Another issue with doing commissions is that they are usually predicated on earlier work, on doing something similar to an already-realized piece. So in a way it can be a struggle to go forward because the commission process is geared toward work that has been made in the past. Personal work—painting,

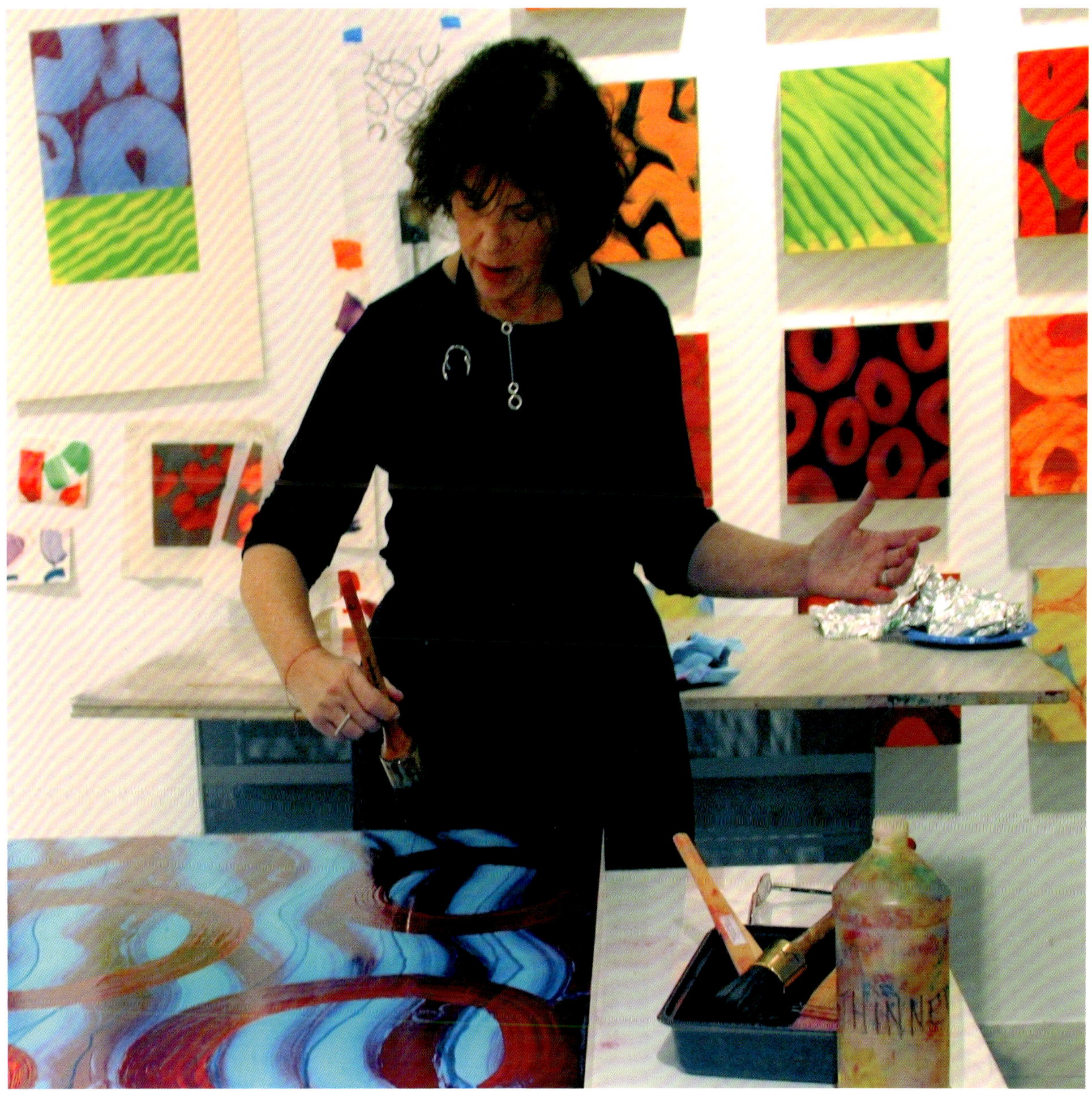

sculpture, printmaking, drawing—has no presumed premise other than what I give it, so there is freedom and intimate engagement, which serves as the impetus for the work.

Having said that, many of the commissions on which I have worked have presented challenging problems that were of great interest to me. Plus, working on commissions always provides a catalyst for new ideas that might not have developed if I were just doing my own work. And, of course, there is the illusion of money that comes from a commission. I am always excited about the execution of a piece, but often end up investing more in materials, time, and energy than the commission fees cover.

You have also completed many installations, modular works that can be expanded or contracted. How did that come about?

I have always worked in some kind of modular, grid-like format. I like to construct; it intensifies my connection to the work. Creating modules provides the opportunity to build a work of art, to expand or shrink it, to move it physically in different sequences or directions. I like the feeling of constructing art. I did a series of module repetition multiples and was able to reconfigure and scale the modules for different site installations *(Kite, Virgula)*. They were based on the concept of bricks—a simple module that can be assembled in many configurations. An interesting aspect of these works was the way the reconfigurations created varying scale, and how the different installations changed the interaction with the viewer.

You have had some interesting experiences with new technologies and the digital arena. How has that affected your work, your creative process?

I have always been intrigued with film, video, cinema. I find film frames fascinating. Even as a young person, I liked the photo booths at Coney Island and on top of the Empire State Building, where you could sit in a cramped little box, pay a quarter, and get a strip of different pictures of yourself. I liked the idea of manipulating action or even forms in units over time. It was modular imagery.

When my friend Michael Jaffe asked if he could film me working on my paintings in the Negev tile factory, I was interested but didn't feel I could take the time away from the work I was doing. But he was persistent and convinced me to get involved with the process (I am always a sucker for process). The experience of organizing the shots, determining the camera's point of view, and finally working in the editing studio was exhilarating. Then, after returning to the United States, Terri Lonier—another good friend and entrepreneur—invited me to accompany her to a Macworld conference in Boston, where I sat in on a session titled "Artists Do CD-ROM." That was it! The film experience with Michael was now combined with a brand-new technology, and immediately, on my way back to New York in the car, I dreamed up a virtual company called HandsOn, which would be devoted to working with the new medium and the arts. All this came at a moment of great stress and trauma in my life. I had just separated from my husband

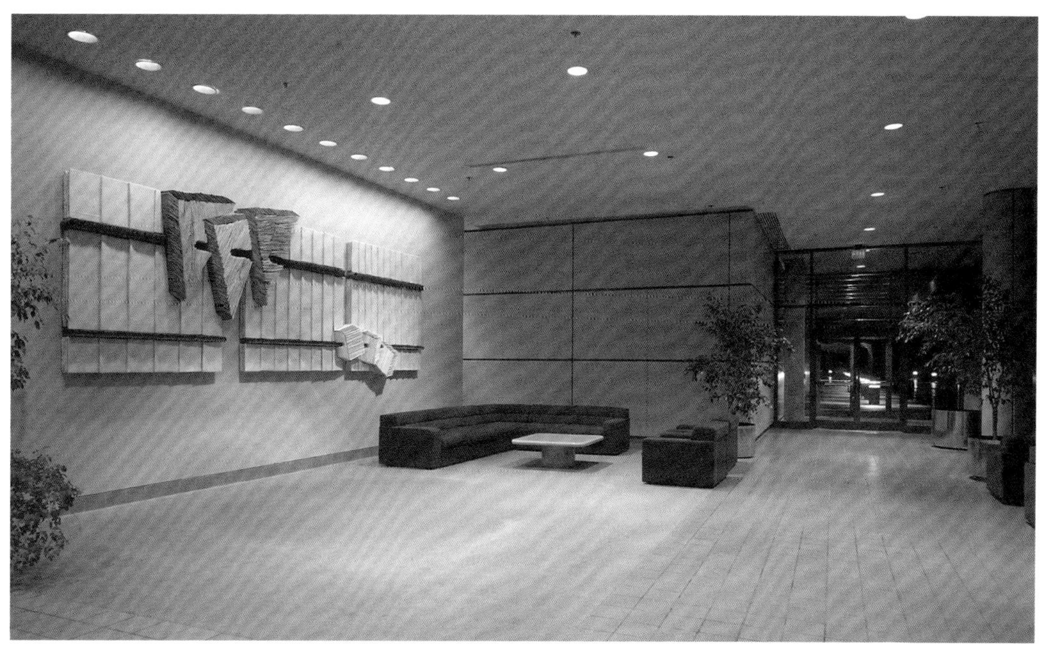

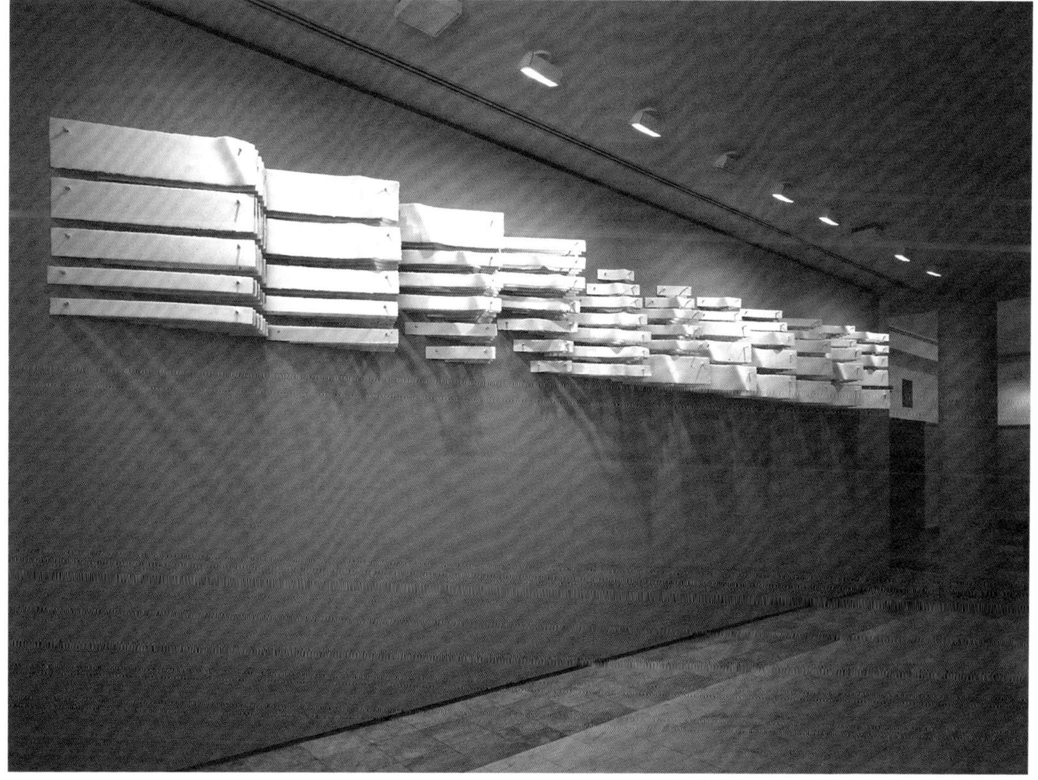

CUBIK THEMES 1981 CERAMIC, METALLIC OXIDE ON PANEL 108" X 240" X 10" IBM, CHARLOTTE, NC

DIAGONAL FRIEZE 1986 CERAMIC AND STEEL 36" X 396" X 18"
STATE OF CONNECTICUT, STATE SUPERIOR COURTHOUSE, ENFIELD, CT

of twenty years, and I wanted a change from the isolation of working in my studio. I wanted to be around people: creative, energetic, smart, innovative people. I needed and wanted to be in a collaborative creative situation. I realized that CD-ROM was a medium that was collaborative by nature and could offer unlimited ways of creative exploration. I had to make a living, and I began to think about the medium in ways that might produce income. In and of itself, trying to make a living from my art was not a new experience for me—but this was a new medium with very exciting possibilities. I began to develop projects around the notion of how artists make art. Recruiting my friends from all the reserves of talented people around me, I embarked on an amazing journey into the brave new world. We felt like we were all in a scene from *Close Encounters* and were moving toward this mountain: nothing had happened, there were no rules, and everything was possible.

It was an exciting time in a nascent industry, when all the movers and shakers were creative talent coming from other fields, defining and generating "The Next New Thing"—and we were it! It was a time of open collaboration, sharing, innovation, and unlimited opportunity. I was given the chance to select a team of programmers, animators, and videographers to digitally develop my concepts and bring them to fruition. As creative director, I worked from artistic imagination and invention and with no preconceived notion of what could or could not be done in this new field, and therefore I was able to direct and inspire truly original, imaginative, and often ingenious projects. These projects won awards and opened doors to all kinds of offers to lead other technology ventures. I was fortunate to be in at the right time, and for a few years I rode the wave, including travel and financial rewards. It was a great ride.

Even though I had been working regularly in the print studio, where I could put to use my new level of understanding of luminous color, I was hungry to get back into my own studio full time. I was filled with a fresh sense of invention and innovative possibilities and was eager to be immersed again in the solitude of my space; isn't that how it always goes?

The experience of the digital domain has, however, actually become a great creative tool that informs the work I do today. What was once more of a conceptual relationship has been refined into an educated and familiar association, where I use a digital eye to reflect, capture, and archive my work. I am always open to new ways of seeing. I recently created a series of large-scale, modular digital-inkjet prints of my studio space for a solo exhibition at the Mississippi Museum of Art called *Work in Progress*.

When did you first know you were an artist?

I now realize that as a small child I saw all things as mutable images. I could look at something and turn it around in my mind; see all sides; imagine it another color, another texture, another scale. I could remember colors, reproduce them mentally—that is, conjure up a color like a smell or a sound. As a child, I thought everyone could, and did, do this. I did it as naturally as breathing, so I thought it was a

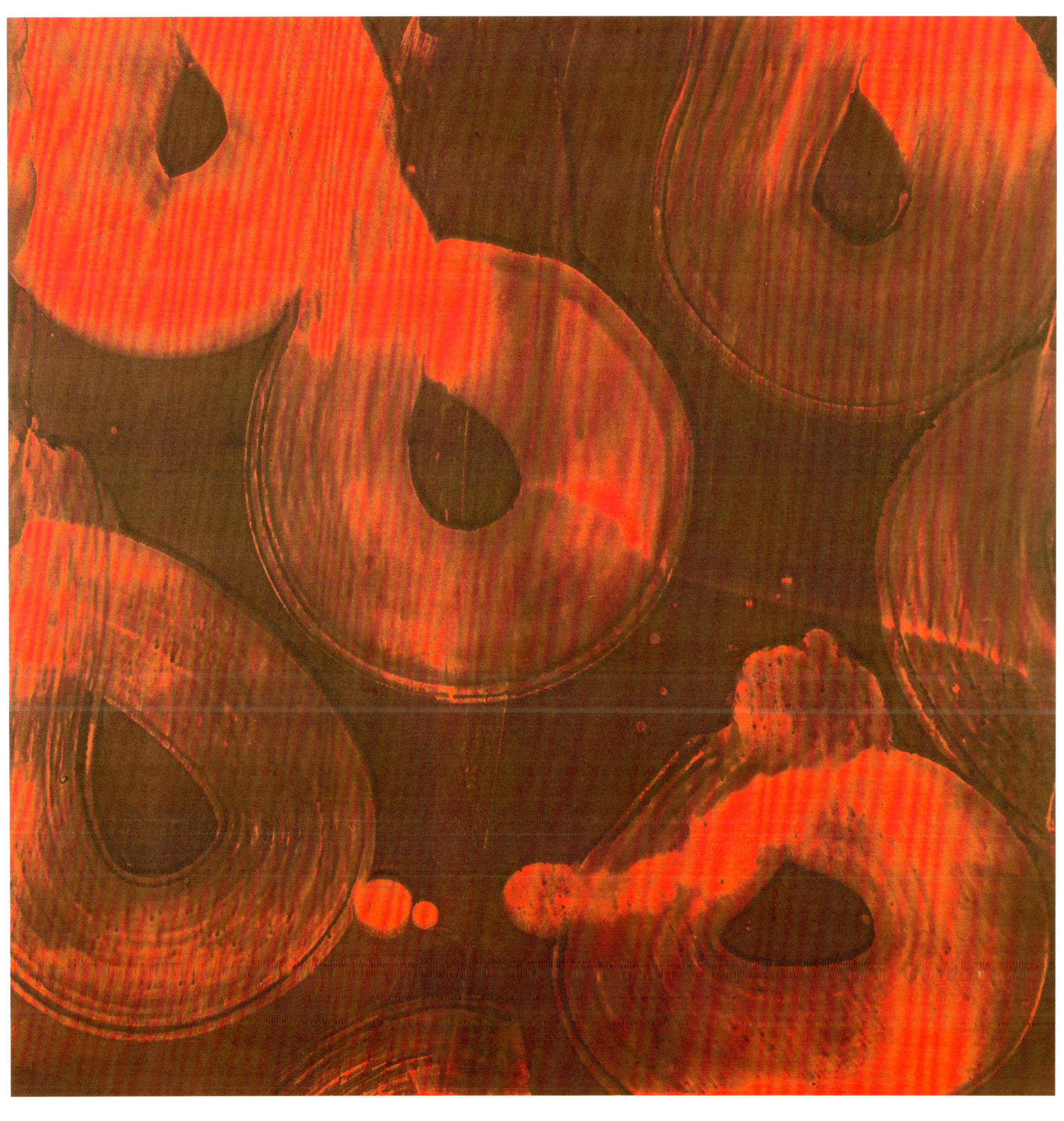

PERSIMMON 1997 OIL ON PAPER 24" X 24"

capricious skill with no redeeming value. When I was maybe eight years old I realized, from interactions with my friends and even some adults, that this was a gift; it was special, and it made me different—it made me an artist.

Did your family recognize this gift and encourage your artistic abilities?

My older sister had been designated "the artist" in the family. She took regular art classes, so I felt that she had that spot covered and I had to find something else. It didn't occur to me that even if she did choose to study art, I could as well. A child sometimes has parochial impressions of things. I was already an artist, but I thought I'd just have to learn to be something else because there was one spot and it had already been filled. Fortunately, my sister ended up choosing another path, so the coast was clear. My parents were surprised when I told them I was going to study art; they thought I would make a good lawyer.

The high school I attended hired a new young art teacher, Ralph Pasquinucci, who offered a fresh, vibrant approach to art. He was tuned in and knew that I was motivated, talented, and committed. He paved the way for me to look at, take in, and begin to conceive of a life as an artist. I began reading about artists and having dreams of going to Paris, studying and living among artists. Modigliani interested me. I wrote an essay about him for my school newspaper. He was a romantic figure with a recognizable personal style.

What attracted you to Queens College?

Well, my options were limited—limited by my parents' financial situation and by their vision of who I was, who I was going to be, and how I was going to live. There would be no art studies in Paris, no life among artists. At that time I really had no support for learning how the world worked and how to put the pieces together on my own. So I had to figure out a way to do everything—explore the world, grow internally, and live within my family's version of my future—while also trying to create my own adventure. You have to understand, it was 1961 and there were distinct stereotypes that we were expected to fit into. I was a girl on the twirling team; in fact, I was selected, with five other girls from my high school, to compete in an Arnold Constable Charm and Beauty Contest. At the time, there were proscribed things young women could aspire to. In my world, being an artist, especially a serious artist, didn't fit; it just wouldn't do. You could of course be a teacher, teach art—that was approved, acceptable. Queens College was nearby, and I was awarded a New York State Regents Scholarship that covered my tuition and book costs. However, it meant that I would be living in my parents' home.

What was it like at Queens College at that time?

Surprisingly, Queens College turned out to be fantastic. It followed the basic Columbia University curriculum, which gave students a strong, academically rigorous liberal arts education and excellent fine arts training. The school was a magnet for accomplished artists as teachers, and I was blessed with some marvelous ones: Barse Miller, Barbara Rose, and John Ferren—a fine artist, a lovely man, and an extremely dedicated teacher. He taught my favorite class, color theory. It was a fantastic experience, working on projects that formed the juncture between theory and practice. In that environment, I began to develop a cultured eye.

As chair of the Arts Study Group, I planned the programs and one semester invited Larry Poons to come and speak. He brought Andy Warhol with him and stirred up the department with his fierce pronouncements about artists not needing to learn to draw or have any formal training or education to be great artists. From Poons on that day, I was introduced to the idea that artists find ways to do what they need to do. Starting then, over time, I developed my own mantra that if you have a strong concept, you will learn whatever it is you need to know in order to bring that concept to life.

After your sophomore year in college, you got married. You were just nineteen...

Why does anyone get married? I met this great guy, Gary Katz, in camp when I was sixteen, and we fell in love. He was handsome, athletic, and planning to be a lawyer, and he liked the fact that I was an artist. He was a partner in every good and wonderful sense of the word, and with him it became safe—and acceptable—to do the things I couldn't do on my own.

After graduating Queens College, you traveled with your husband to Israel and then to Europe. How did that influence your art? How was that important to you as an artist?

In every way. We wanted adventure. My cousins had joined the Peace Corps, and we thought about that before deciding to go to Israel as Olim, new immigrants. I had just read *Exodus*. We were to be the new pioneers, and we were. We lived in an absorption center, with other immigrants from all over—Romania, Poland, Russia, Morocco, Tunisia—and a group of young American archaeology students. We were forging a new path as part of a group; we had a mission and wanted adventure. We were doing something for the world and for ourselves. Because we arranged officially to go to Israel as Olim immigrants, the government helped with our arrangements; provided an initial place to stay; and placed Gary, who was fluent in Hebrew, with an accounting firm in Jerusalem. We traveled by Vespa all over the country, slept on the beach at Haifa, and climbed Masada before sunrise. It was an exciting and wonderful time.

I was looking to continue studying painting and was introduced to Ruth Bamberger, who was an admired Israeli artist. I went every day to visit her in her old Arab house in Mea Shearim, the ancient part of the city. She took me under her wing. She is the one who taught me how to cook with olive oil, how to eat artichokes, and how to bargain in the souk, the Arab market. Most of all, she provided me with a vision, a time line of how life could be: that I could be a woman, an artist, a wife, and a mother. She also taught

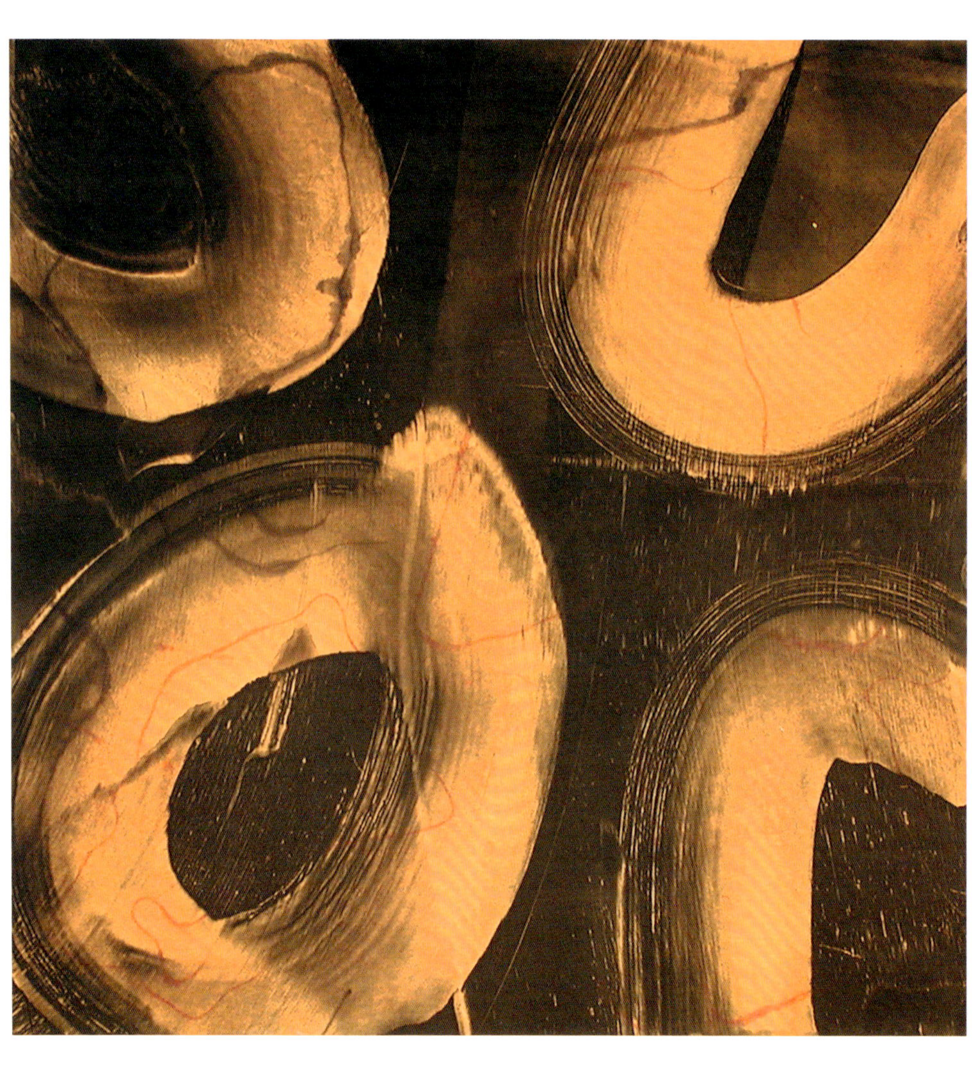

GOOD & PLENTY XIV 2002 OIL ON PAPER MONOTYPE 32" X 32"
THE MUSEUM OF FINE ARTS, HOUSTON, HOUSTON, TX

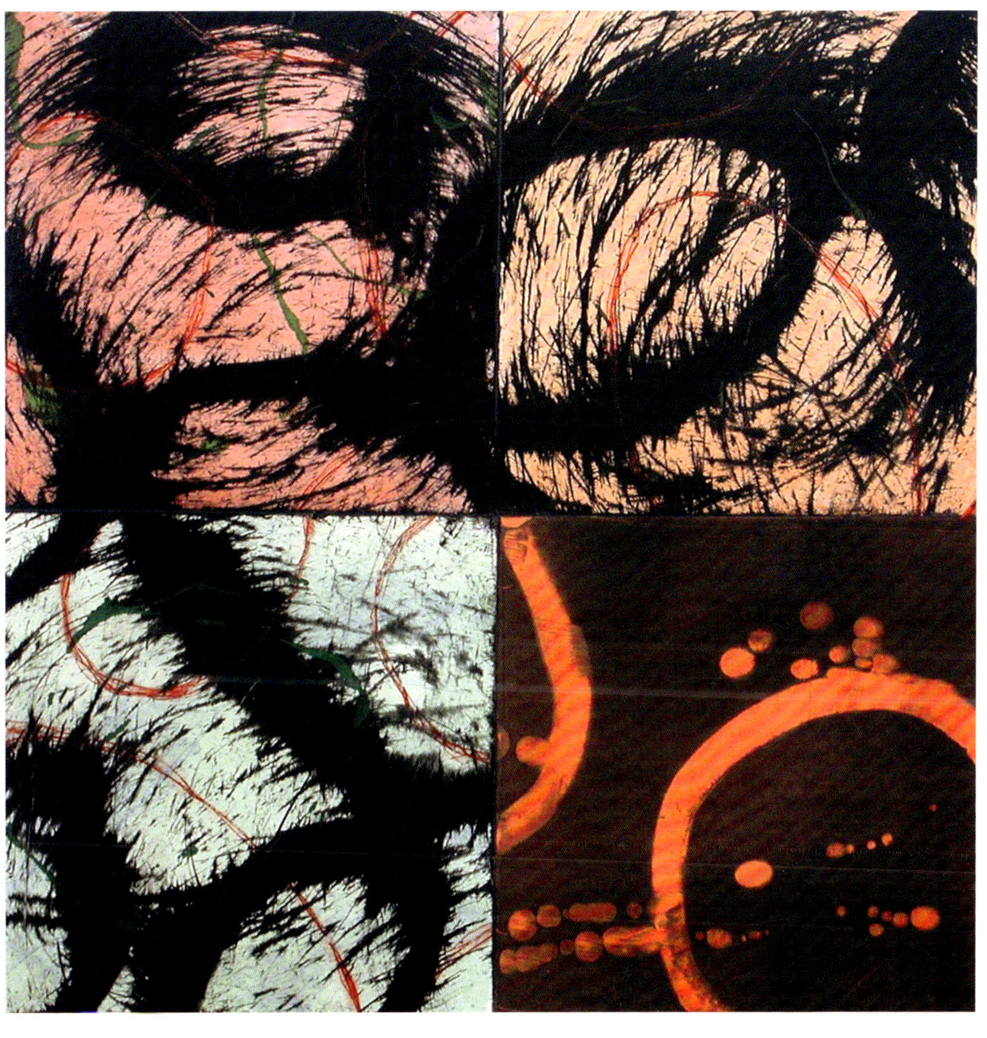

ACANTHUS QUATTRO XXVI 2002 OIL ON PAPER MONOTYPE 32" X 32"
MINNEAPOLIS INSTITUTE OF ARTS, MINNEAPOLIS, MN

me patience, that I had time; that the urgency of creating work or a career was something that happened over time, not all at once. She was a role model. We sketched together; we studied etching together; we talked about art together. I relaxed and leaned into all these experiences.

What do you wish for the viewer who encounters your work?

I have no preconceived idea of what I want a viewer to see; if anything, I am more concerned about what the viewer feels. I think the emotional aspect of the work is a way in, an access, if there is any connection at all between artist and viewer. A goal is that the work resonates on some basis with each viewer, or engages a viewer on a visceral basis. The act of painting is a very intimate affair. It is my opportunity to be totally in a world of my own making, my own controlled reality. The paintings represent the outer limits of my desire to share that world, or to offer the viewer an access to his or her own private world. I set up the parameters, I create the rules of engagement, and I am the supreme commander. How many times in life do you get to do that? If the work is good, if the paintings are real, the viewer's encounter with them will take care of itself.

What's next?

I am always tying to figure out how to make color impactful, which is not the same thing as trying to make it bright or loud or even intense or noticeable. It's about creating a reaction, a memory, an experience. It's about bringing a primal recollection to the conscious or visceral surface of life.

Many of my recent paintings have been done in clear colors and high-value compositions. I'm thinking the next group will be more monochromatic, with softer hues and quieter values that will nonetheless possess vibrant intensity.

I like working where the degree of difficulty is high, the work is ambitious, and there is no clear or preconceived path to success. I need to stay in the moment—I can't just call it in. I am currently in the middle of a long group of paintings, which are stacked up in my head like airplanes waiting on a clear night to land at La Guardia. So that's what I'll be doing for a while. ⊞

(OVERLEAF) **DETAIL** PAGE 69

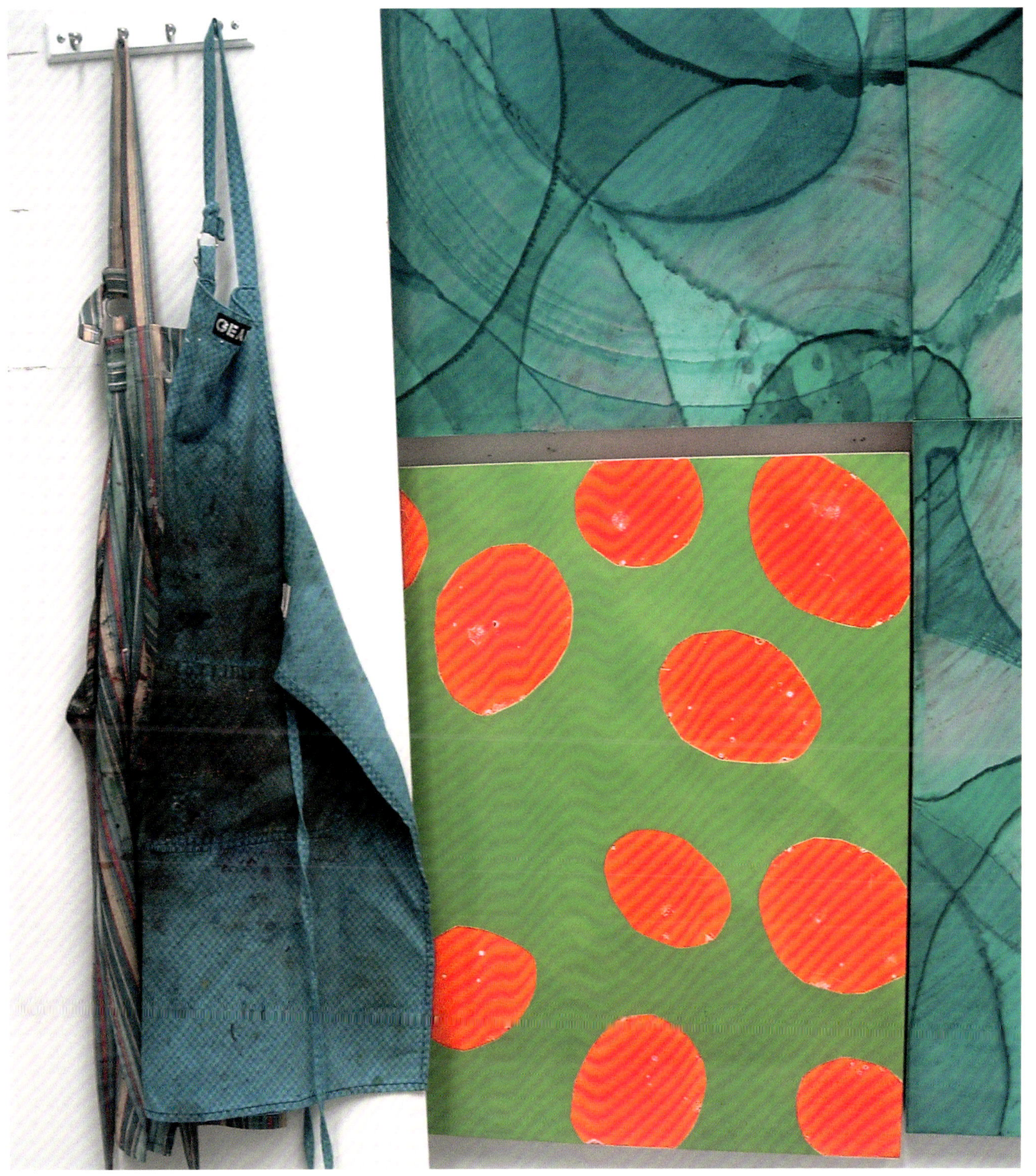

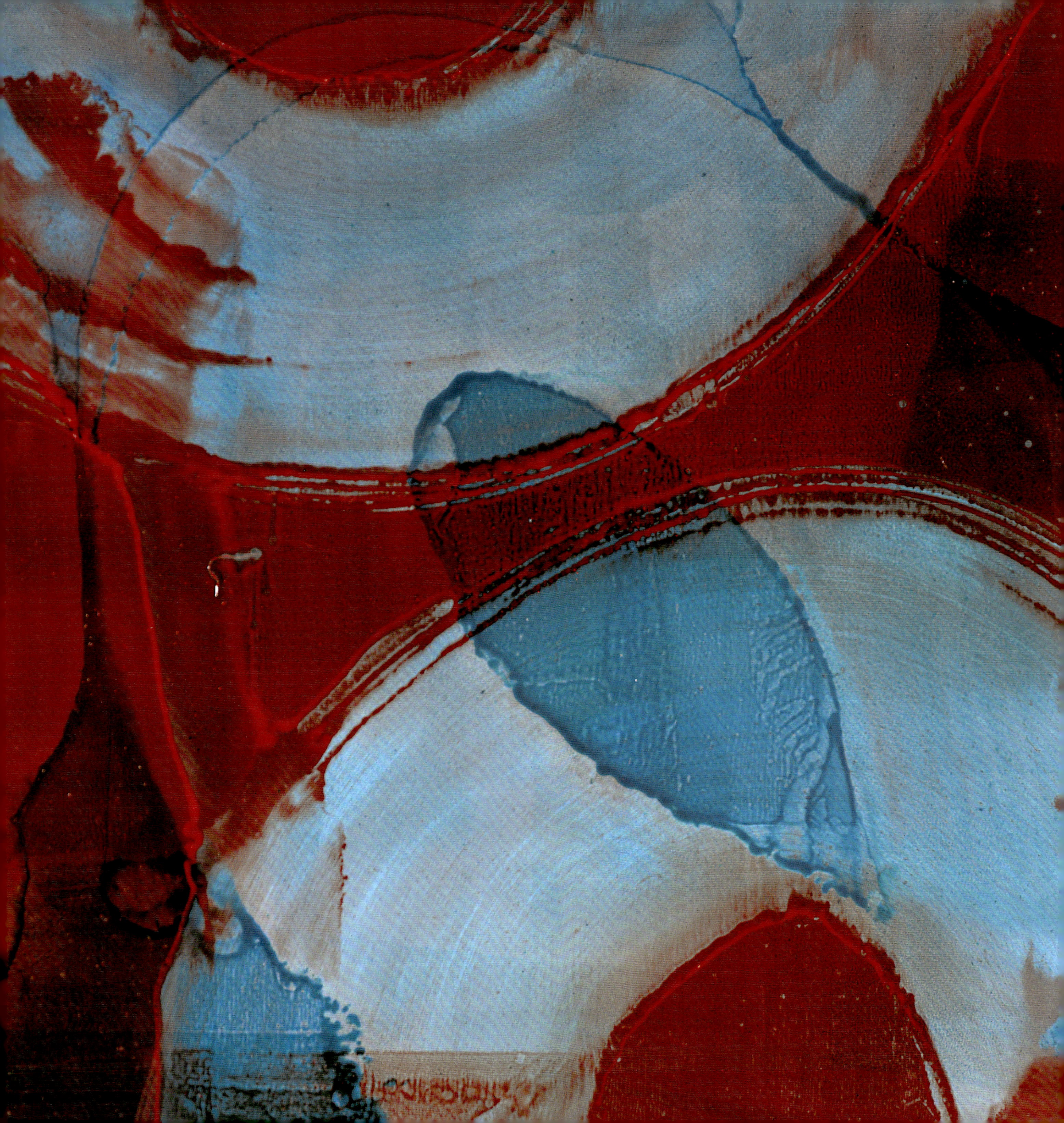

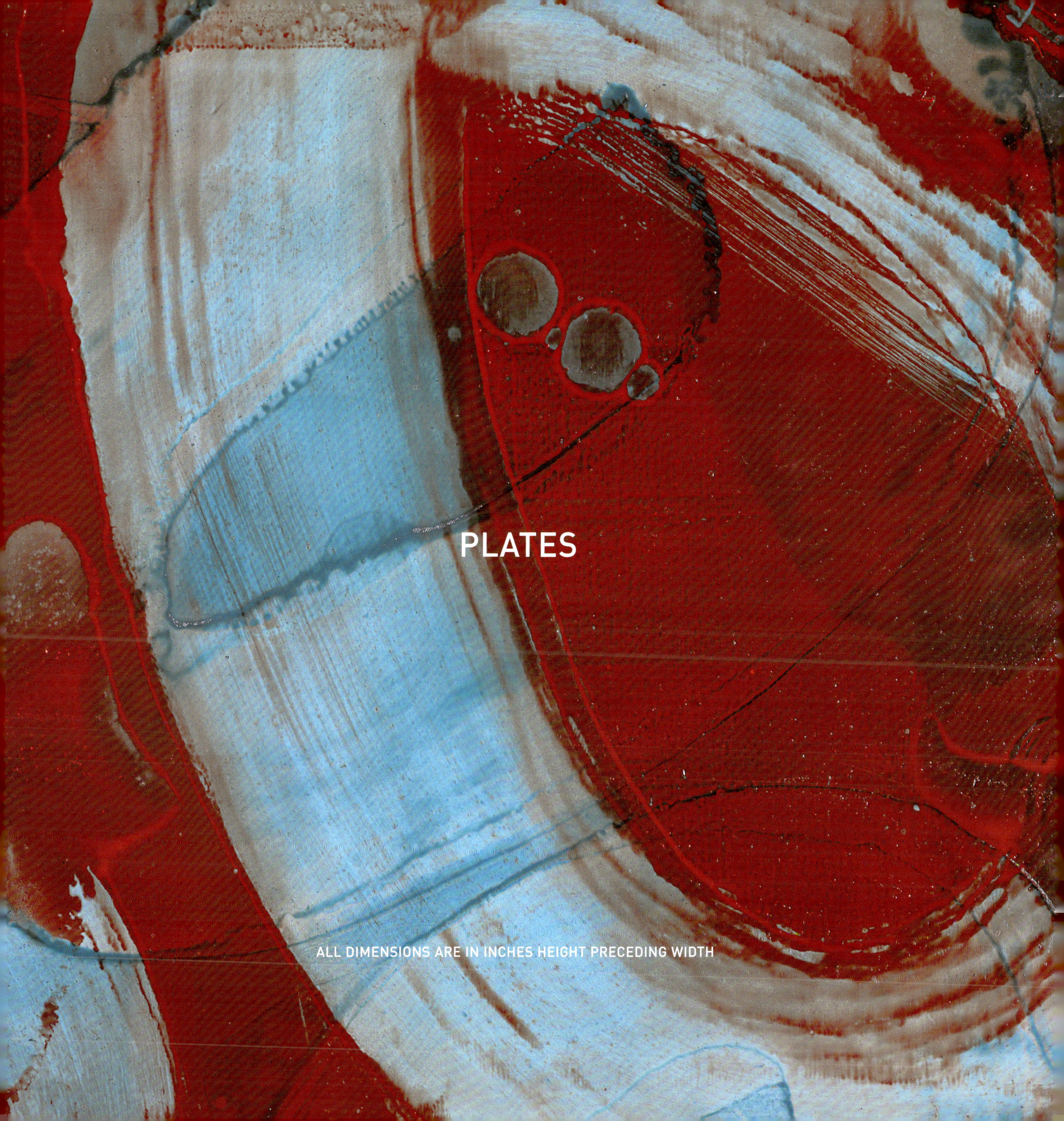

PLATES

ALL DIMENSIONS ARE IN INCHES HEIGHT PRECEDING WIDTH

BOSSA NOVA 2002 OIL ON STYRENE 48 X 48

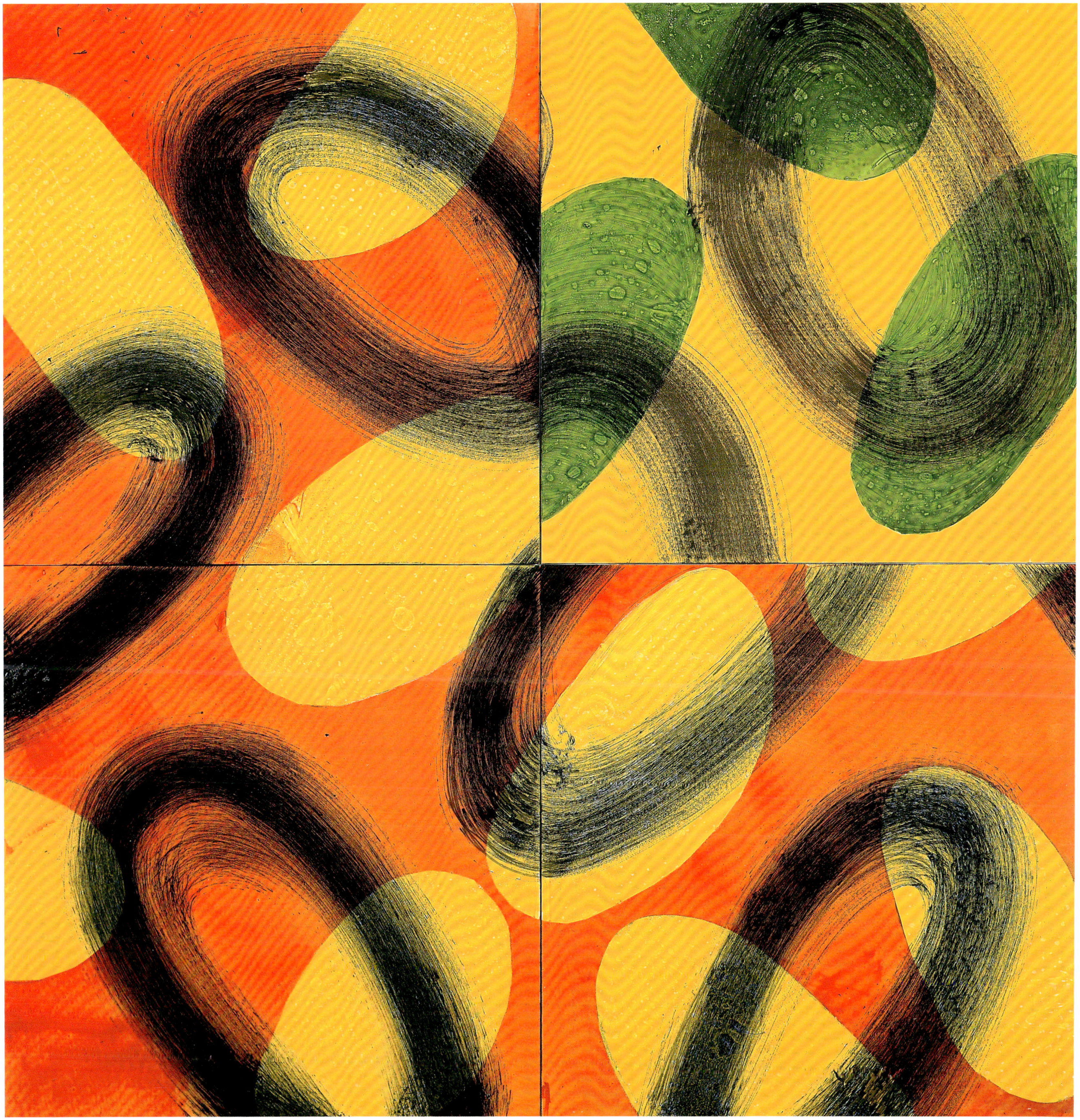

MAMBO 2002 OIL ON STYRENE 48 X 48

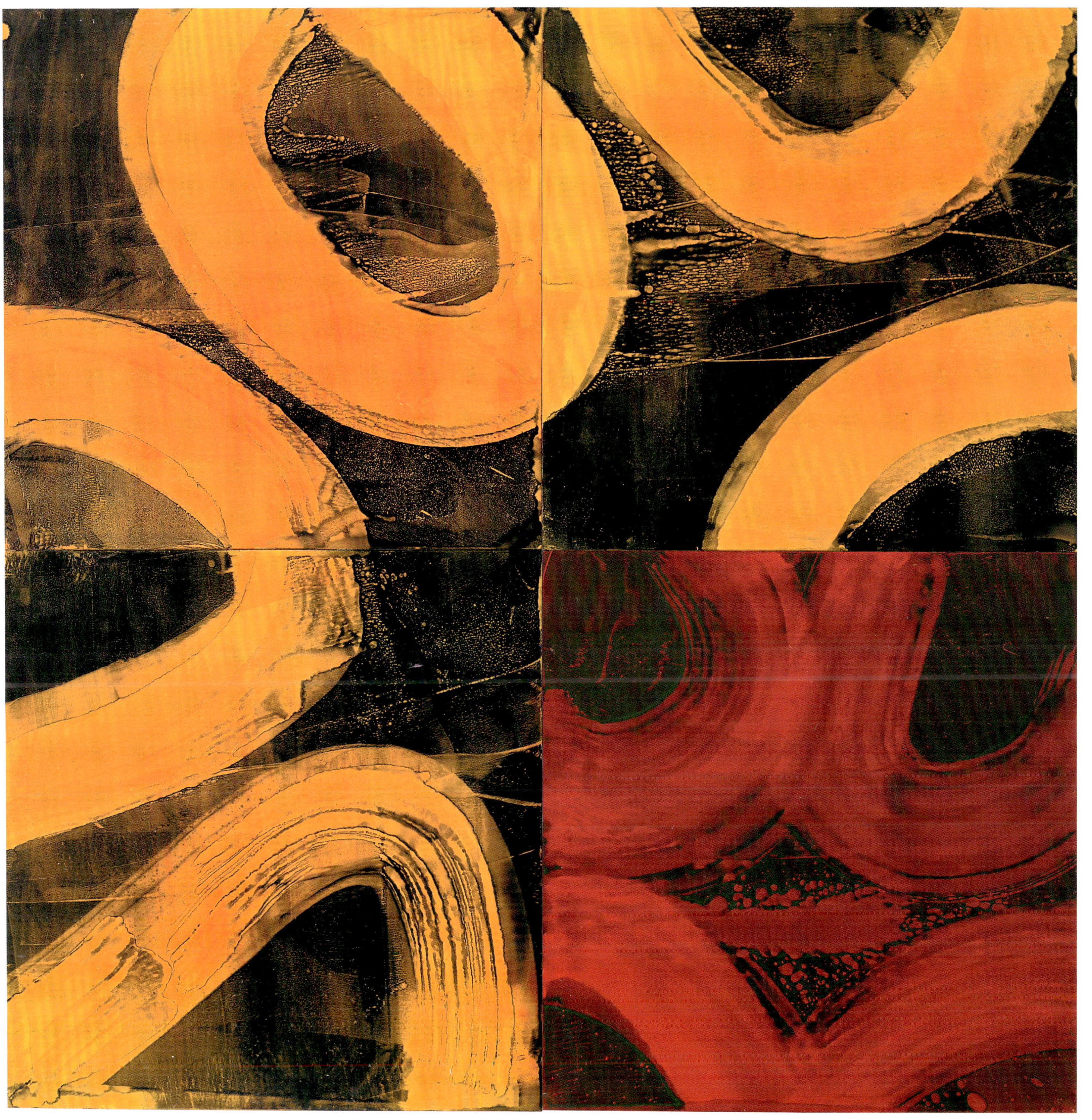

53

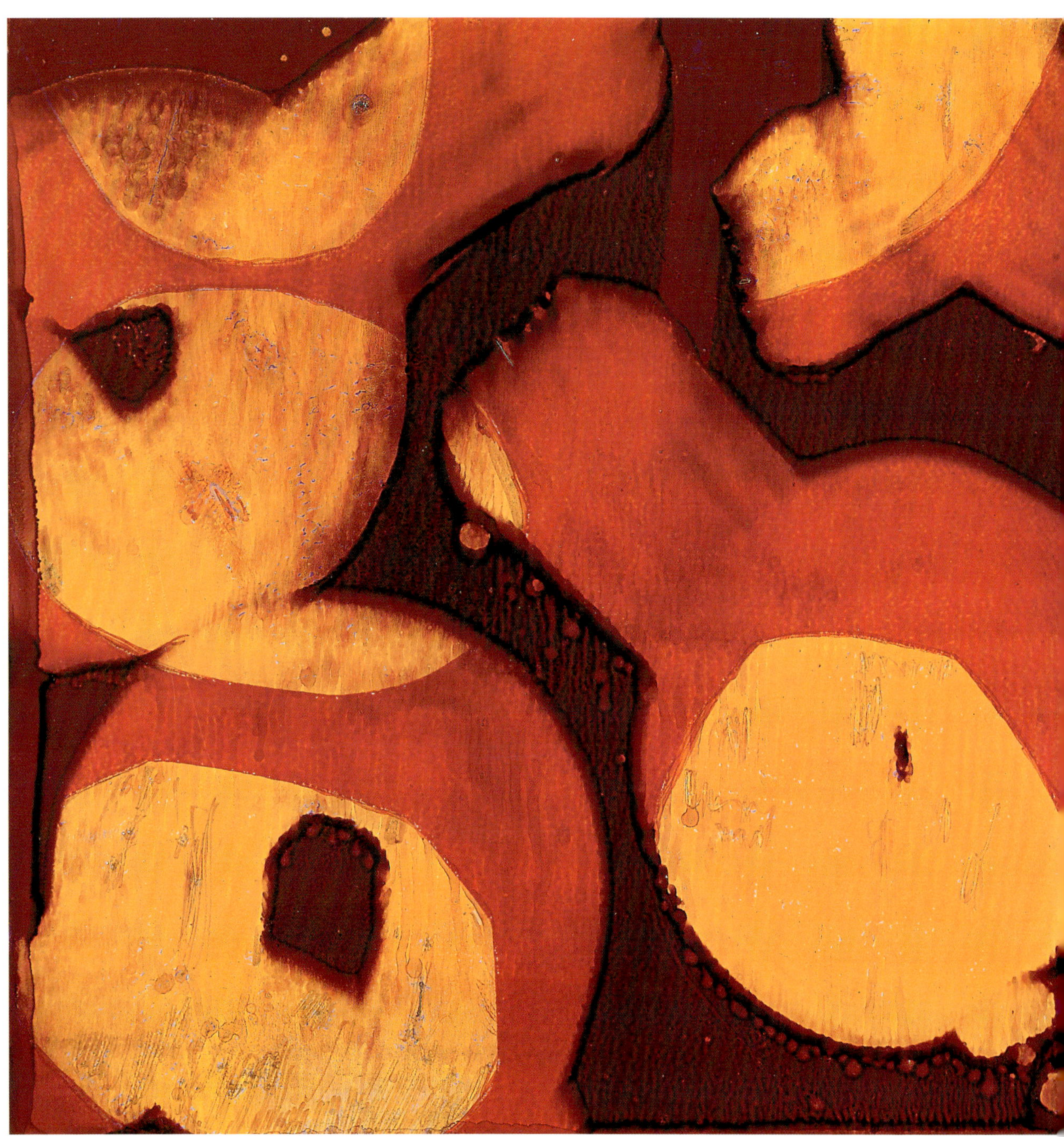

DUET: VERONA 2002–2003 OIL ON PANEL 12 X 24

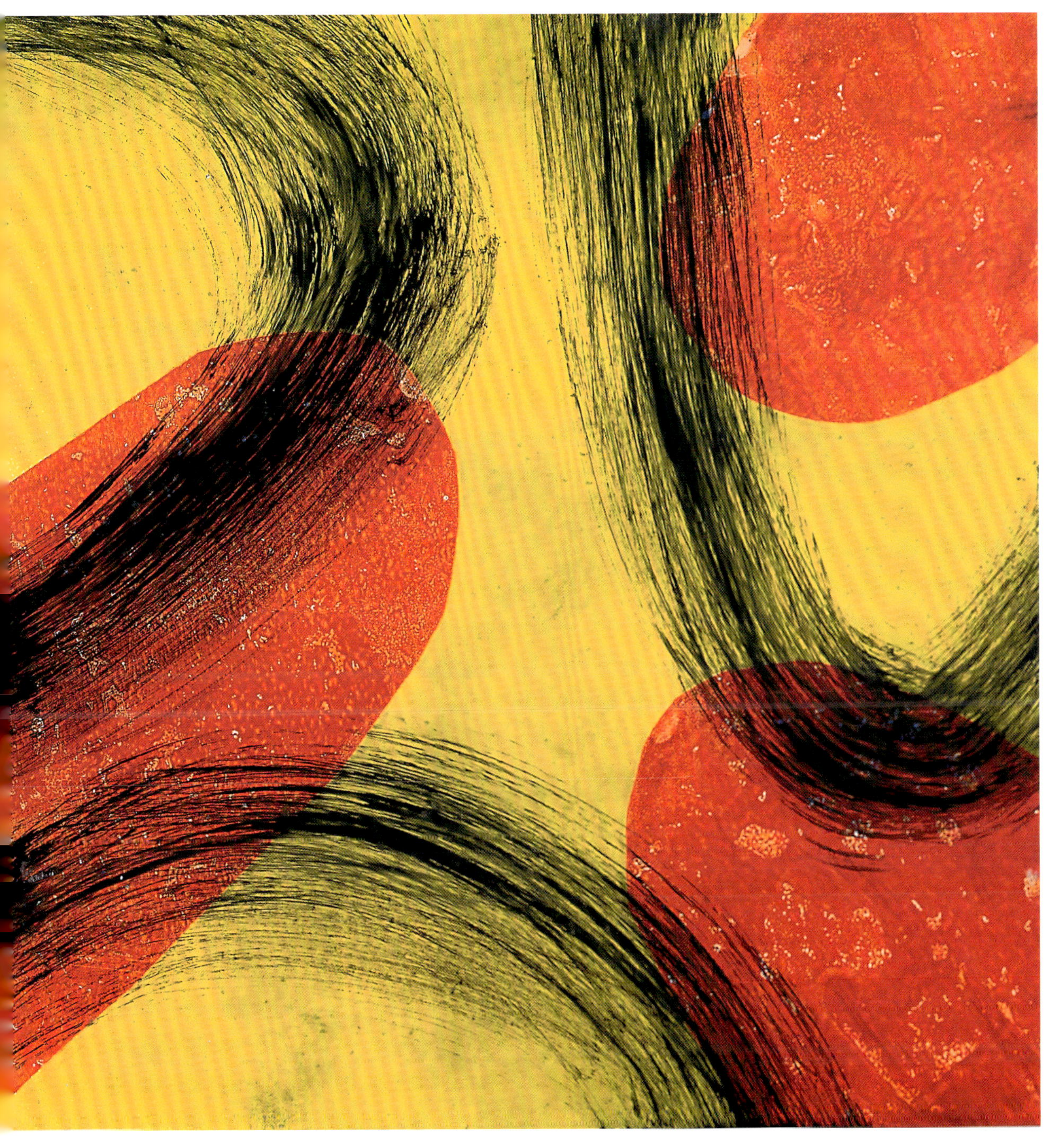

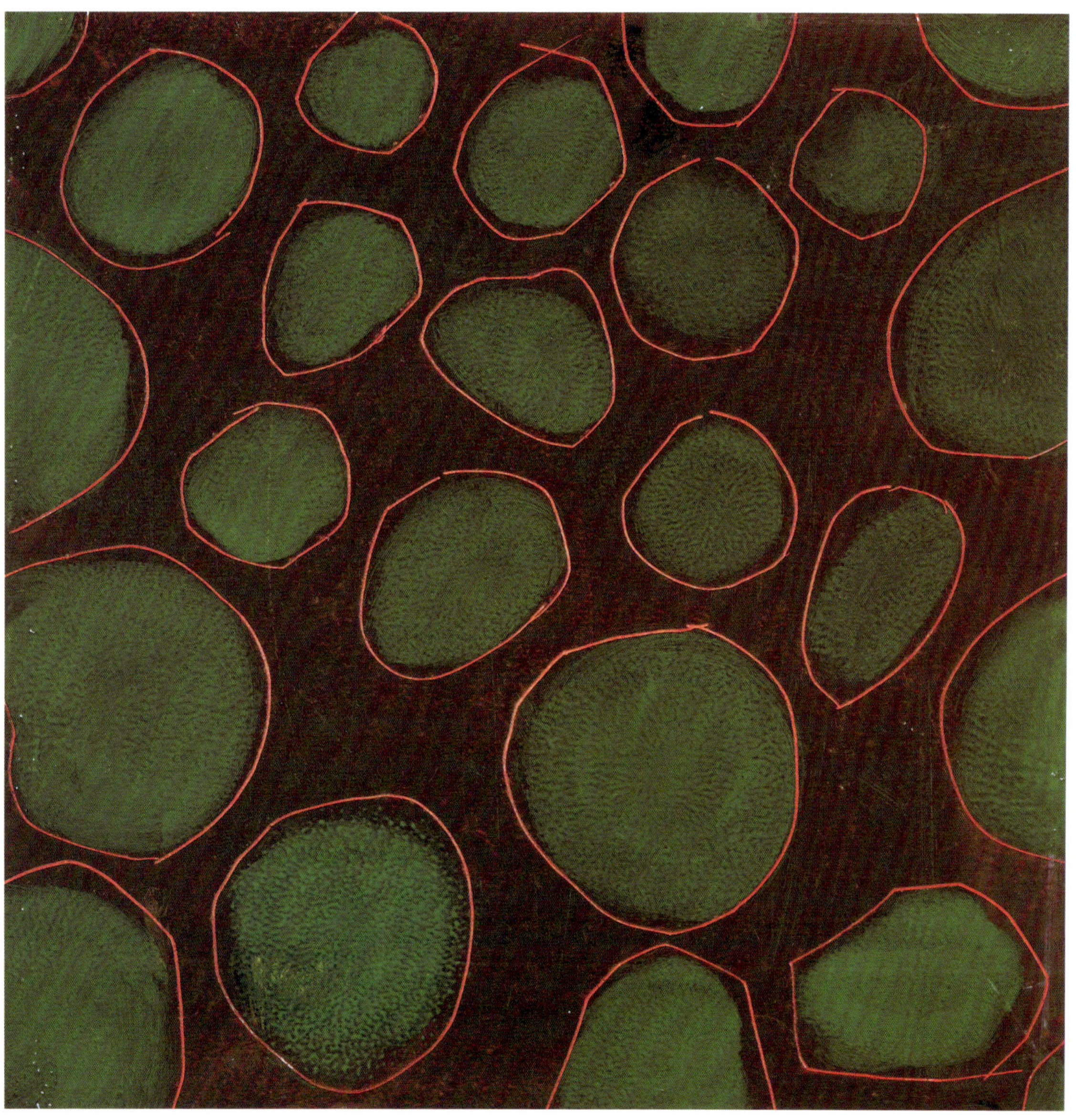

MOSS STONE 2003 OIL ON PANEL 8 X 8

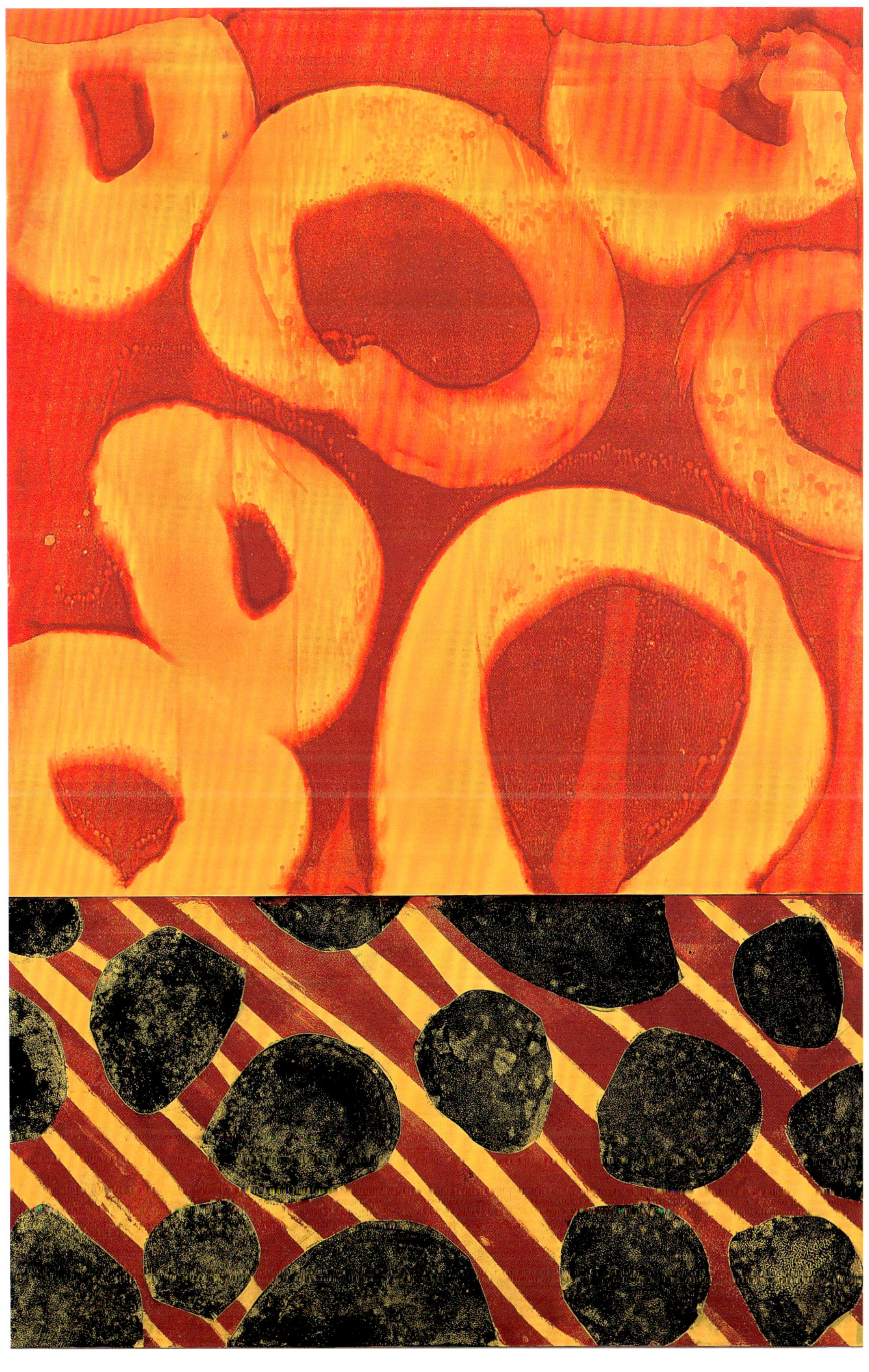

ROOTS & SHOOTS: ANATTO 2003 OIL ON PANEL 36 X 24

DO THE HUSTLE 2002 OIL ON STYRENE 48 X 48

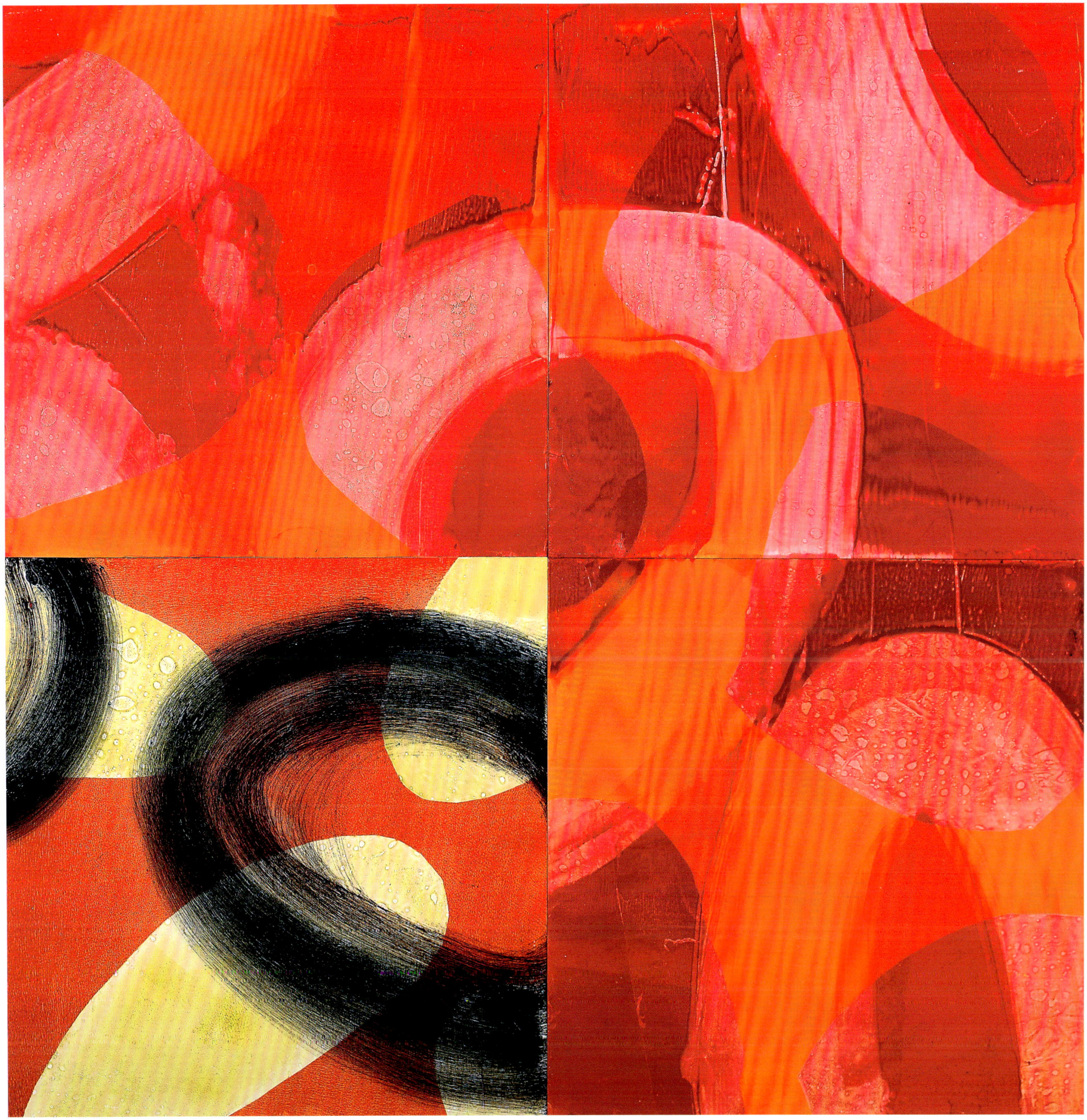

60

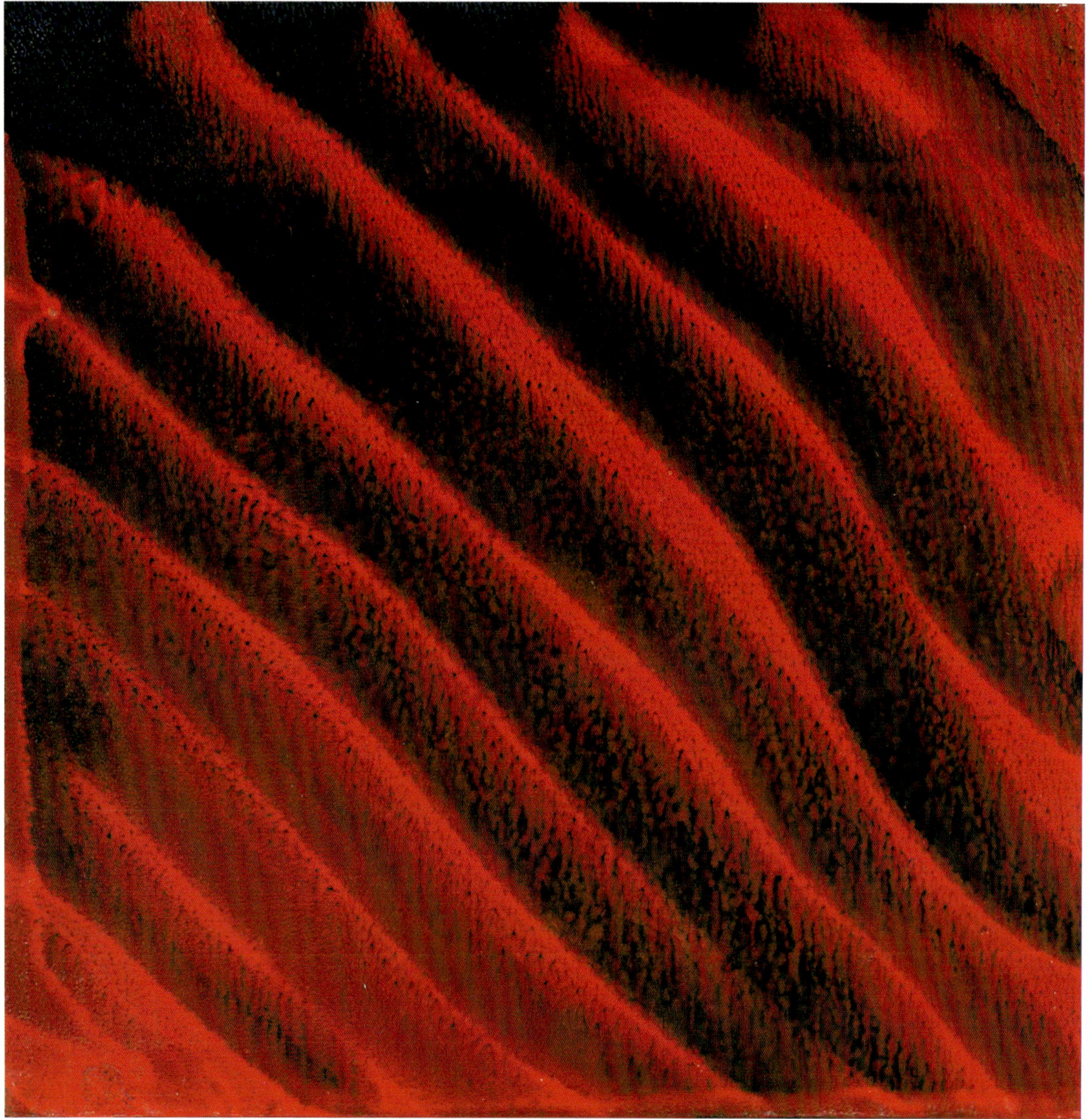

UNO STROLL 2003 OIL ON PANEL 8 X 8

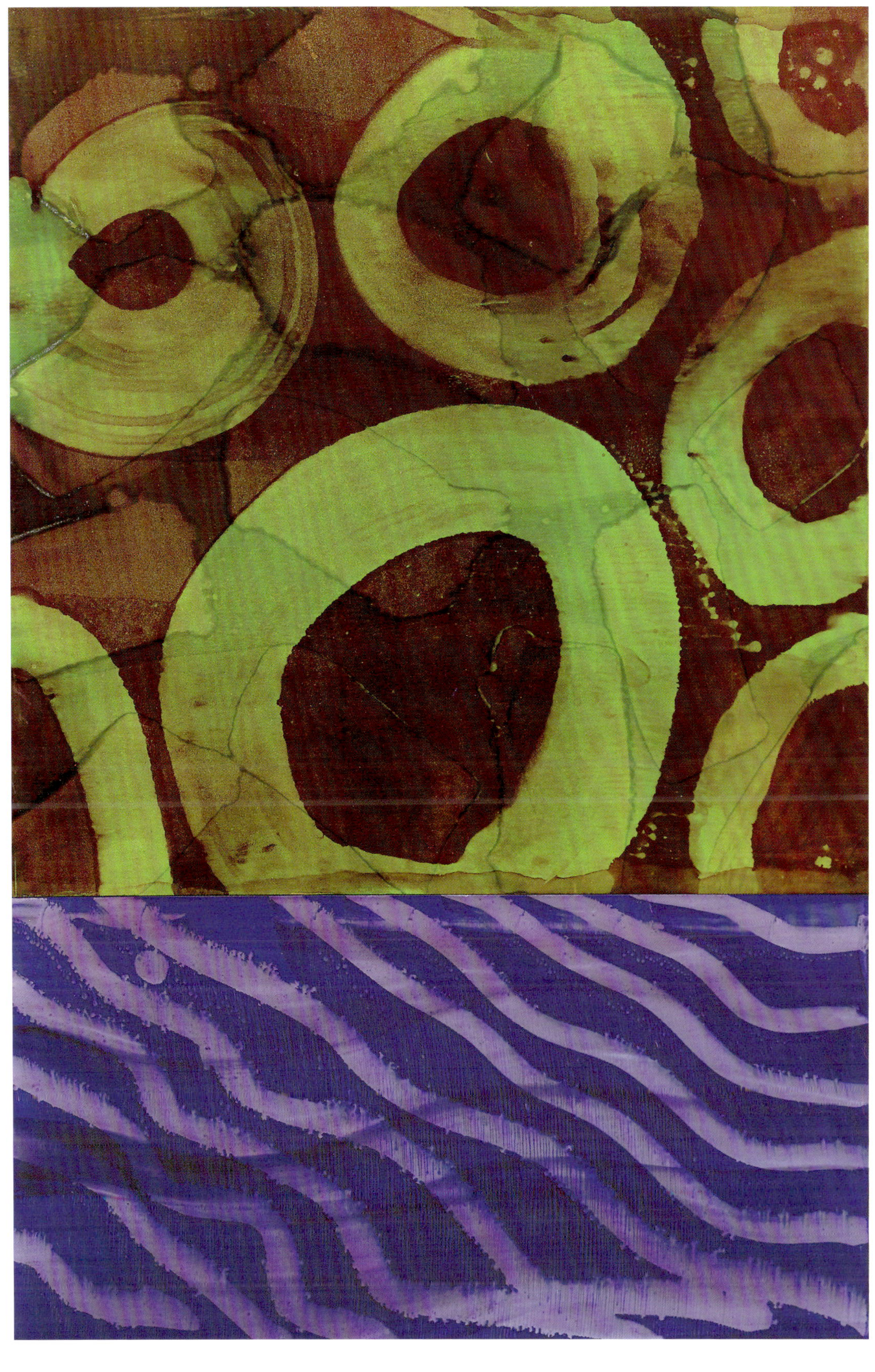

ROOTS & SHOOTS: COLEUS 2005 OIL ON PANEL 36 X 24

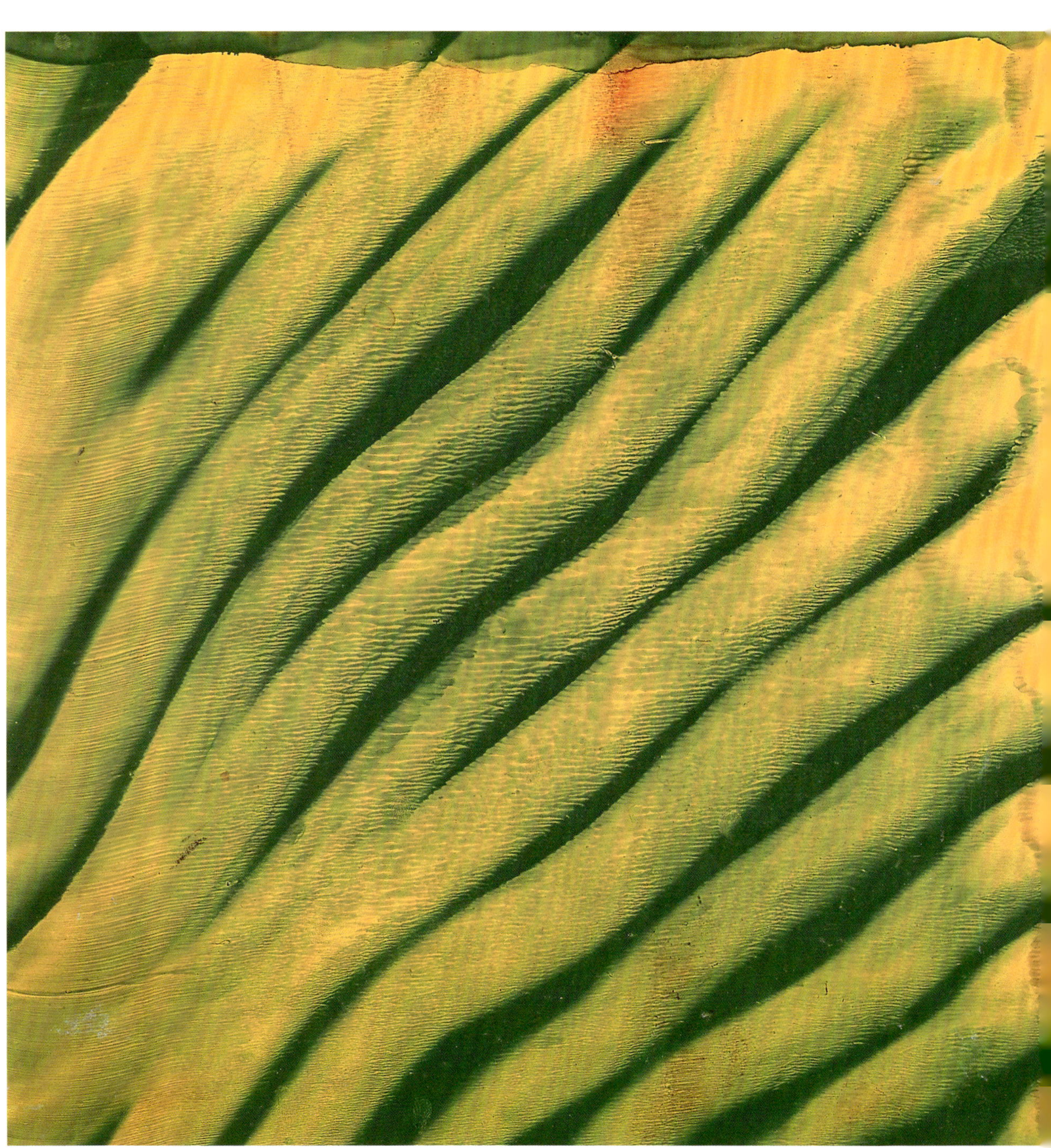

DUET: STAVANGER 2004 OIL ON PANEL 12 X 24

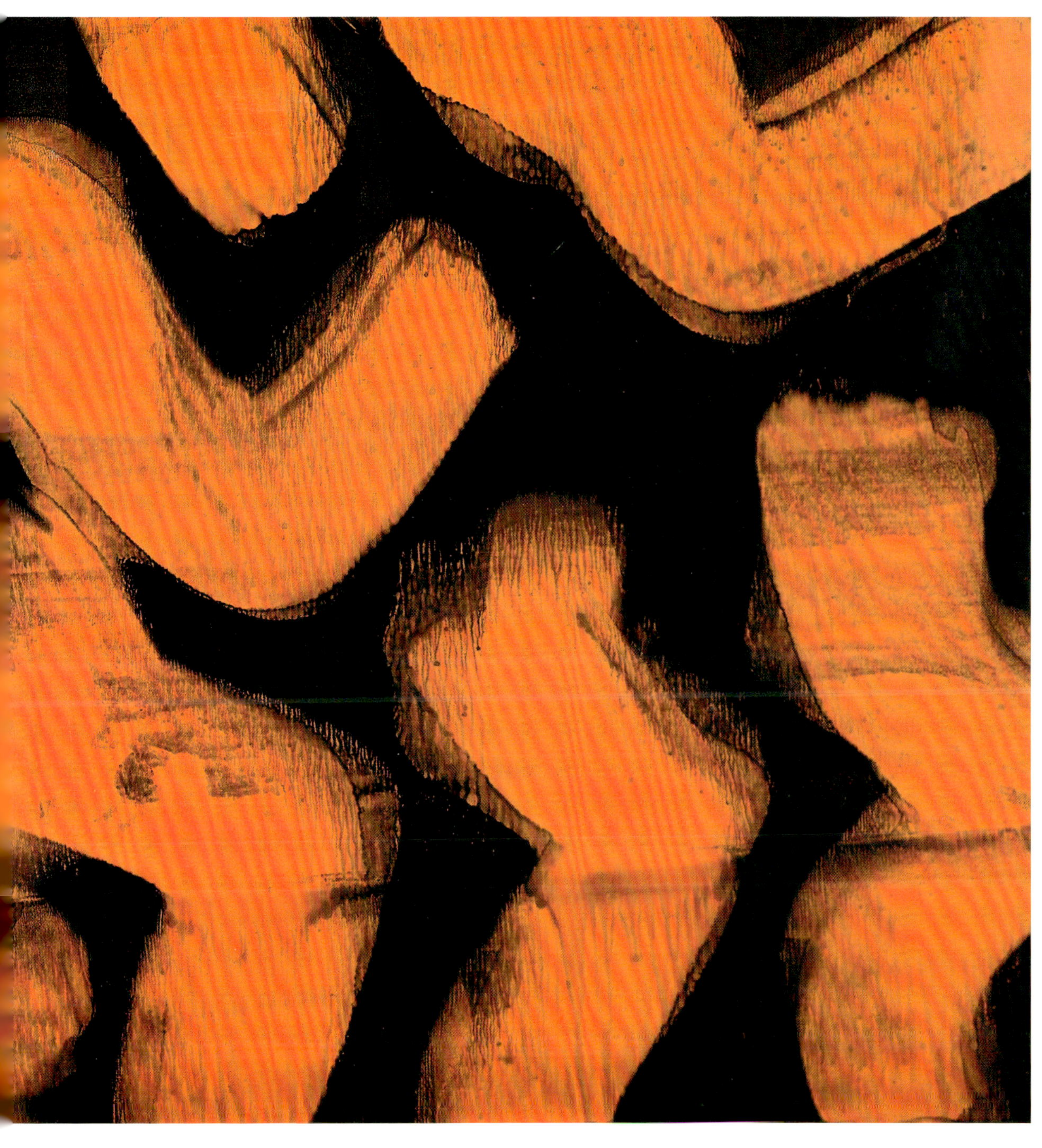

BOULDER CONSTELLATION 2004 OIL ON PANEL 48 X 48

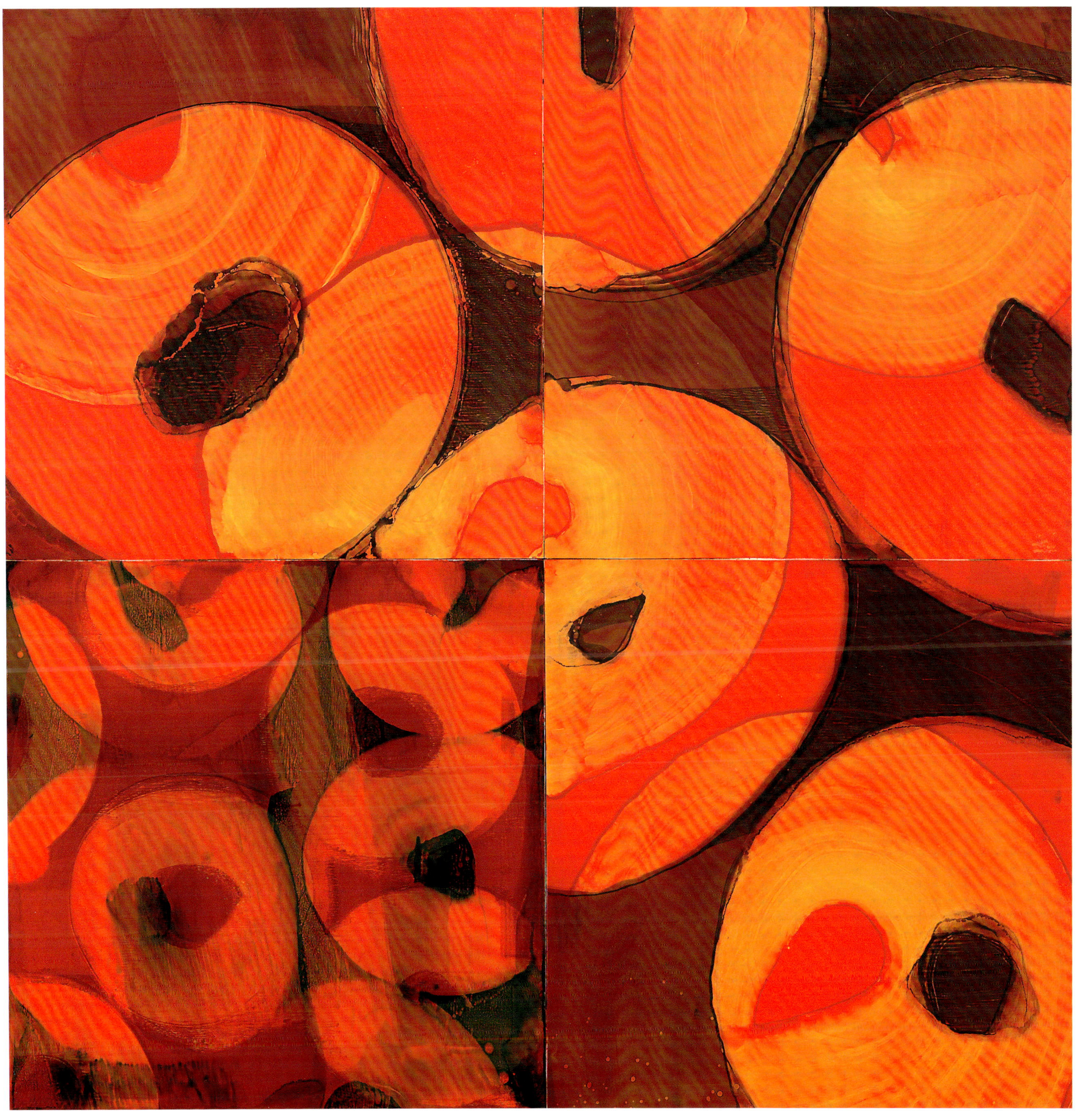

BLOOD ORANGE & CITRUS SKYY 2004 OIL ON PANEL 48 X 48

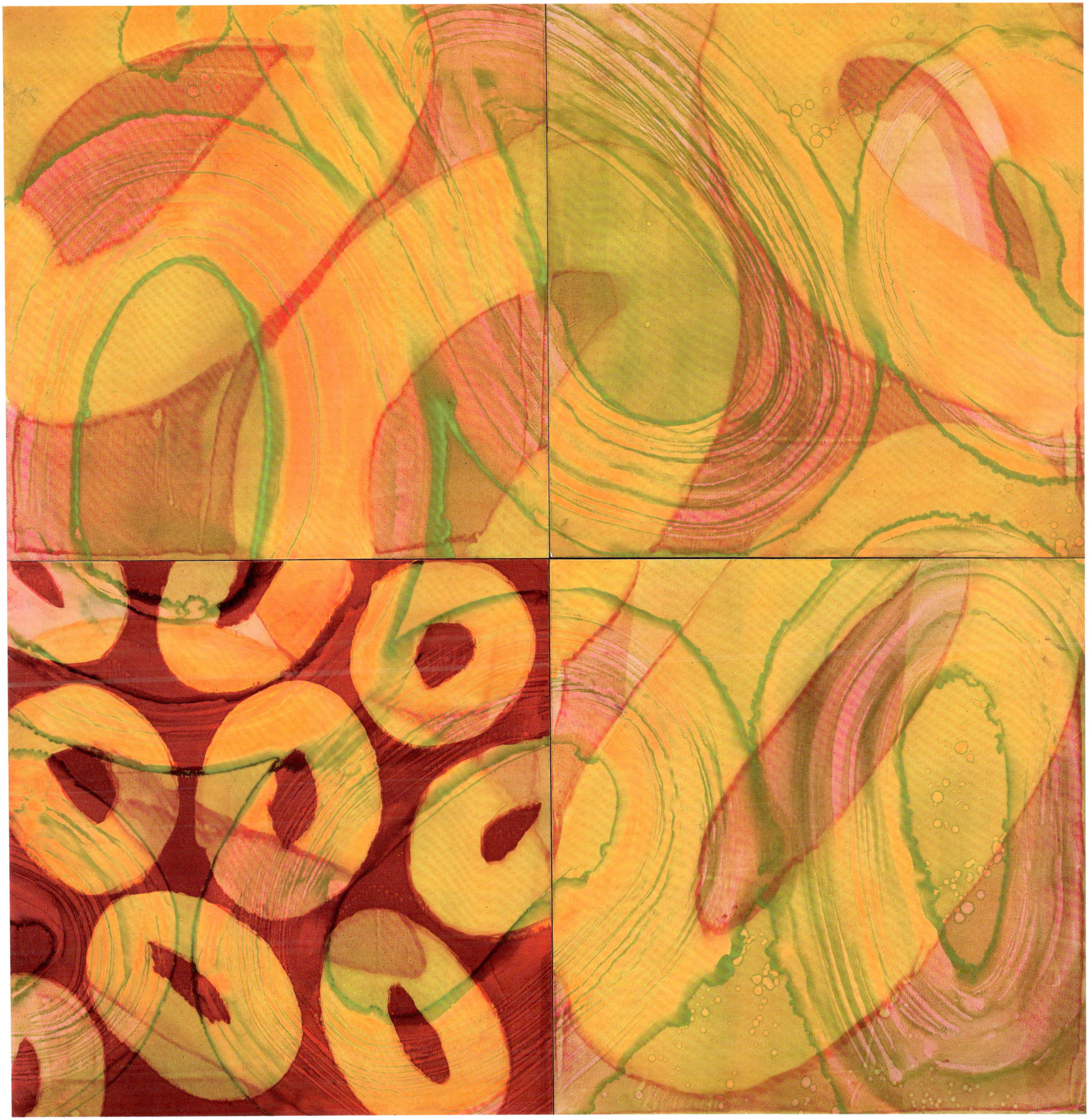

UNSPOKEN REFLECTION 2004 OIL ON PANEL 48 X 48

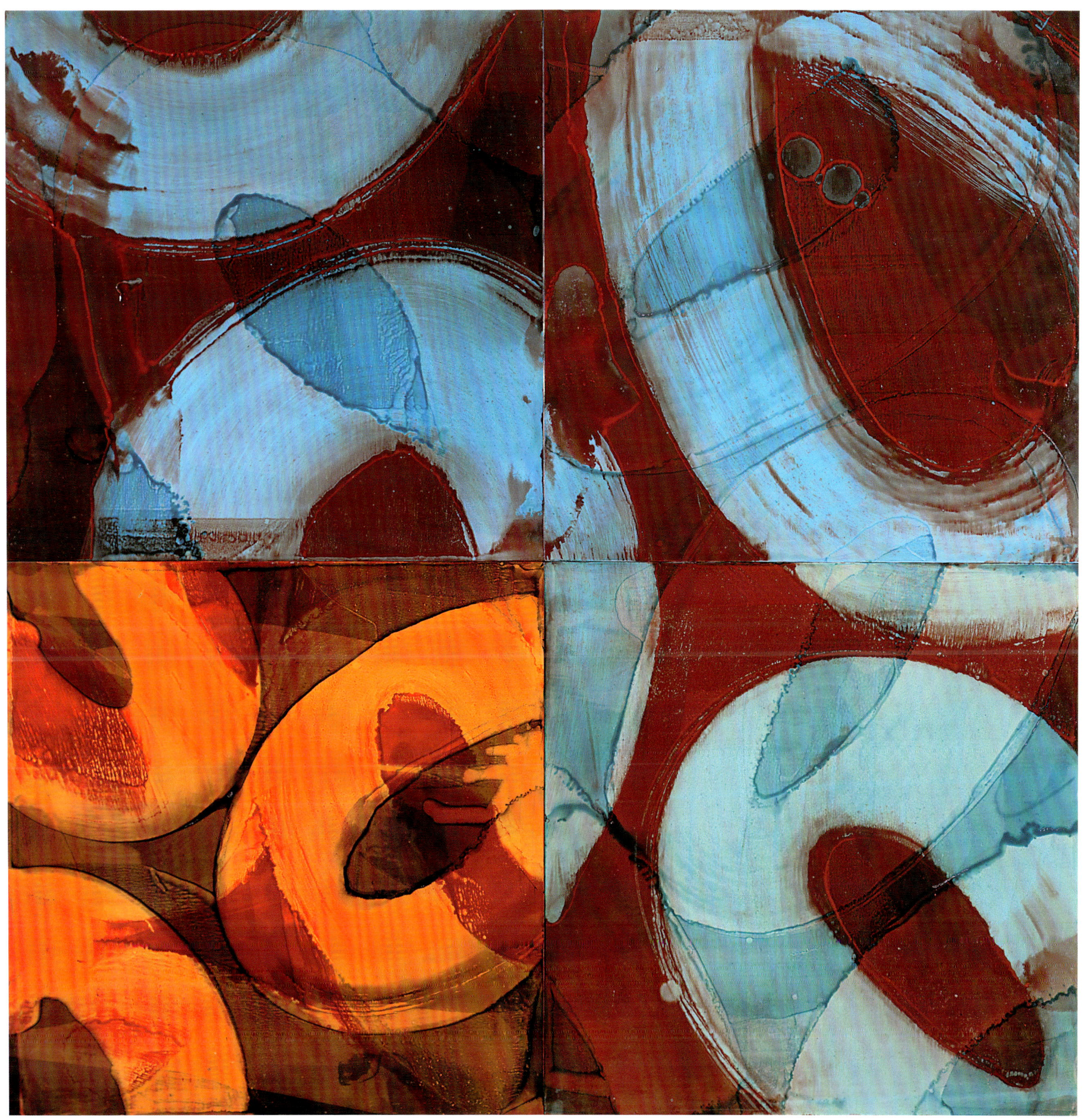

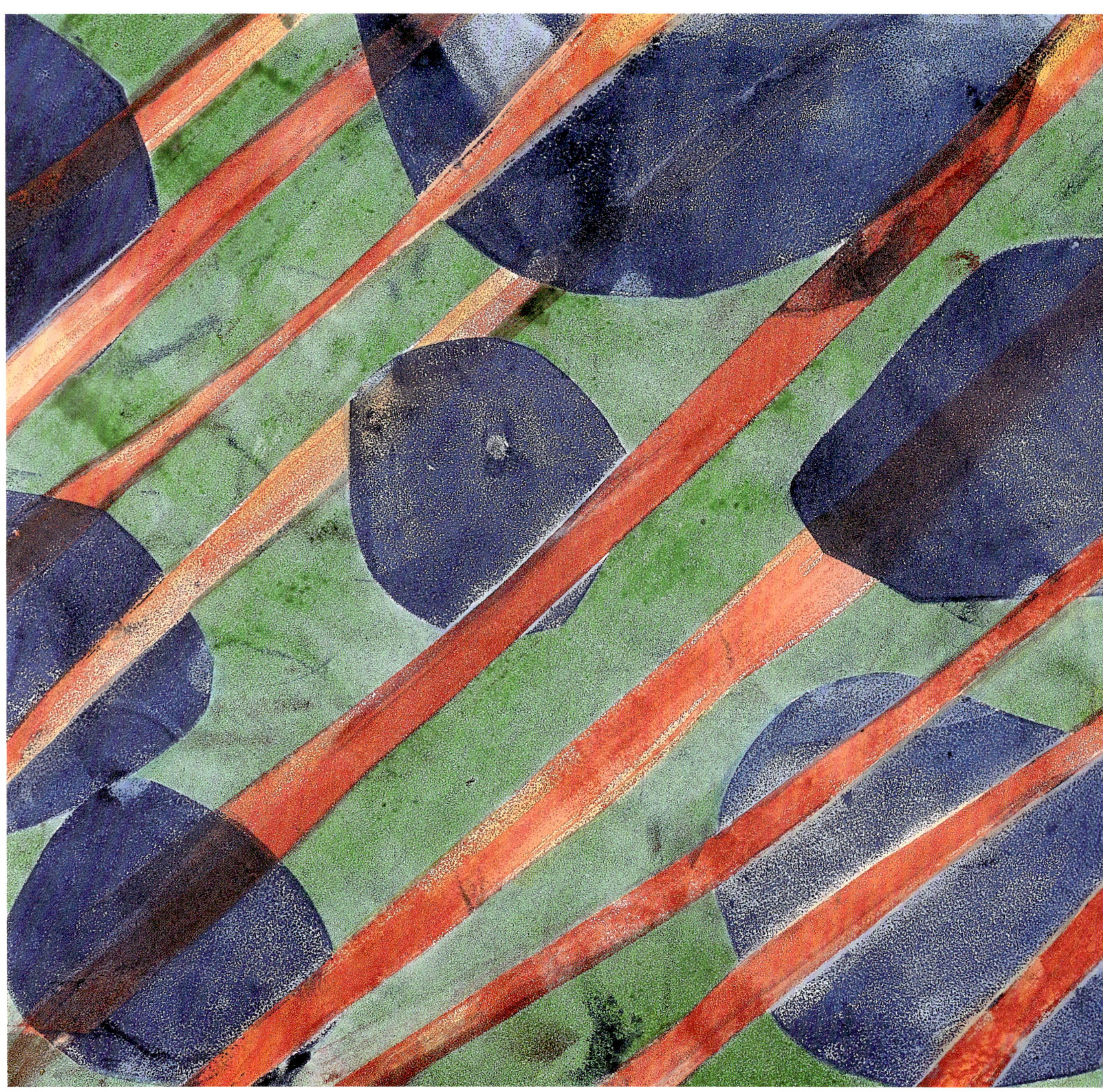

DUET: COMO 2004 OIL ON PANEL 12 X 24

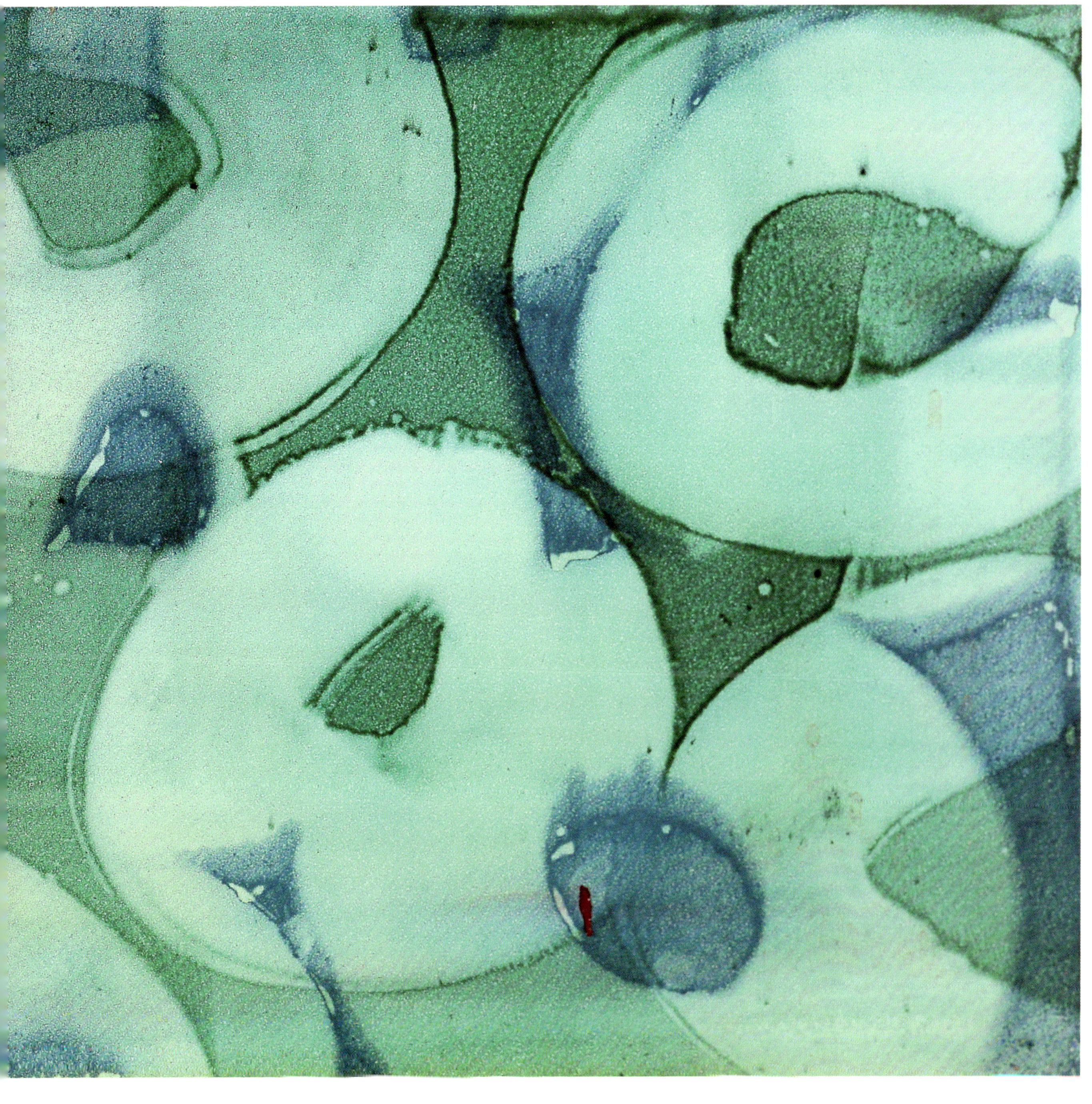

UNO: WEST COAST 2004 OIL ON PANEL 8 X 8

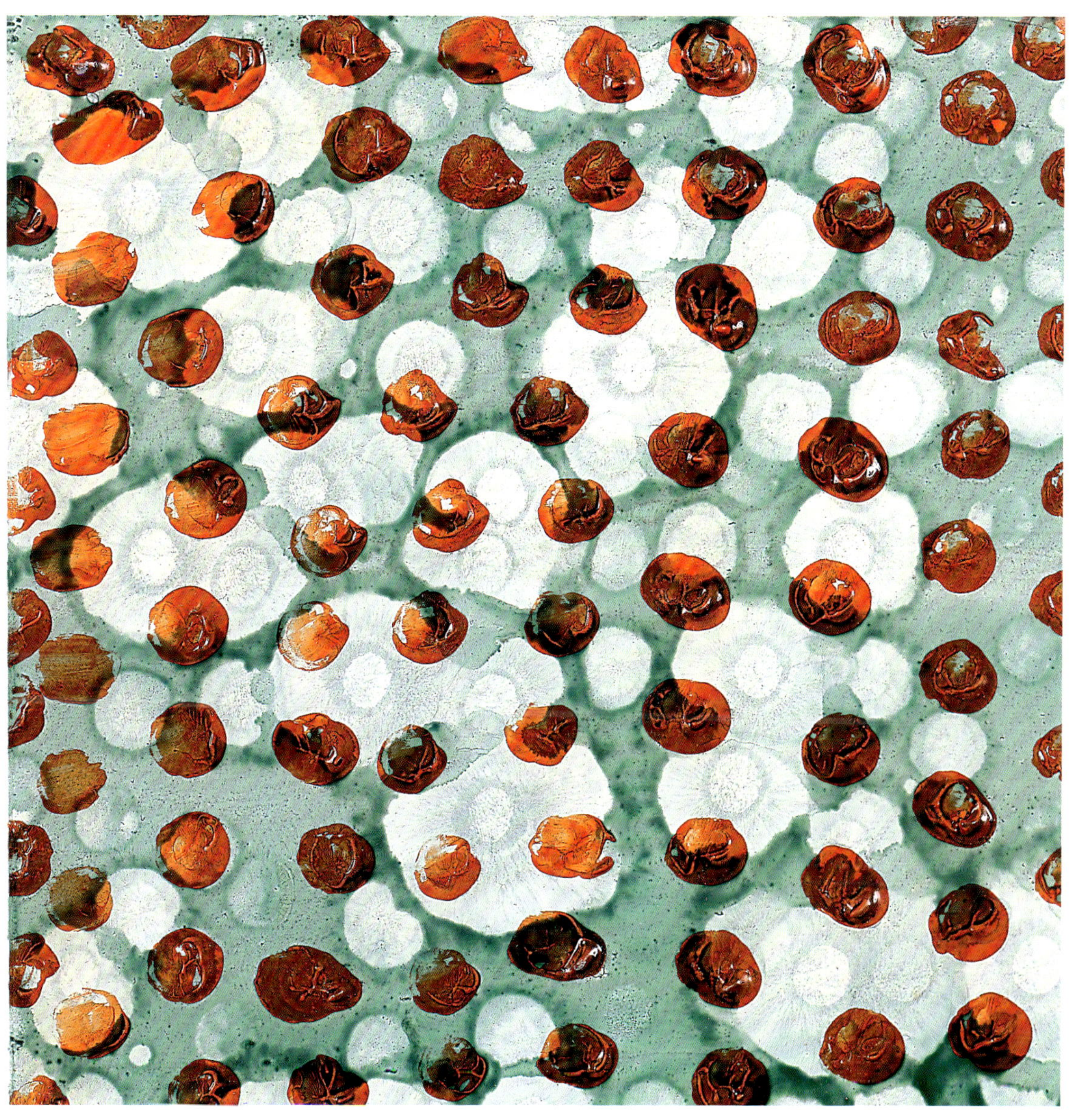

UNO: MERENGUE 2005 OIL ON PANEL 8 X 8

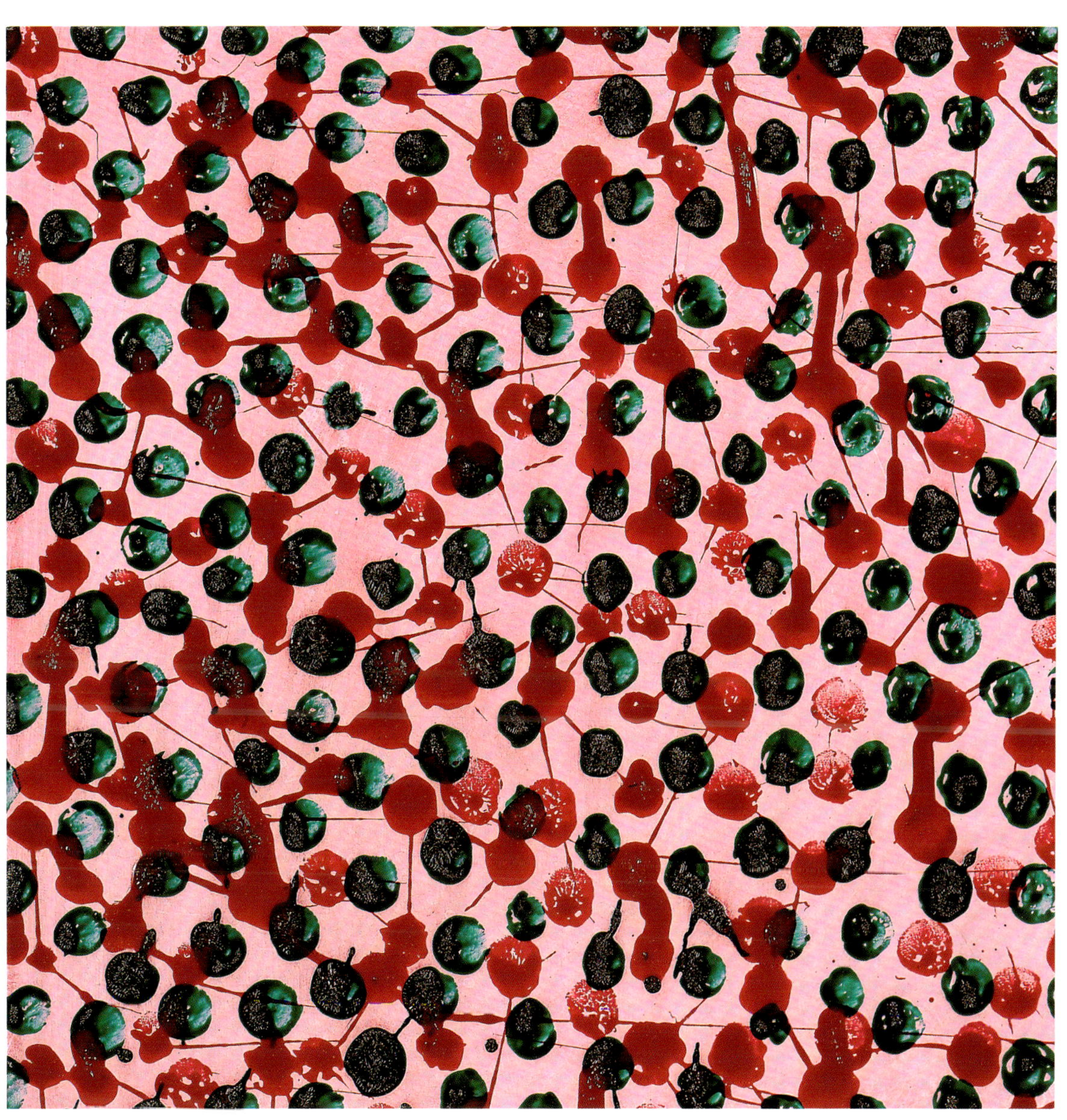

CLEAR & COPIOUS 2005 OIL ON PANEL 30 X 30

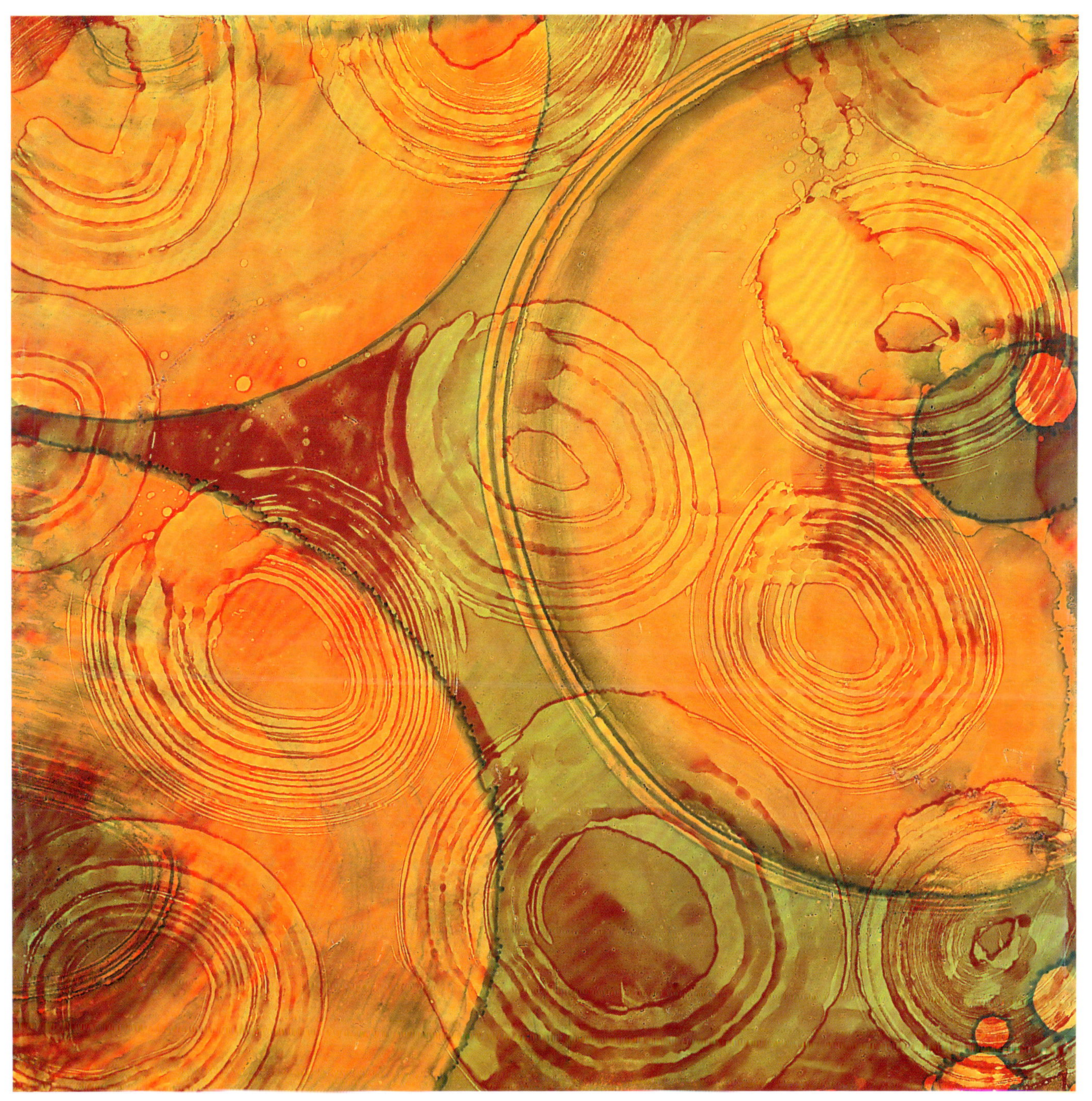

DECIDUOUS IN DENVER 2005 OIL ON PANEL 48 X 48

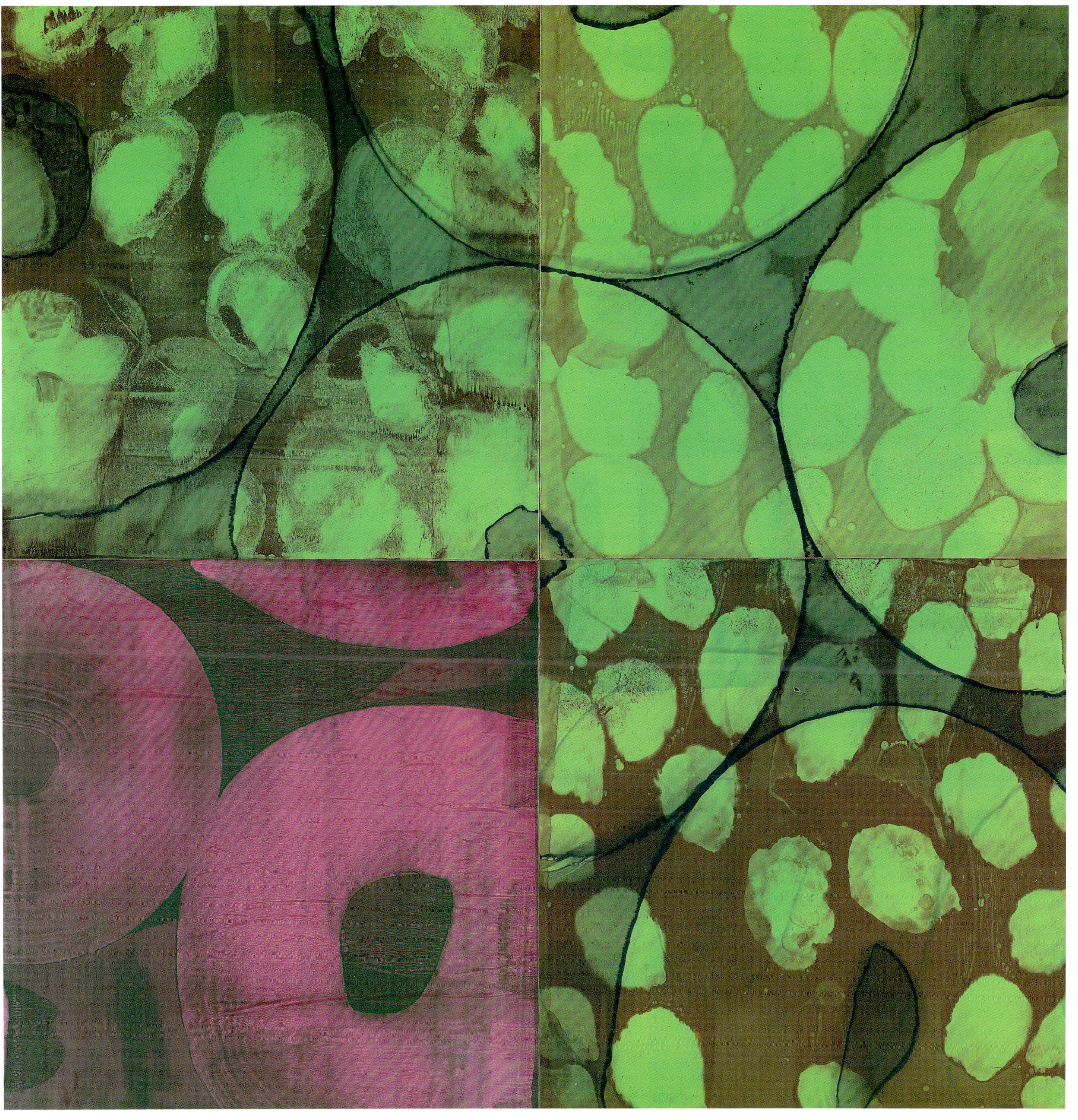

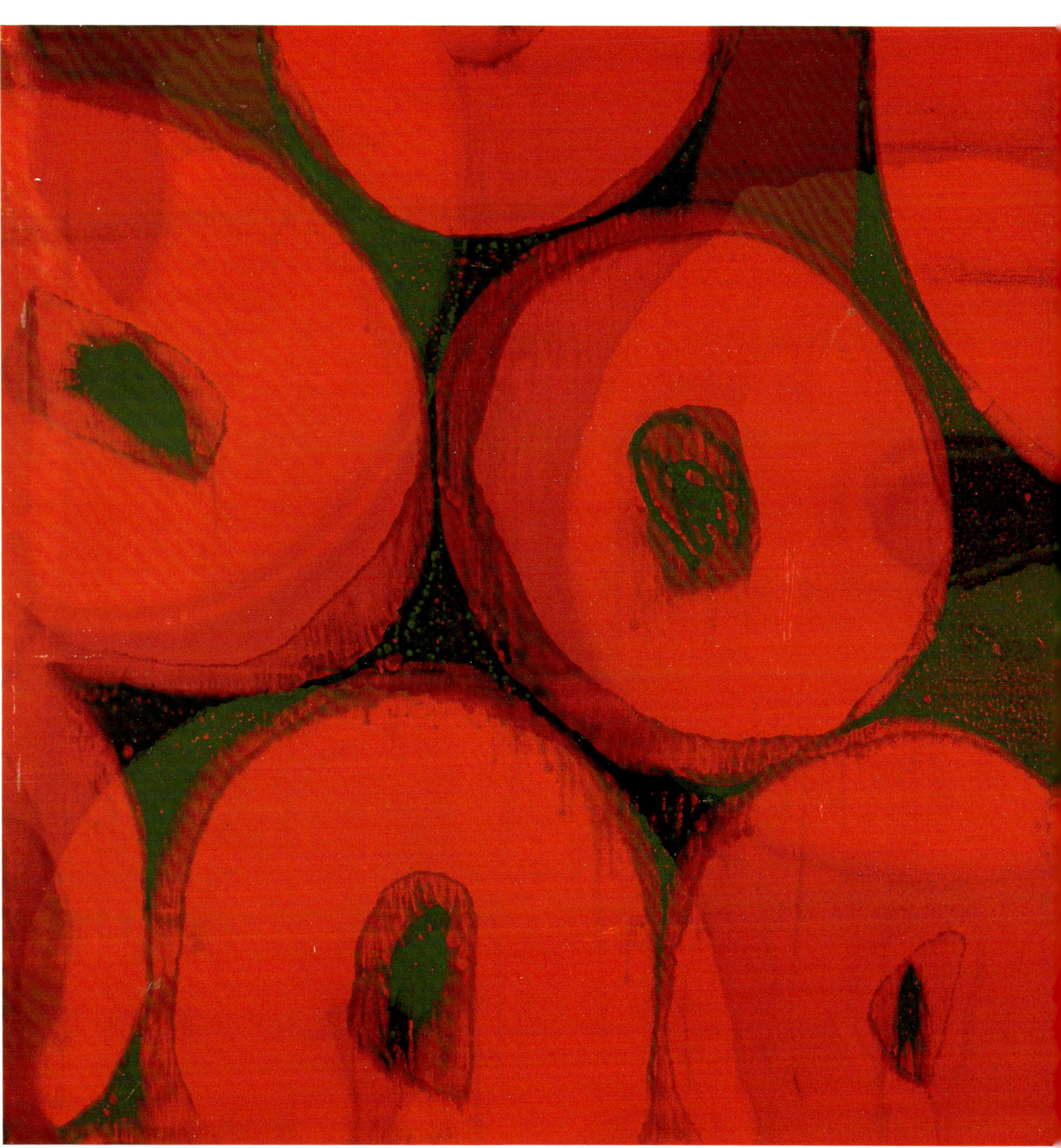

DUET: ROUEN 2005 OIL ON PANEL 12 X 24

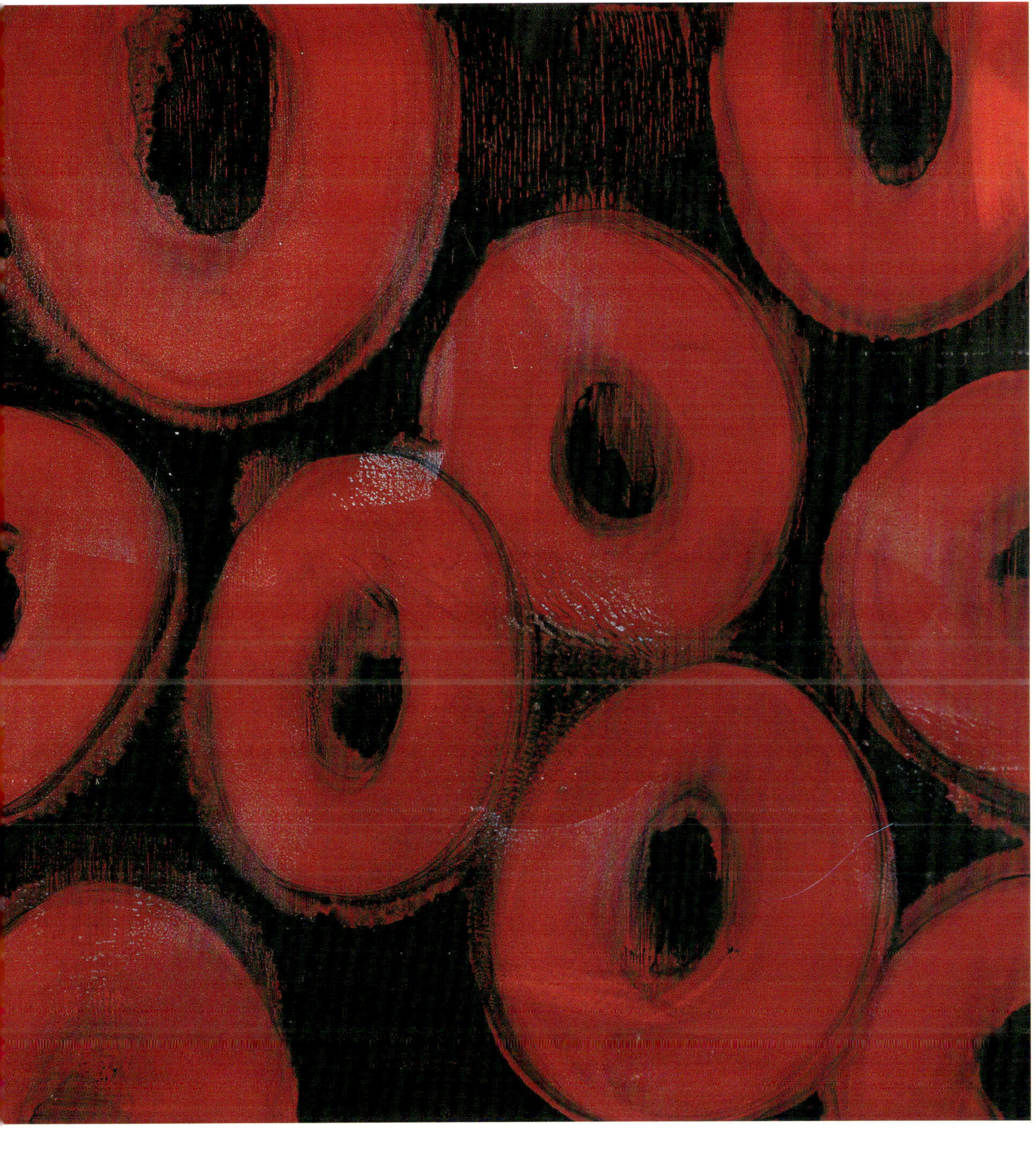

82

ROOTS & SHOOTS: SUMAC 2005 OIL ON PANEL 36 X 24

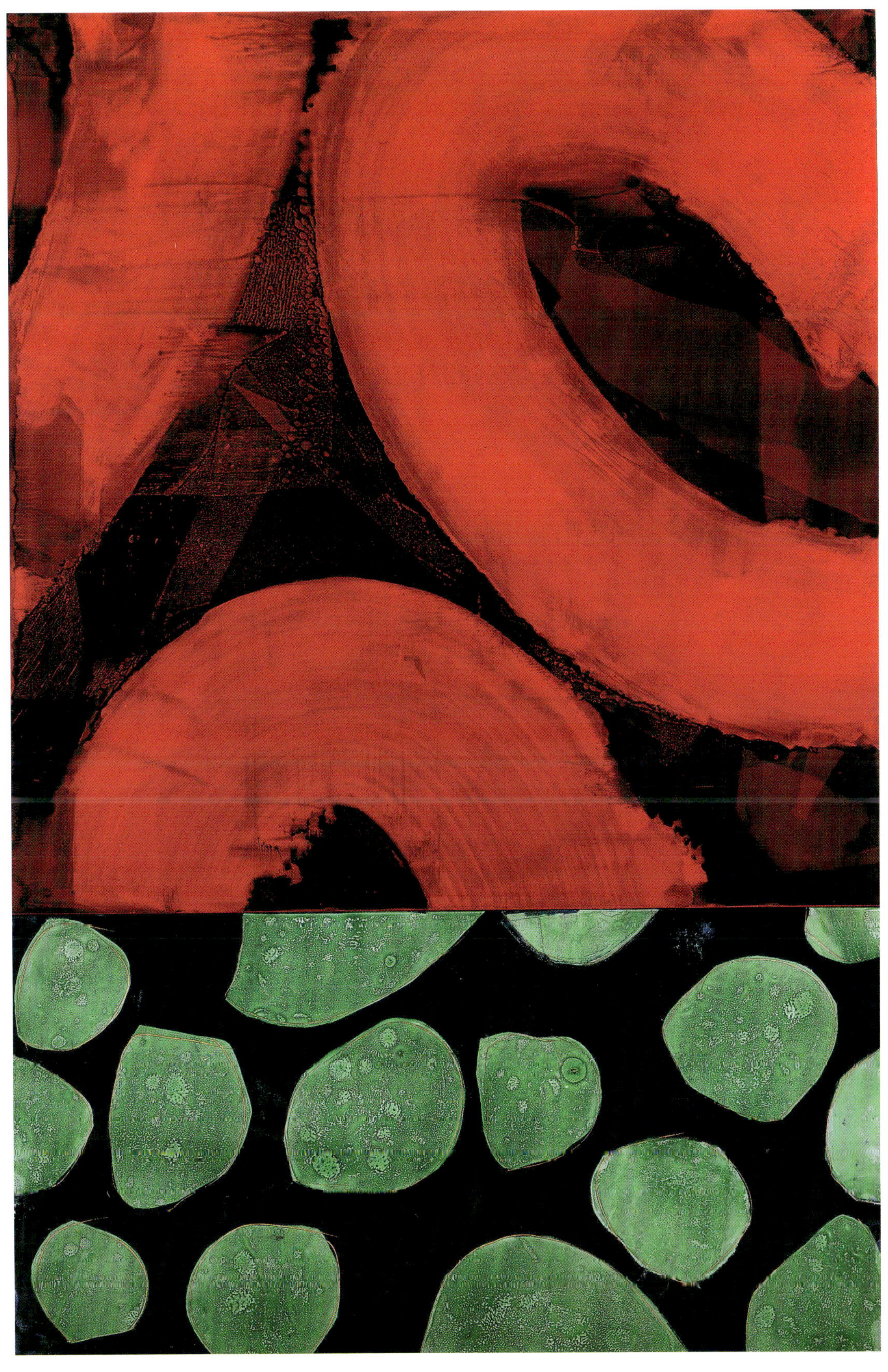

SOLO: CADMIUM 2005 OIL ON PANEL 24 X 24

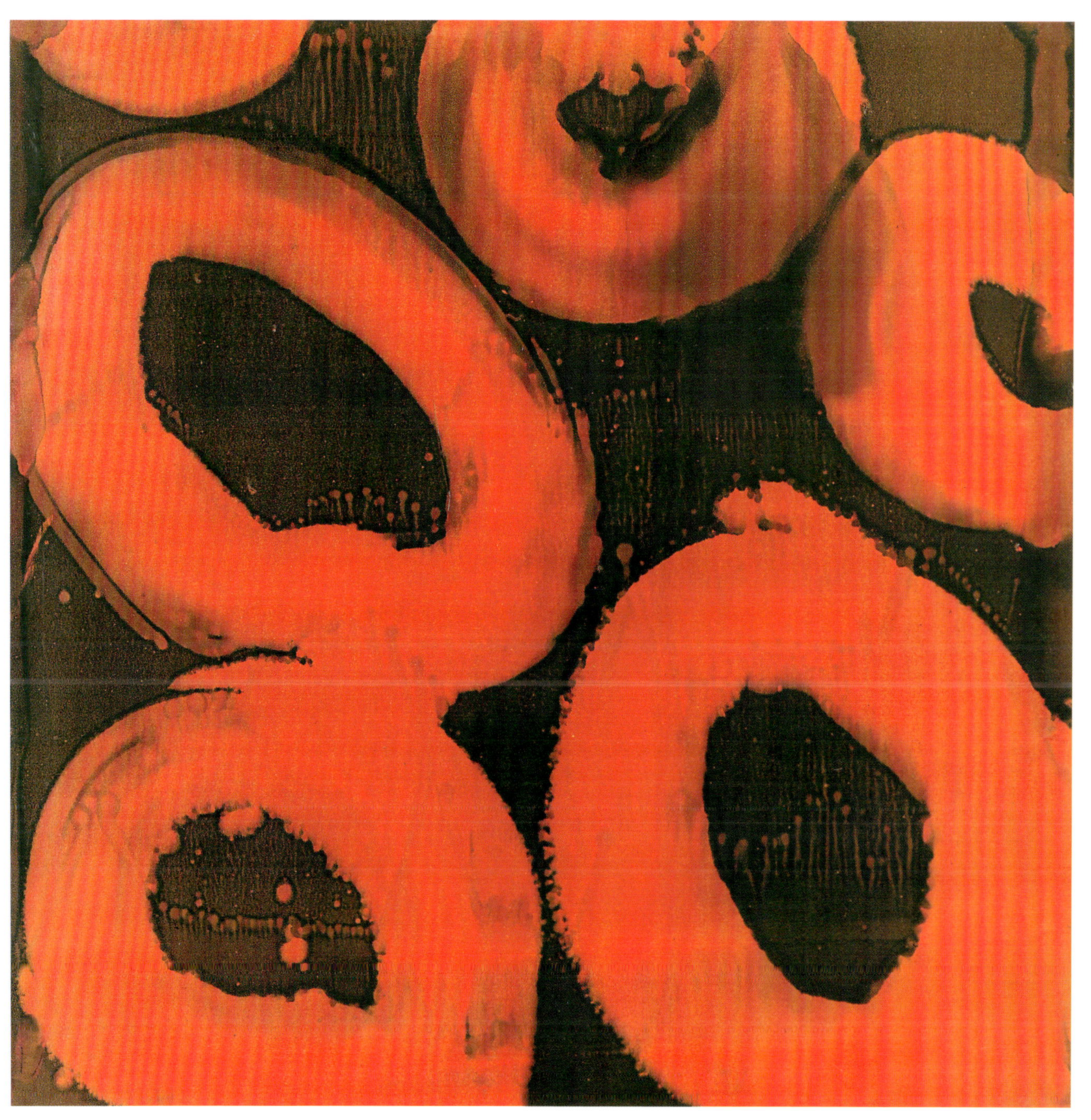

86

DAISY CHAIN 2005 OIL ON PANEL 48 X 48

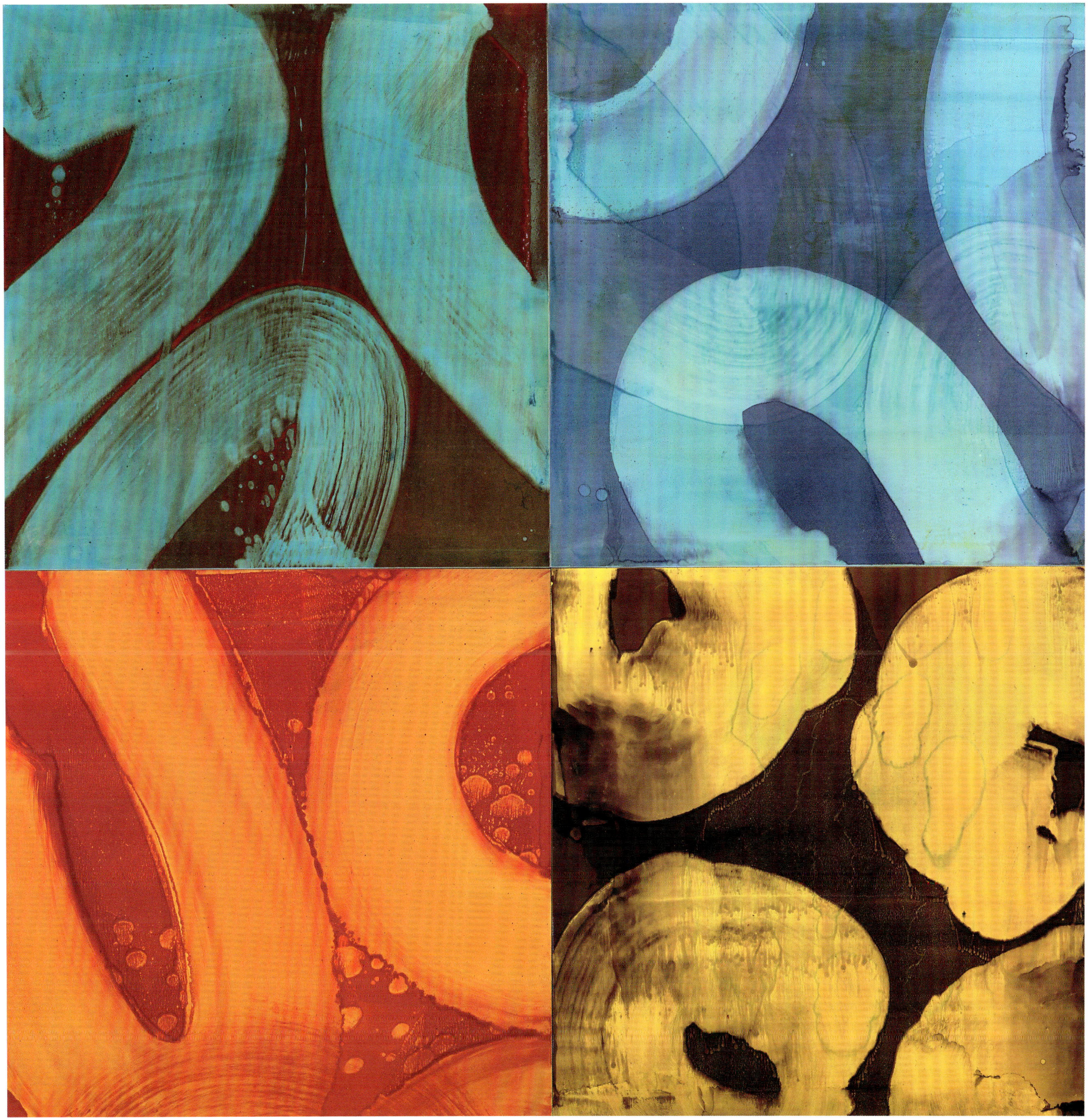

HIGH HEATER 2005 OIL ON PANEL 48 X 48

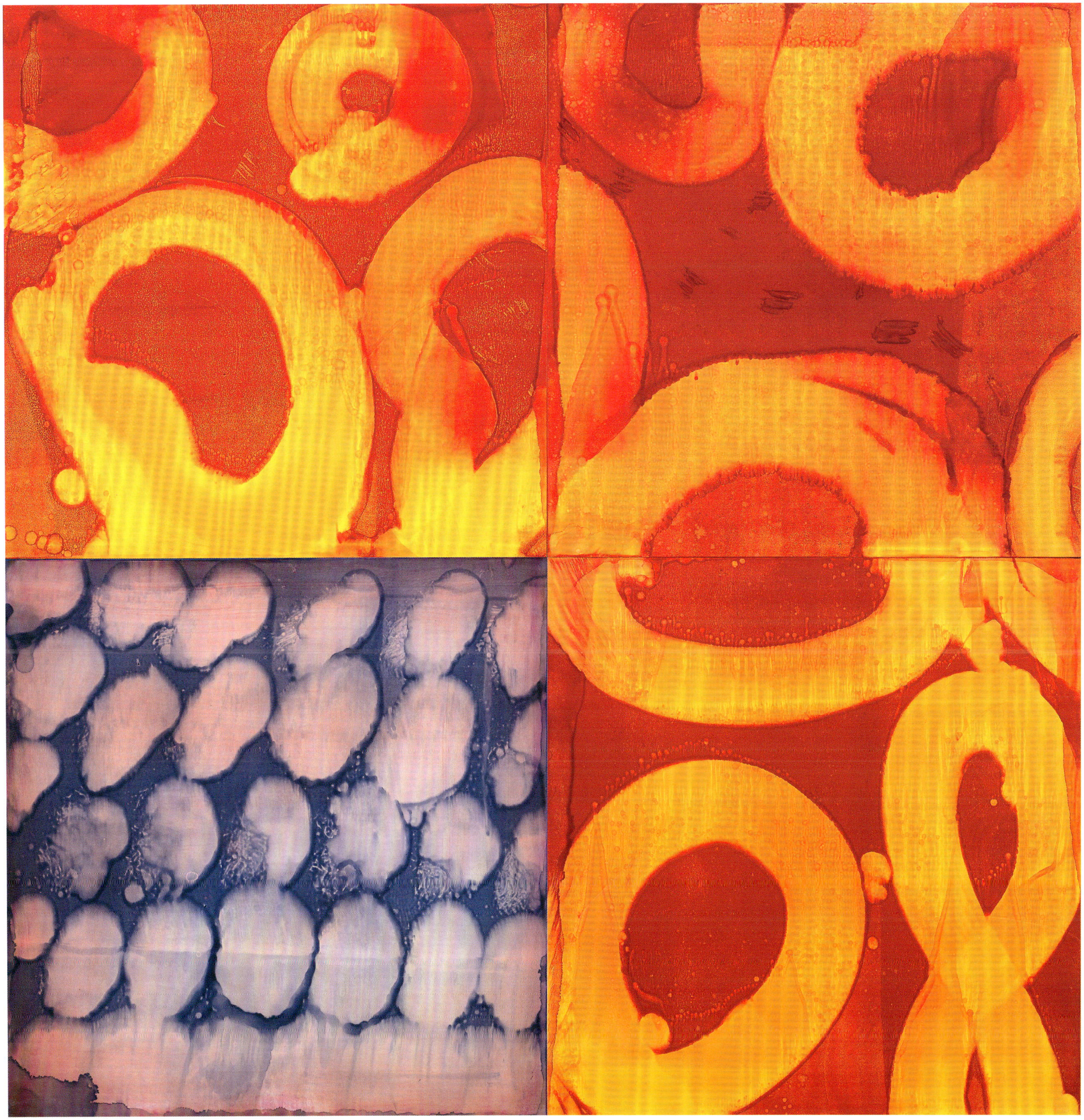

COLLATERAL CLEAVAGE, ALVEAR PALACE 2005 OIL ON PANEL 60 X 60

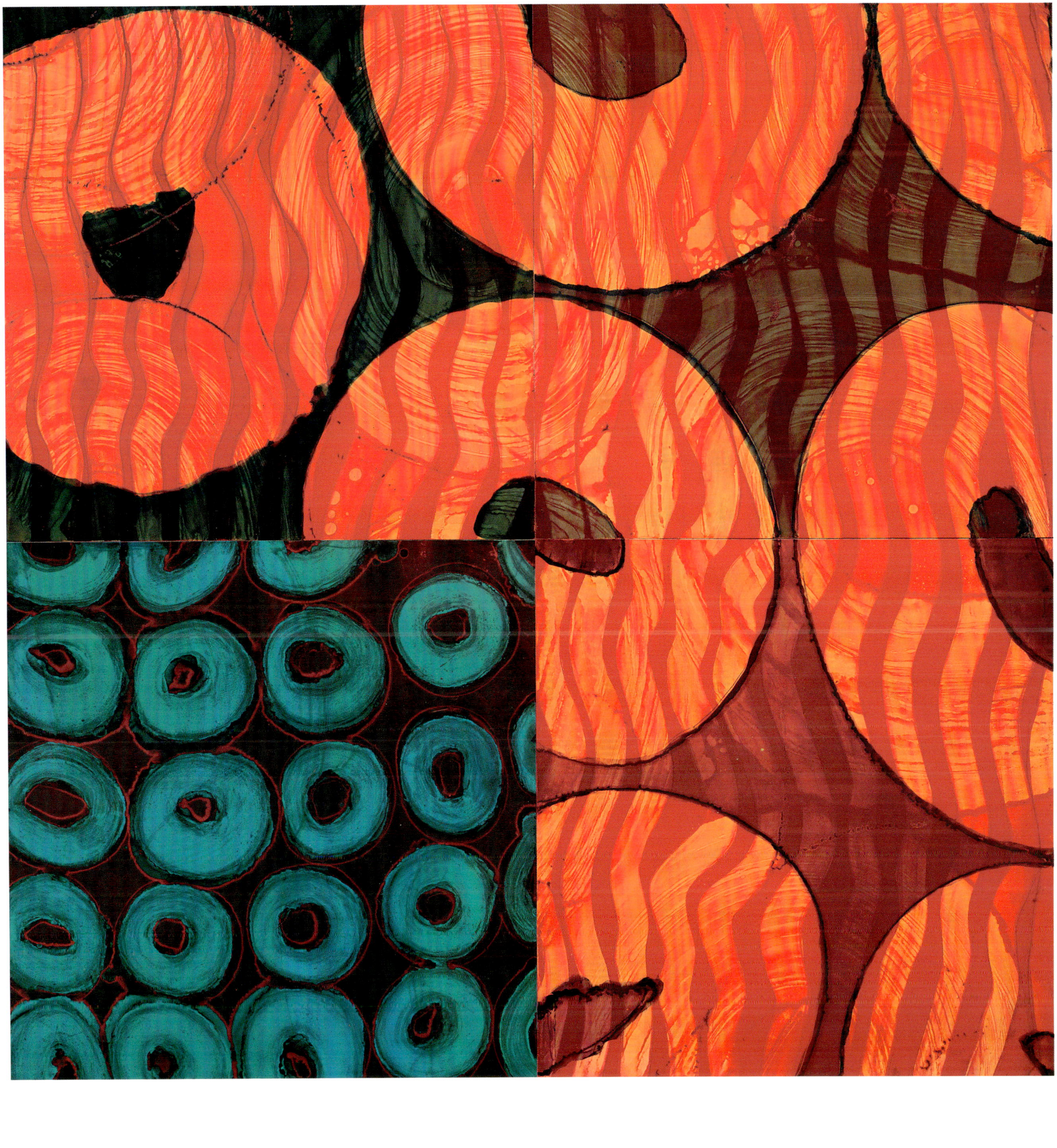

GOOD & PLENTY: ULTRA BLUE 2005 OIL ON PANEL 48 X 48

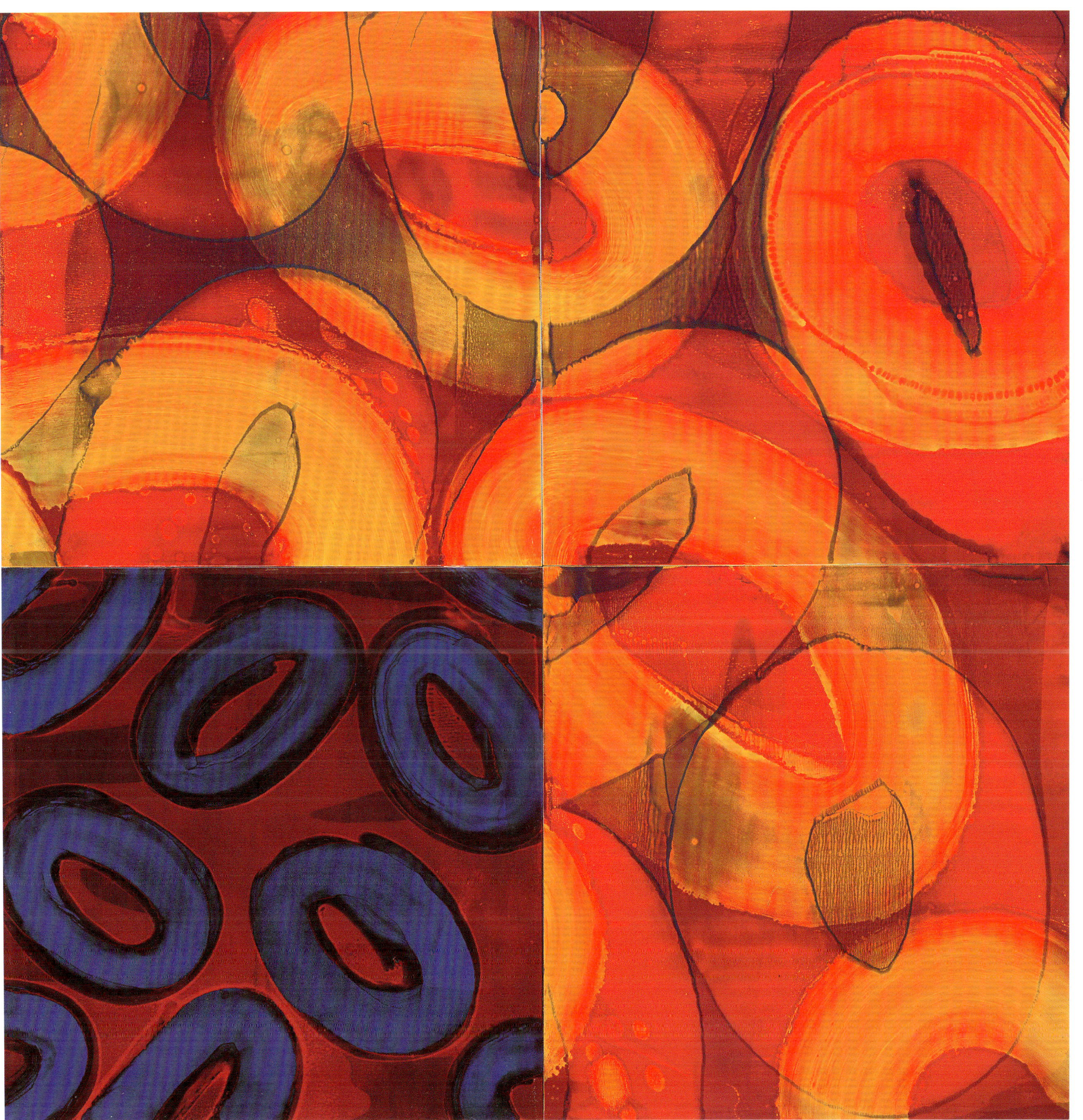

BIG EASY SAX 2005 OIL ON PANEL 48 X 48

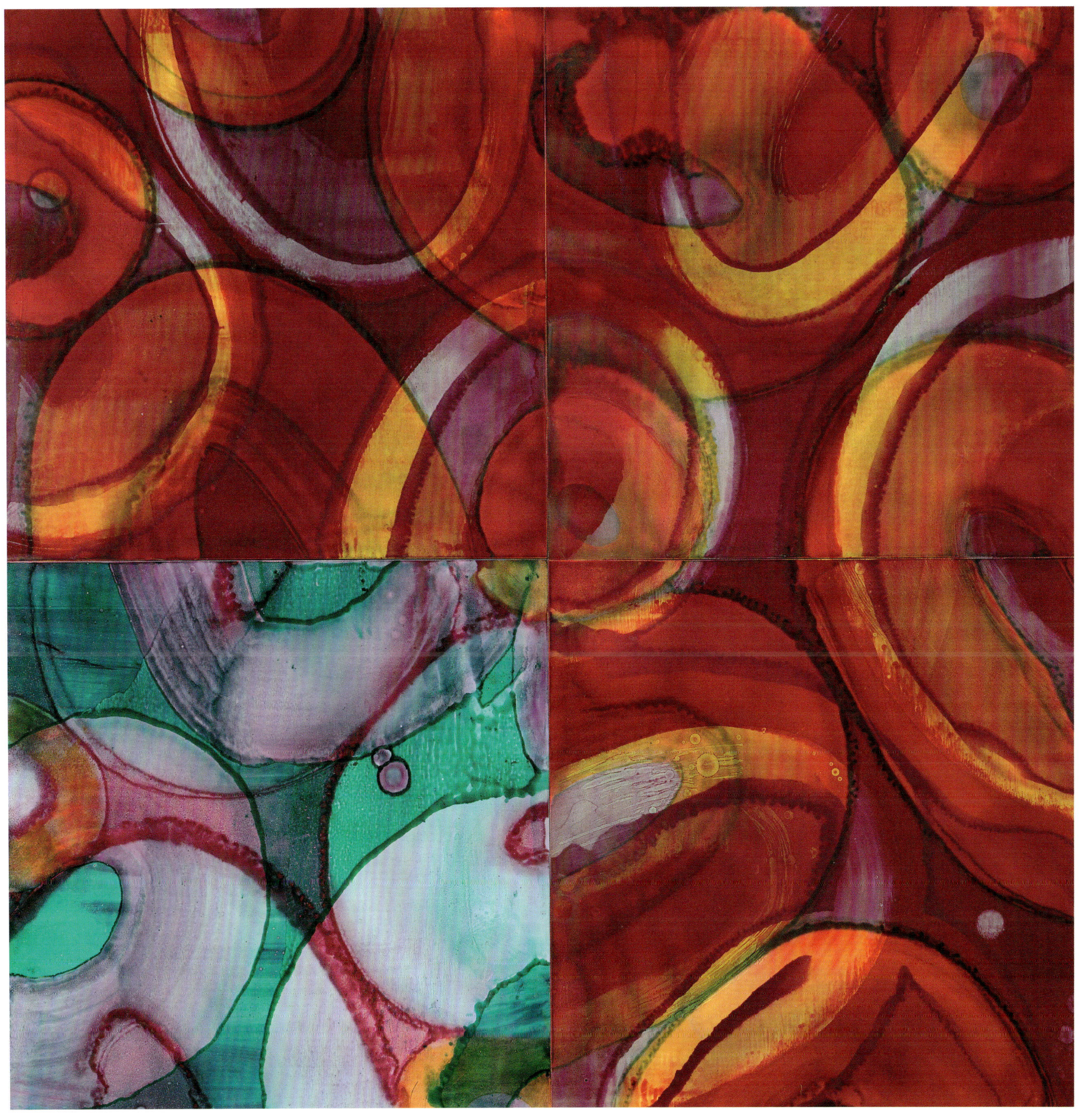

RHUBARB & SUPREME GREEN 2005 OIL ON PANEL 48 X 48

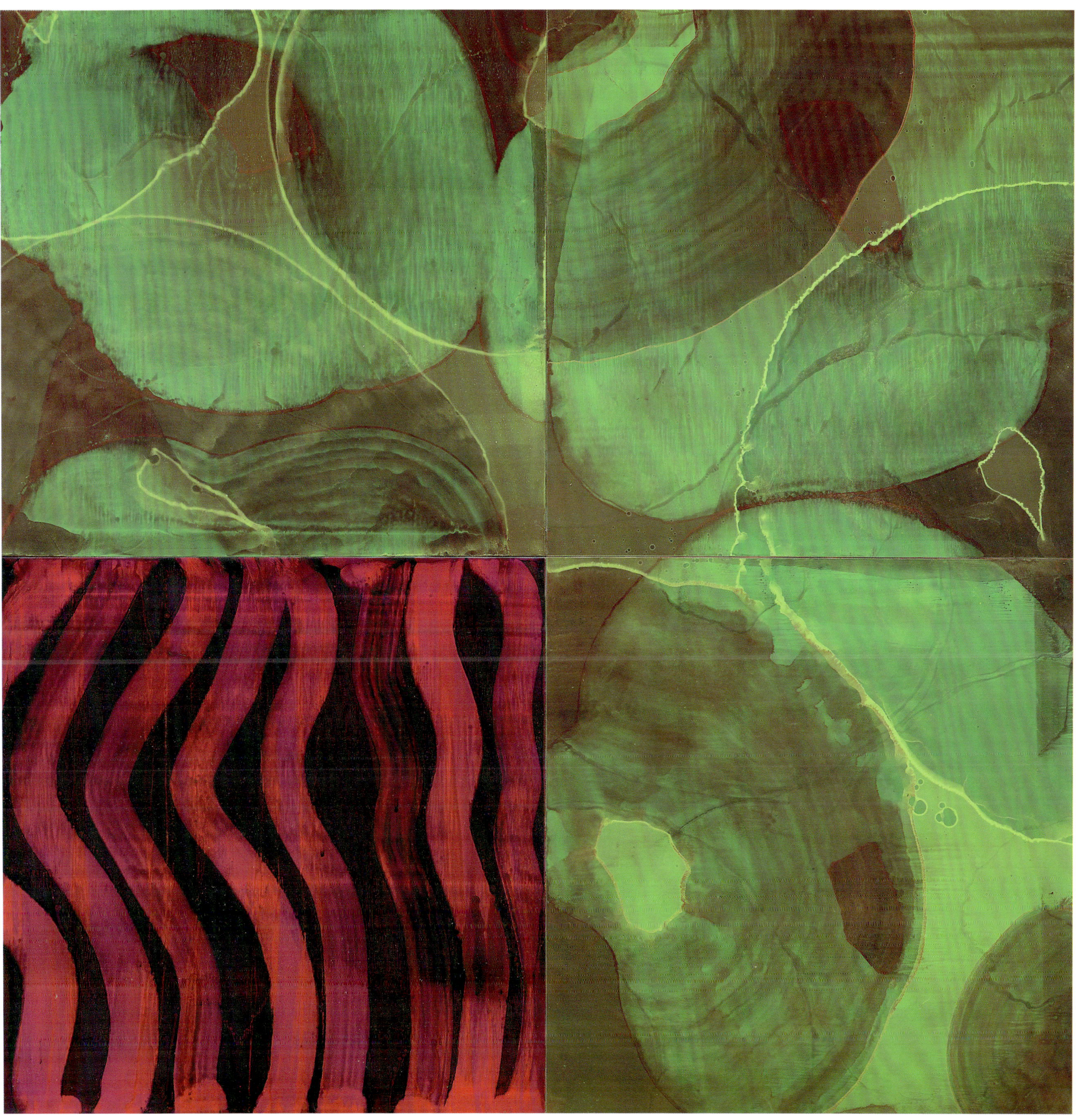

COVERT HUES 2005 OIL ON PANEL 48 X 48

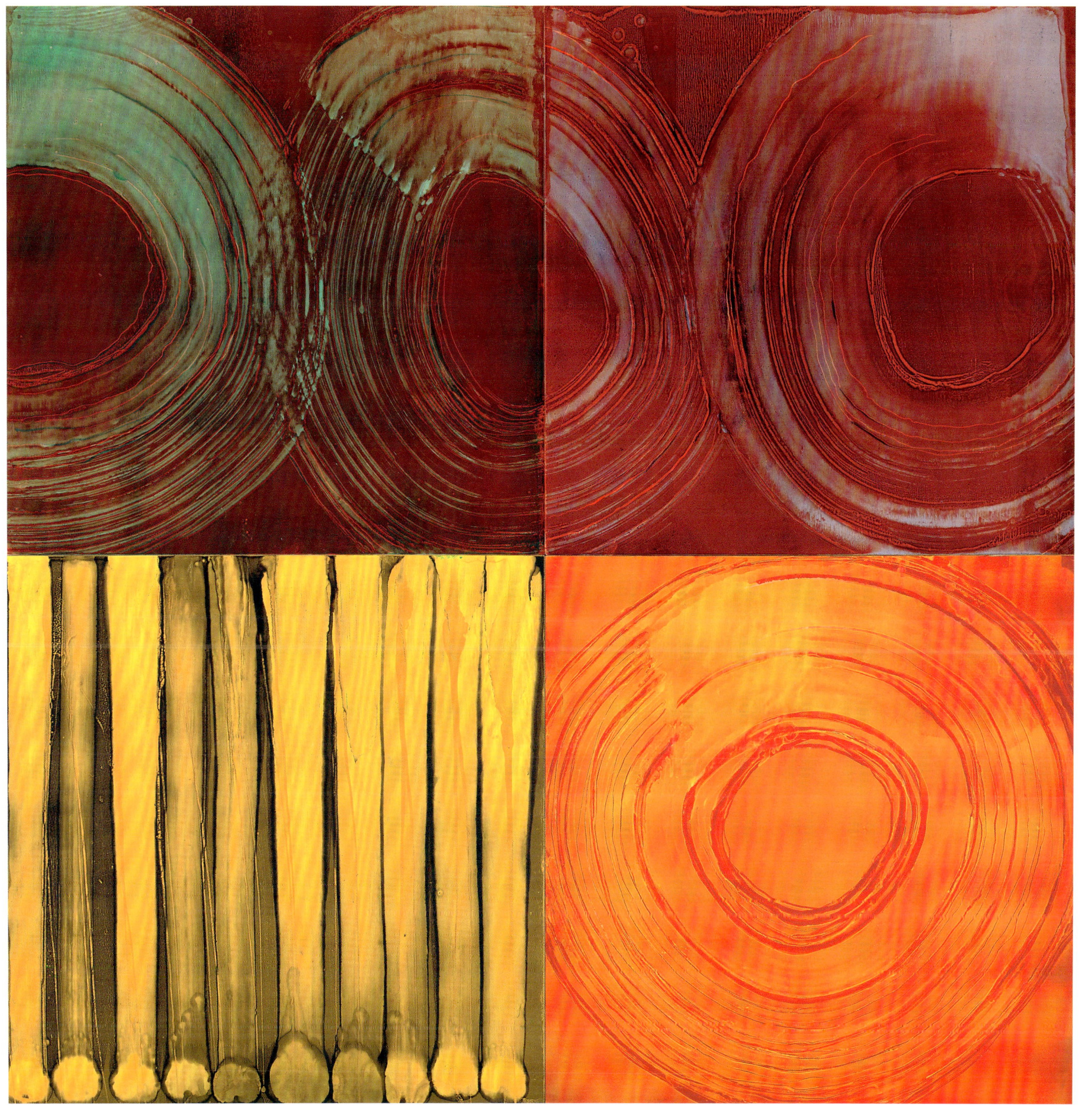

SOLO: THALO 2003–2006 OIL ON PANEL 24 X 24

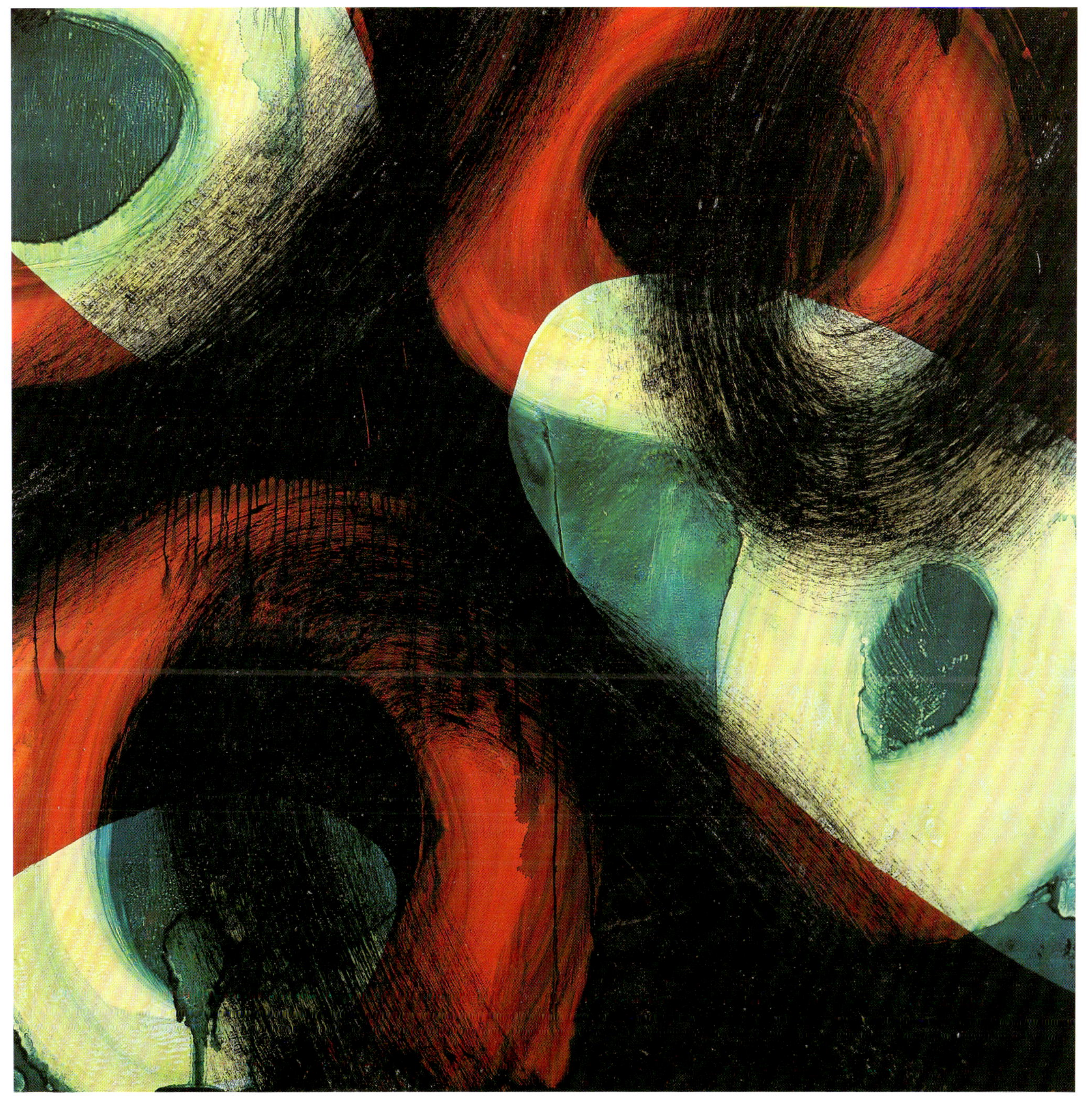

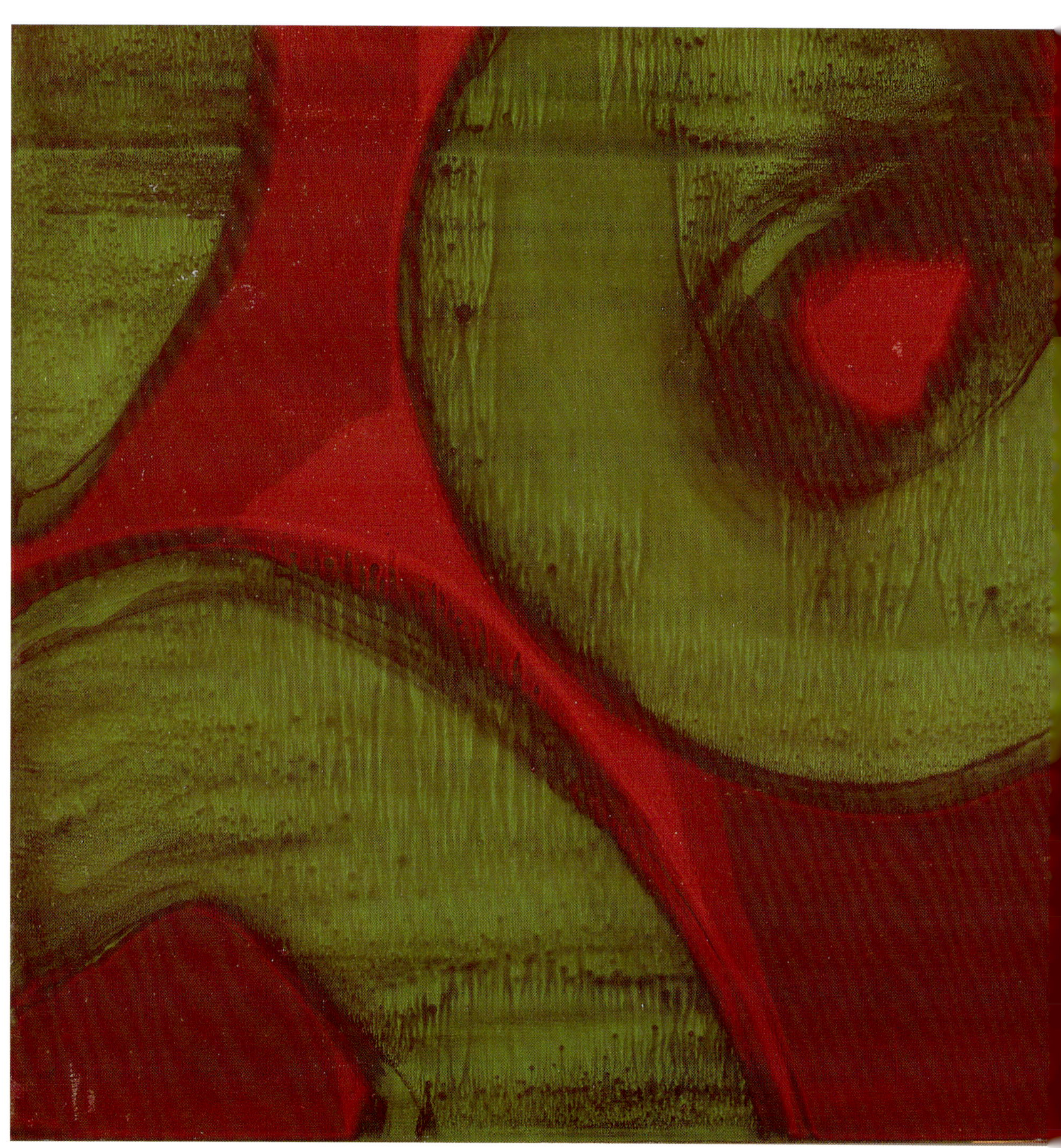

DUET: MALMO 2006 OIL ON PANEL 12 X 24

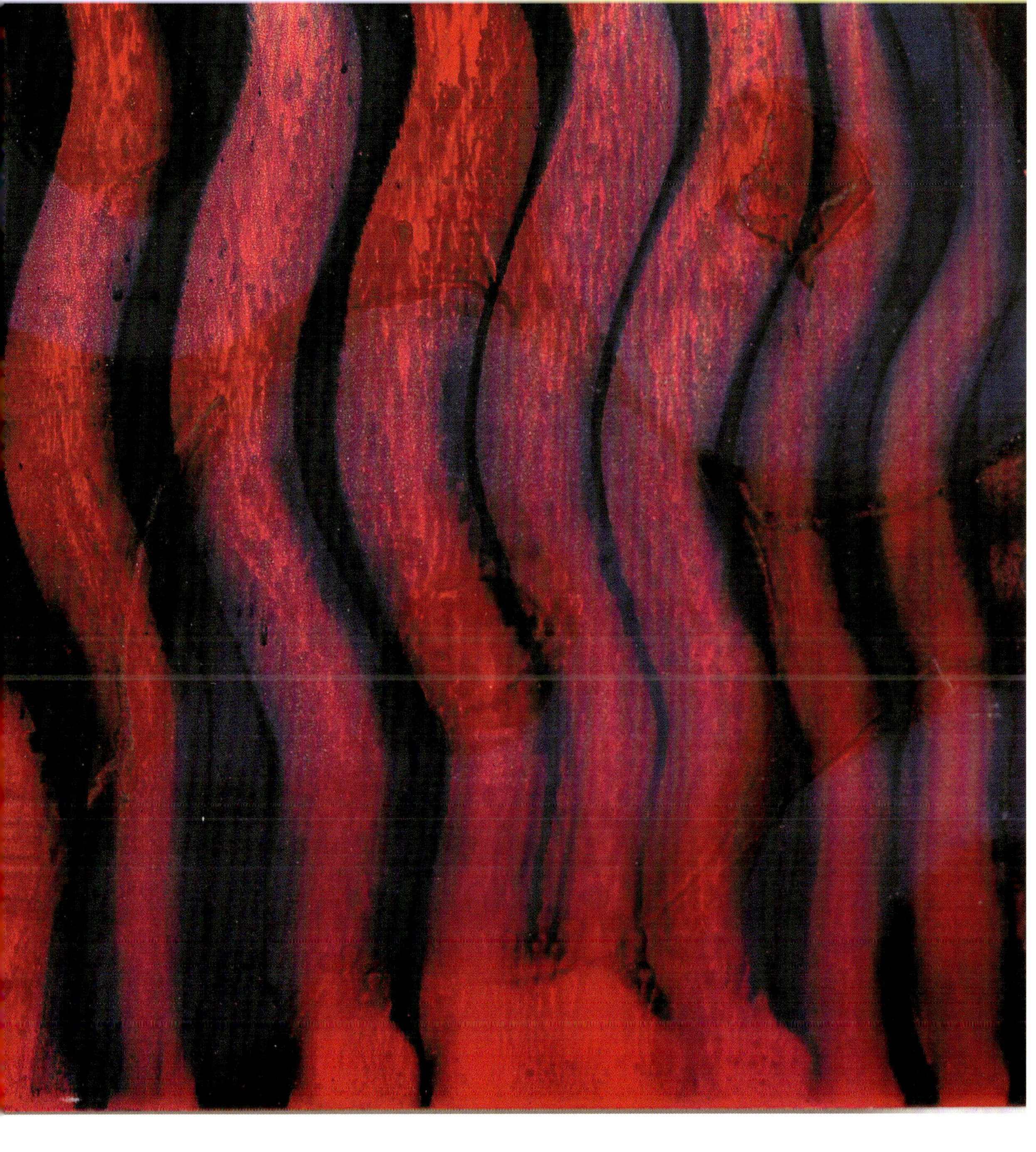

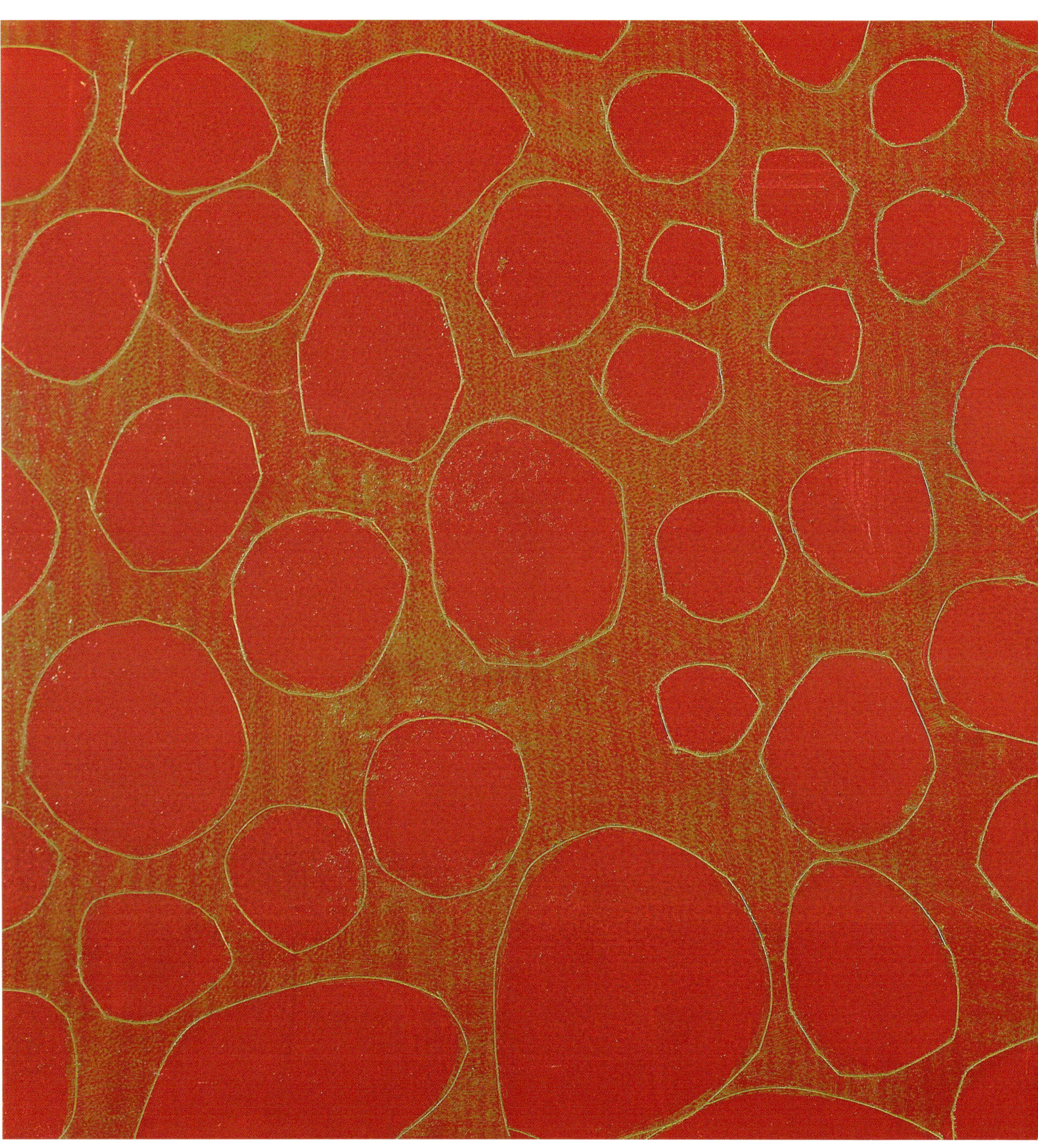

DUET: SIENNA 2006 OIL ON PANEL 12 X 24

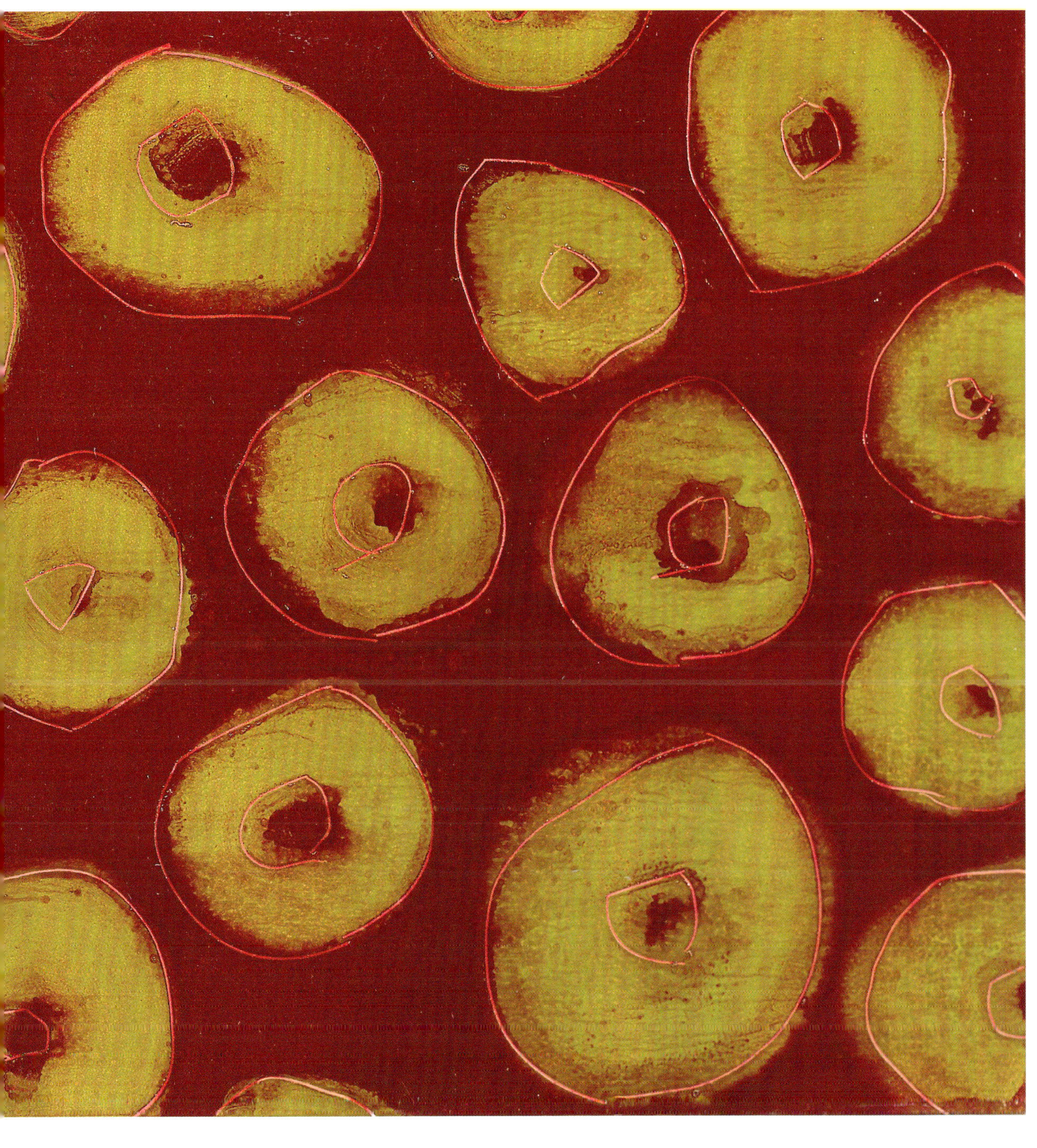

106 **TRANSMIT LeWITT** 2006 OIL ON PANEL 48 X 48

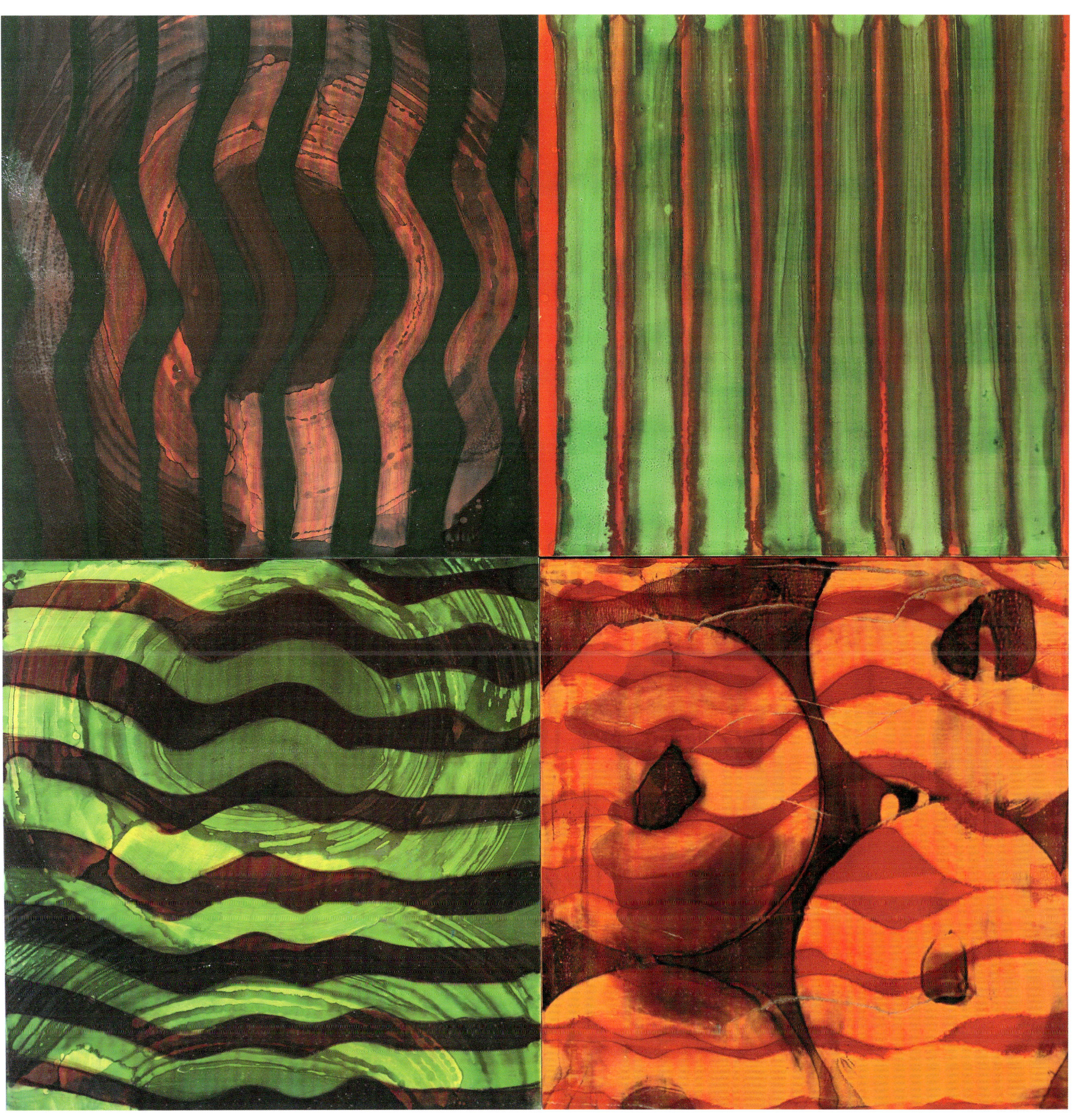

RETORT TO ROUAULT 2006 OIL ON PANEL 60 X 60

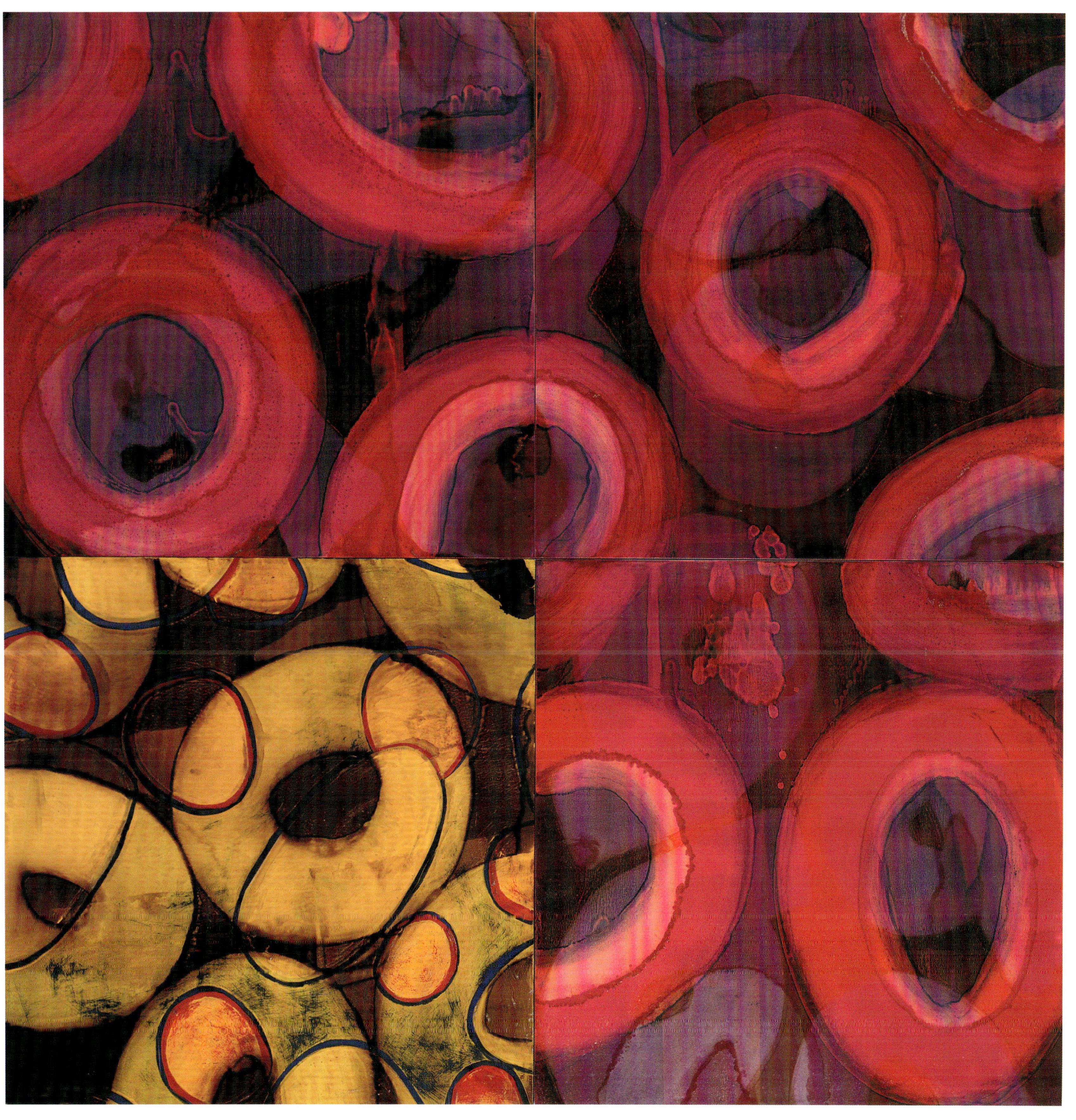

ROOTS & SHOOTS: TANGELO 2005 OIL ON PANEL 36 X 24

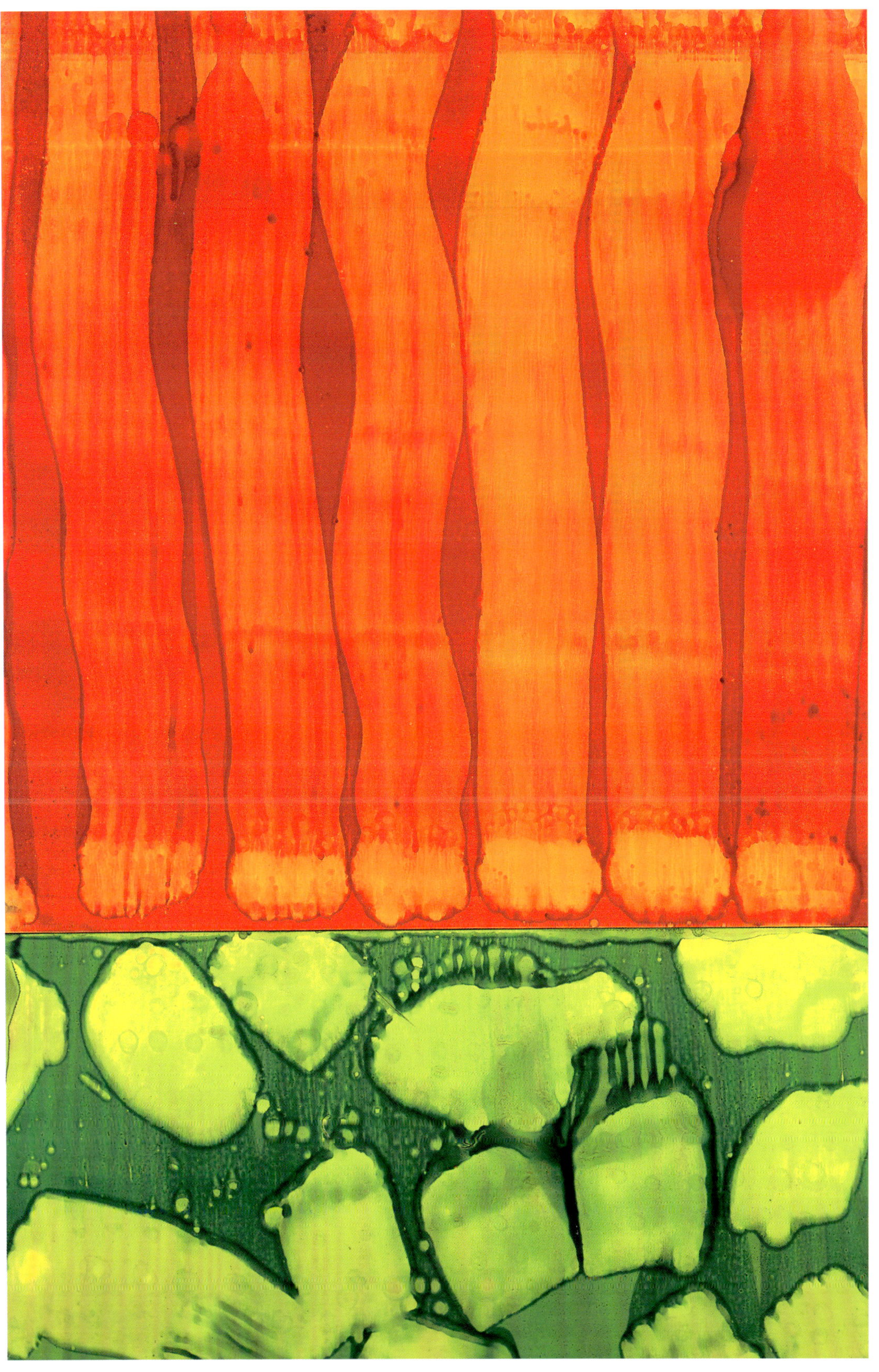

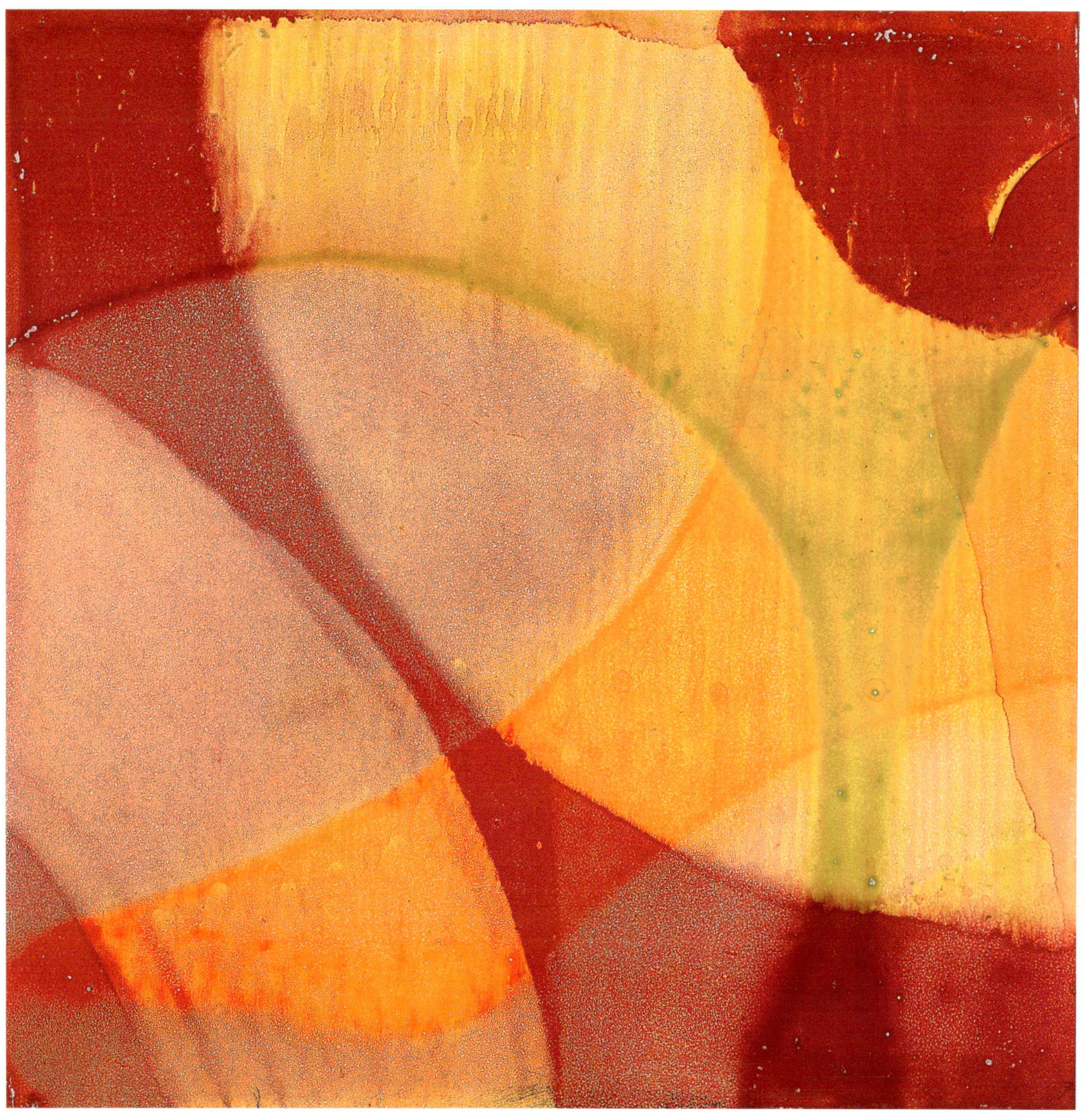

ILLUMINATED MANNEQUIN 2005 OIL ON PAPER 8 X 8

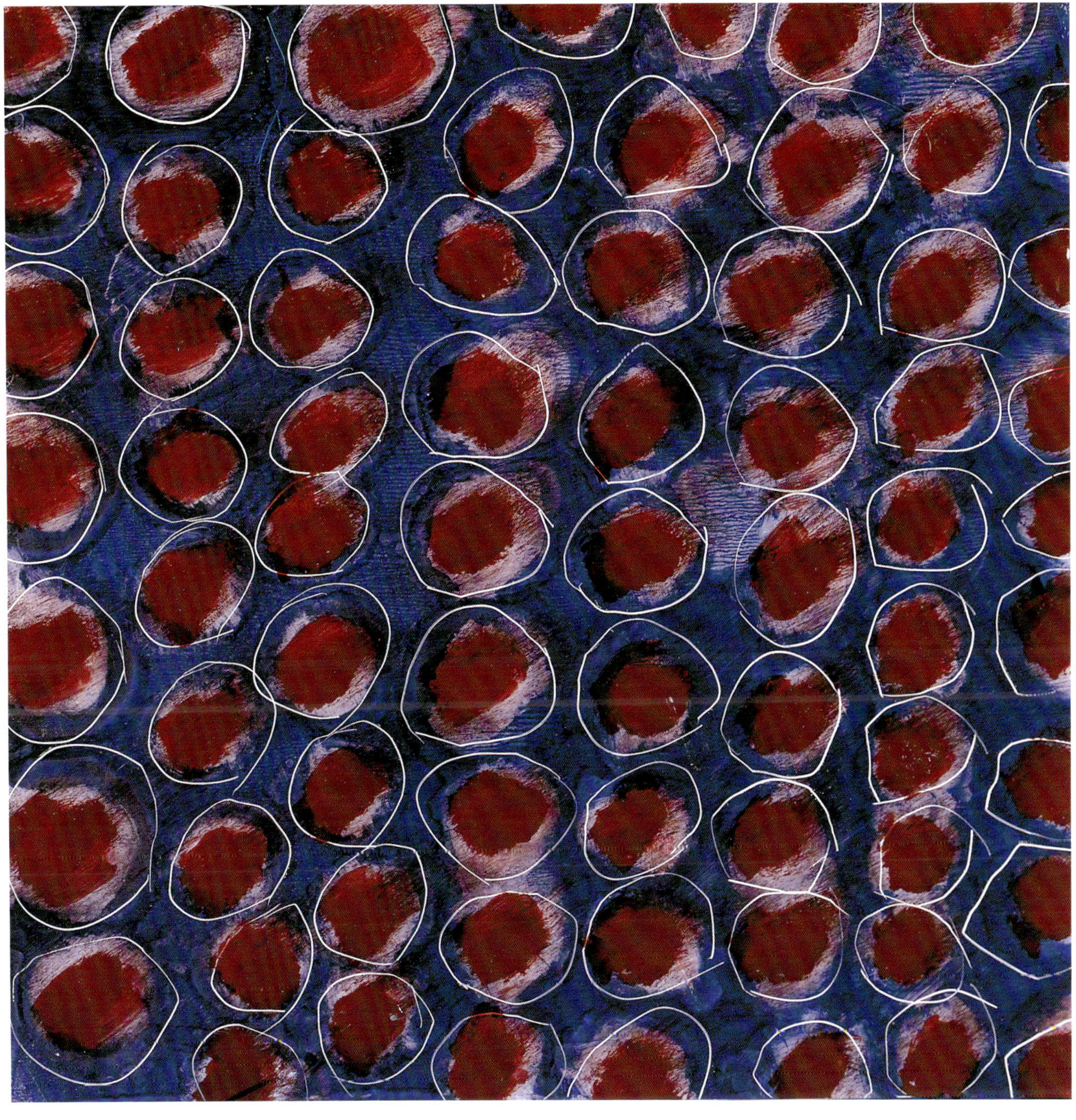

CONGENIAL SPECTER 2006 OIL ON PANEL 8 X 8

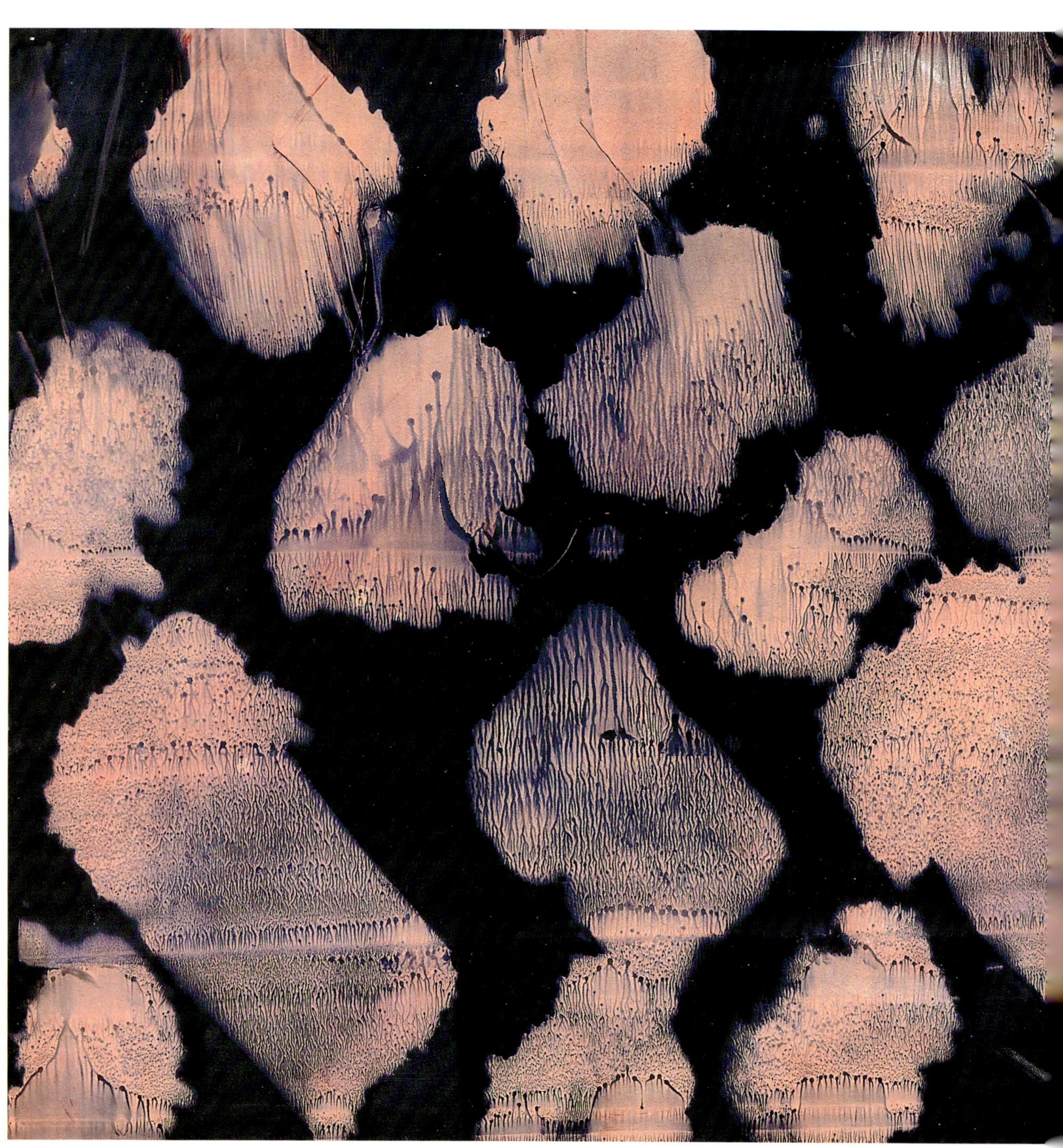

DUET: BOLOGNA 2006 OIL ON PANEL 12 X 24

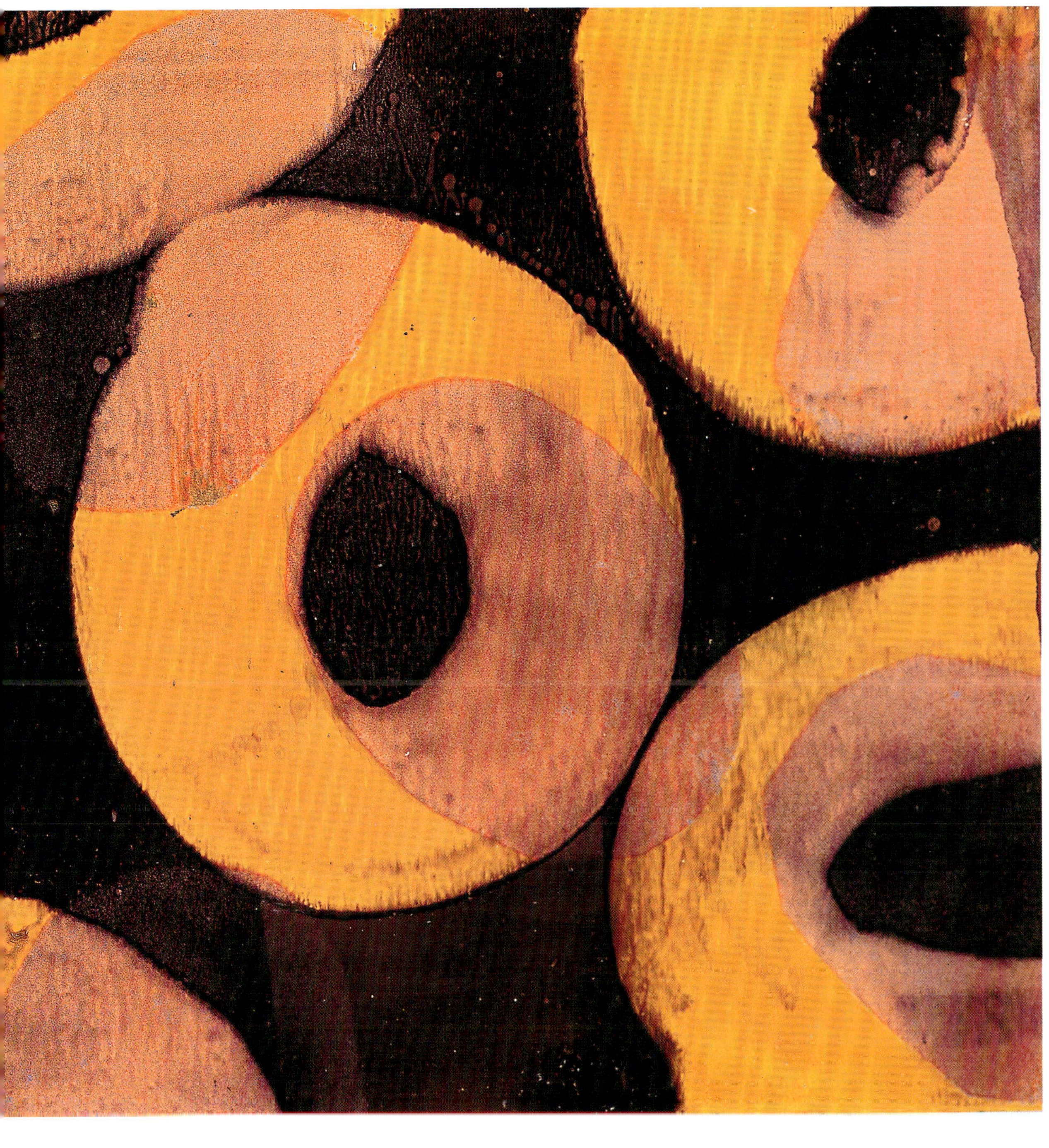

AMBER SKY & TANGERINE MOON 2004 OIL ON PANEL 48 X 48

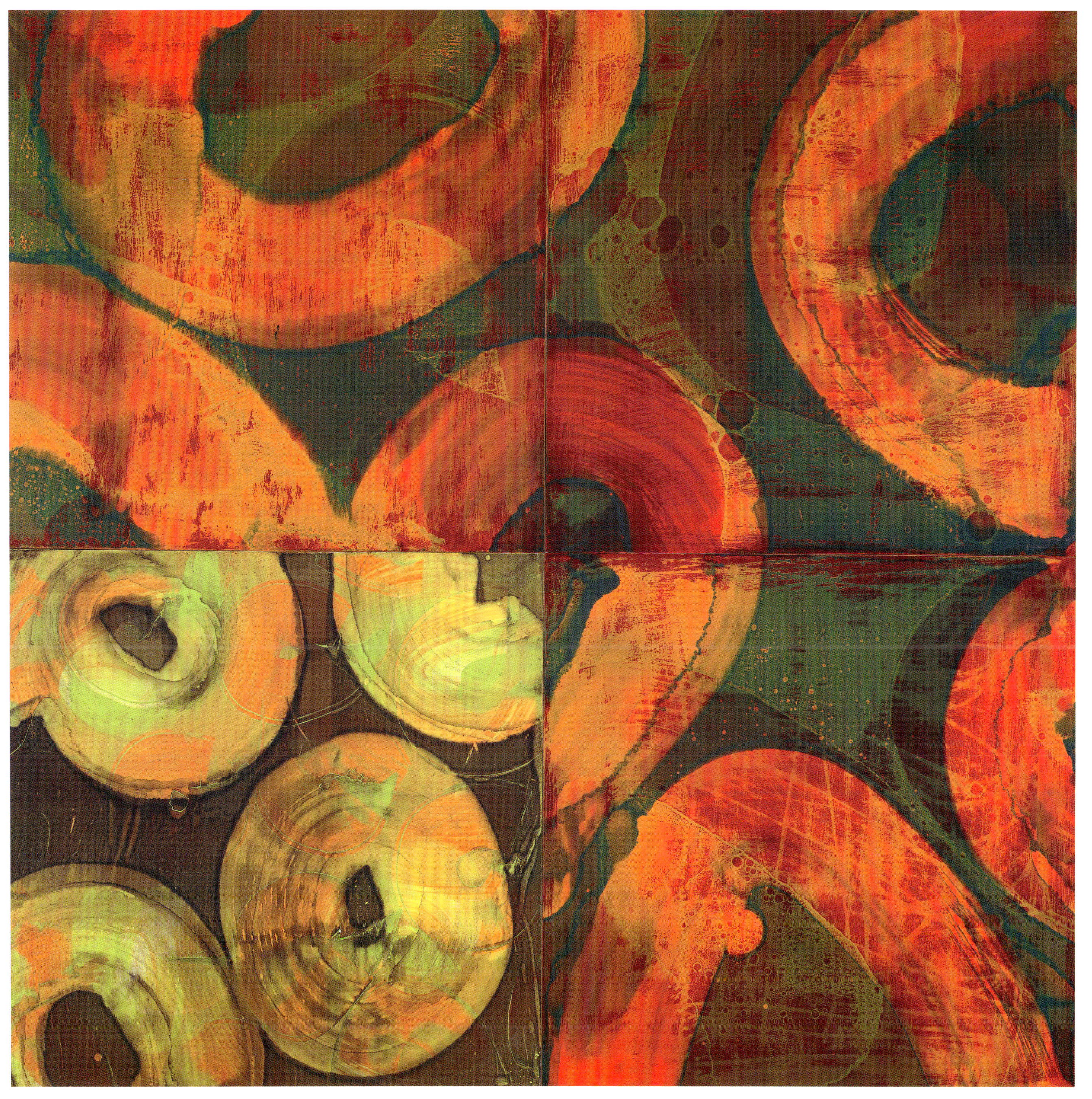

117

BOMBAY SAPPHIRE, NIGHT 2005 OIL ON PANEL 60 X 60

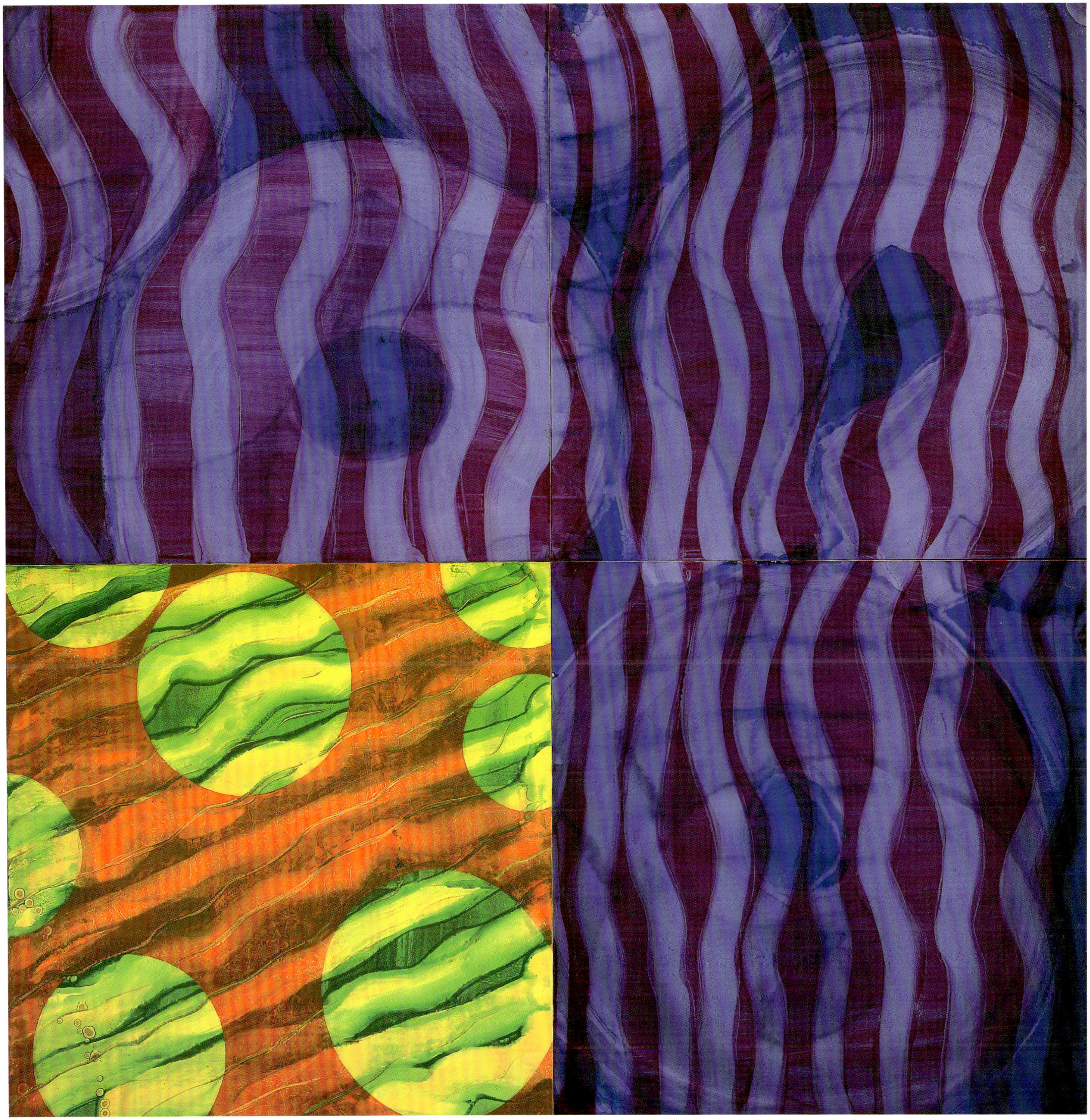

DIFFUSION ALLUSION 2006 OIL ON PANEL 48 X 48

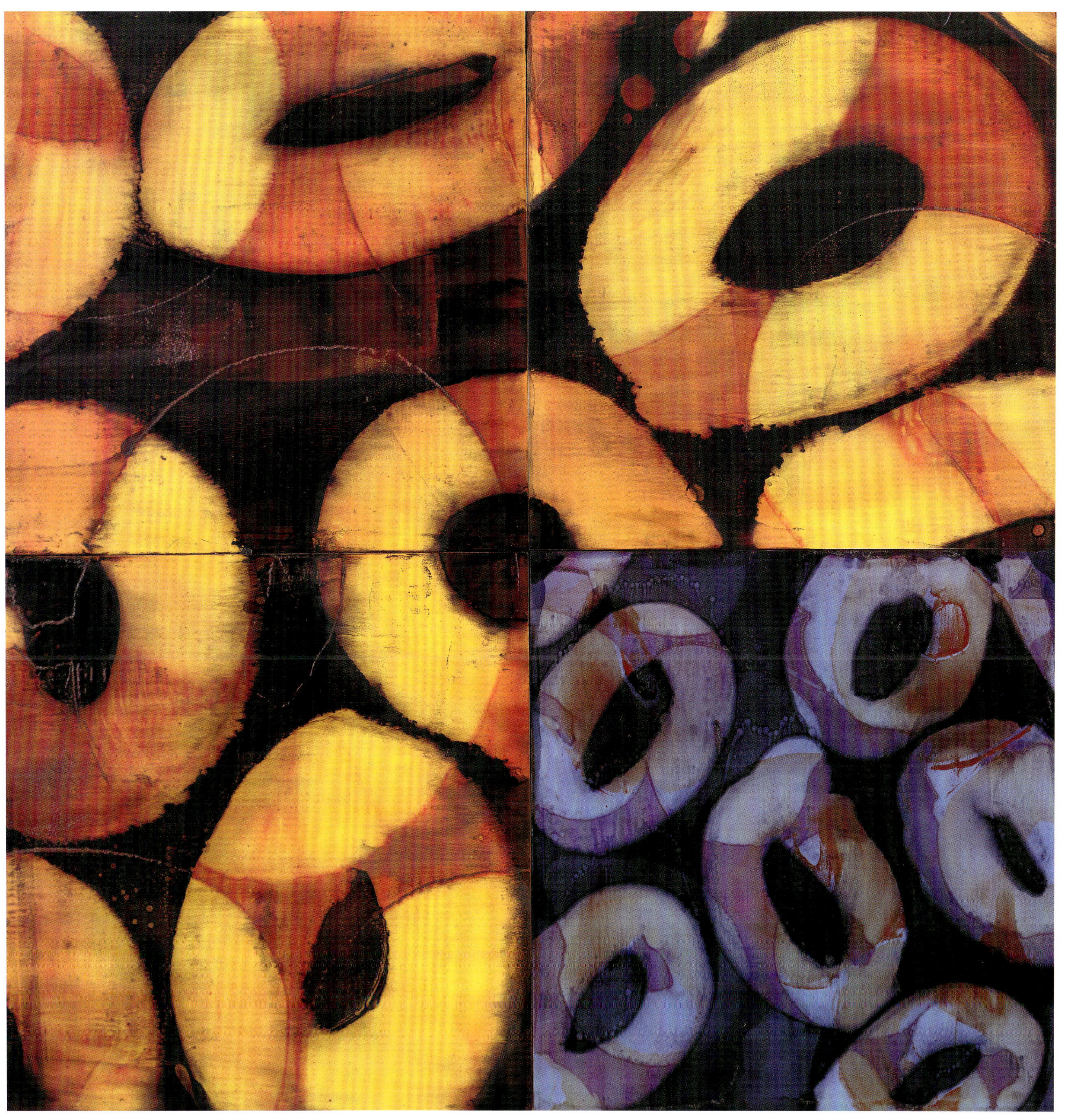

LYRICS FOR CARLOS GARDEL 2006 OIL ON PANEL 60 X 60

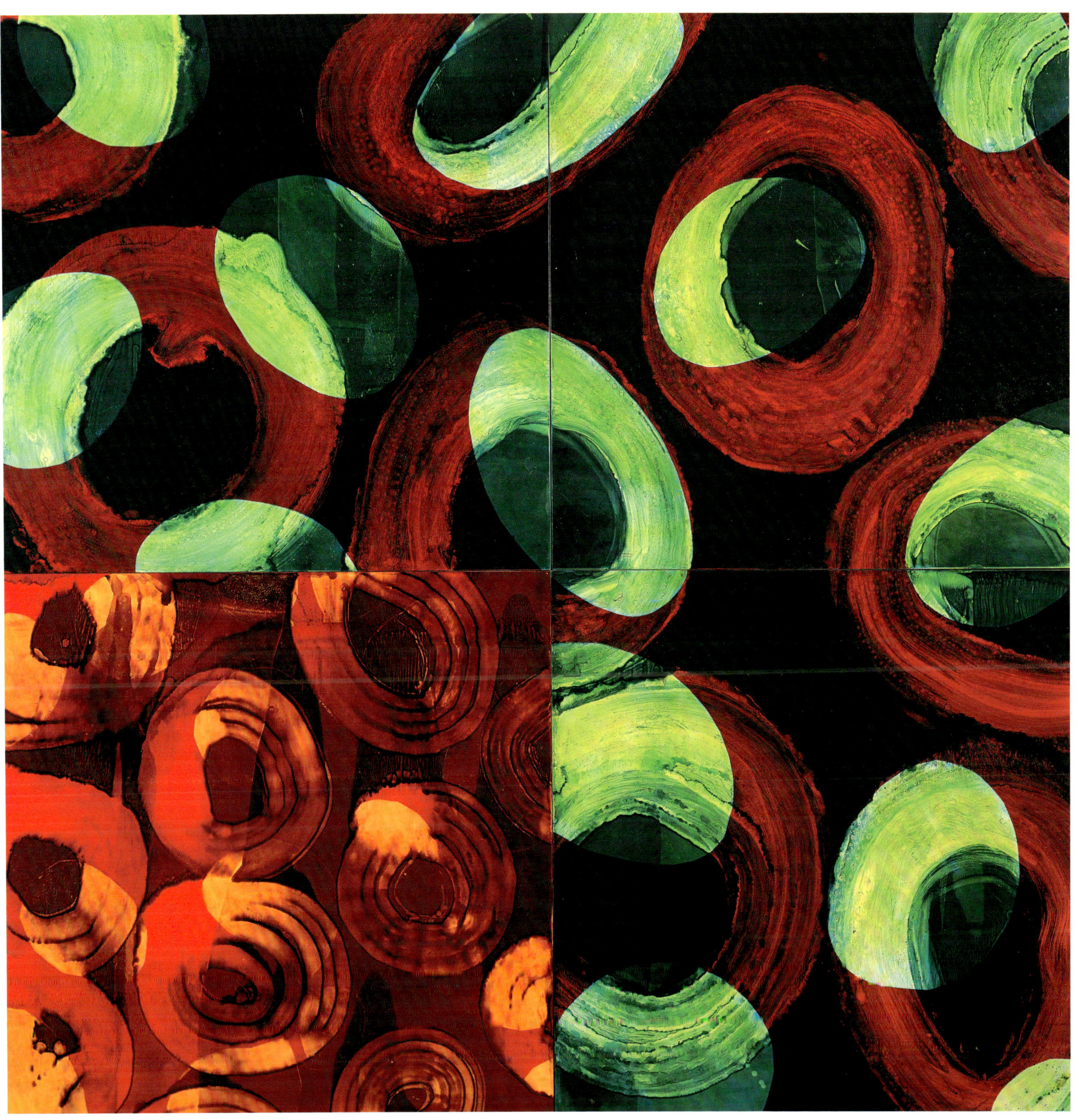

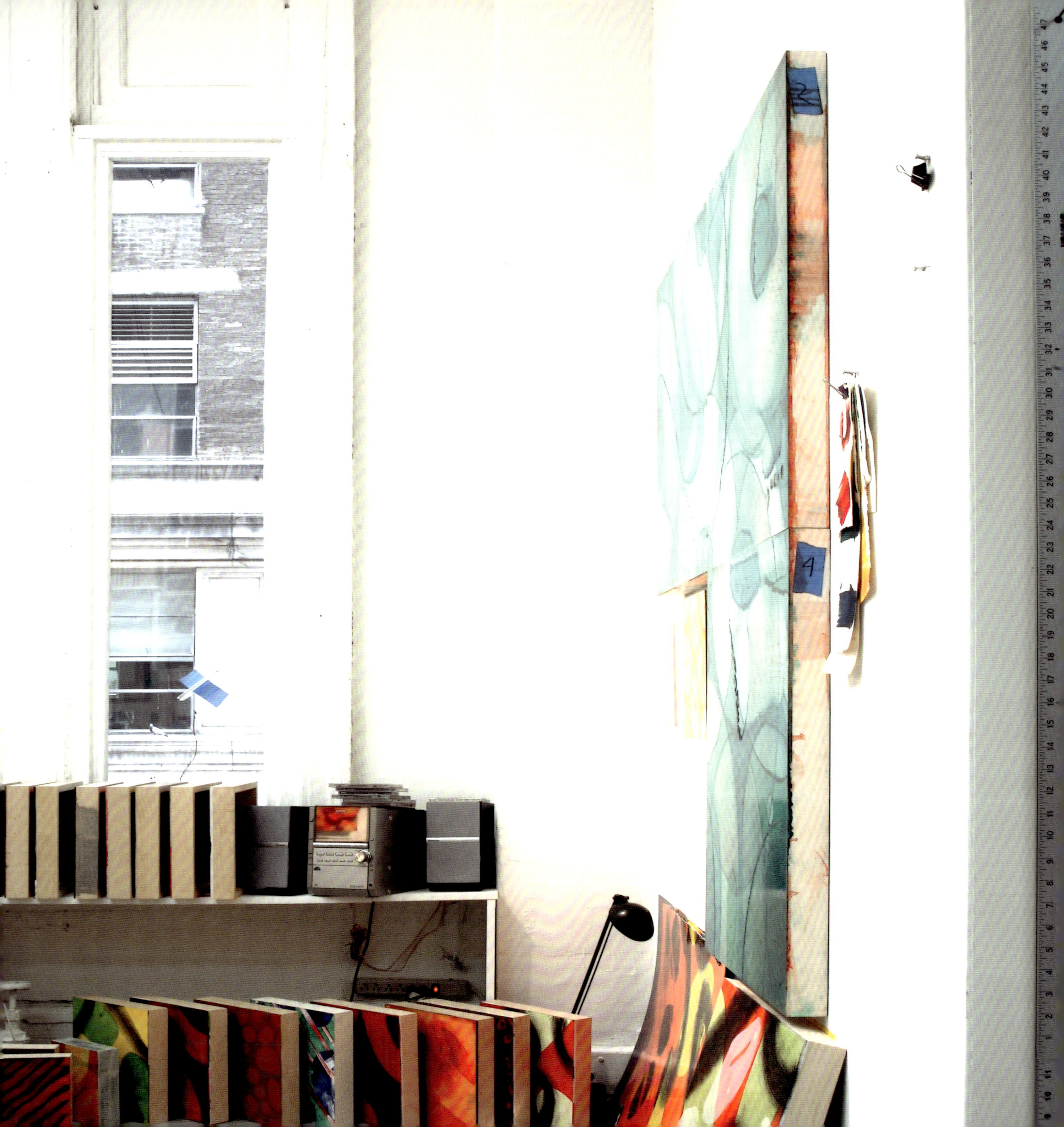

CHRONOLOGY

1943 Born in Brooklyn, New York, to Ruth Keisler, a graduate of New York University, and Dr. Julius Dintenfass, a pioneering chiropractor who holds the New York State Chiropractor's License Number 1.

1950 Family moves to Woodmere, Long Island.

1957–61 Attends Lawrence High School in Lawrence, New York.

1960 Takes summer job as arts counselor at Woodcliff Camp in Woodstock, New York. Visits art galleries and meets other artists. At Woodcliff, meets Gary Katz—the camp's head of waterfront—and begins romance.

1960–61 Writes arts features for the Lawrence High School newspaper and takes classes with Ralph Pasquinucci, a young art teacher and encouraging mentor.

1961 Graduates from Lawrence High School.

1961–65 Attends Queens College. Receives traditional fine arts education. Studies with John Ferren, Barse Miller, Elias Friedensohn, and Barbara Rose, who introduce Dintenfass to contemporary art and artists, including Frank Stella.

Develops strong interest in Stuart Davis, Morris Louis, Ad Reinhardt, and Mark Rothko.

1963 Marries Gary Katz, who is enrolled at New York Law School. The couple settles in an apartment near Queens College.

1963–64 Chairs Arts Study Group at Queens College. Arranges campus visits from artists, including Larry Poons, who arrives accompanied by Andy Warhol. A heated debate ensues on the importance of classical training for artists, and Poons states his belief that there is no need for an artist to learn to draw. The discussion lingers in Dintenfass's mind, and she embraces the idea of making art on one's own terms.

1965 Graduates from Queens College with a Bachelor of Fine Arts.

Travels to Israel with Katz and studies with painter Ruth Bamberger (1904–76) in Jerusalem. Takes etching and drawing classes with Bamberger.

Receives first commission: to design Pop Op Disco, Jerusalem's first discothèque.

1966 Creates a series of etchings of sites in and around the Old City, Jerusalem.

Gary Katz receives U.S. draft notice. Before returning to New York, the couple travels extensively in Switzerland, Italy, France, Belgium, The Netherlands, and England.

Returns to New York City. Accepts short-term third grade teaching assignment at PS 4 in the Bronx, New York.

Gary Katz passes the New York State Bar examination.

1967 Couple moves to New Rochelle, New York.

Son Robert Allan Katz born.

Establishes small studio within family apartment. Teaches at a local arts center.

1969 Son Marc Adam Katz born.

1970–71 Rents Judith Weber's temporarily unused ceramics studio and begins experimenting with and integrating ceramic media into her artistic repertoire.

Retuns to Israel with family and travels extensively. Renews mentorship with Bamberger.

Exhibits, Mamaroneck Artist's Guild, Mamaroneck, New York, *1971 Open Juried Show*.

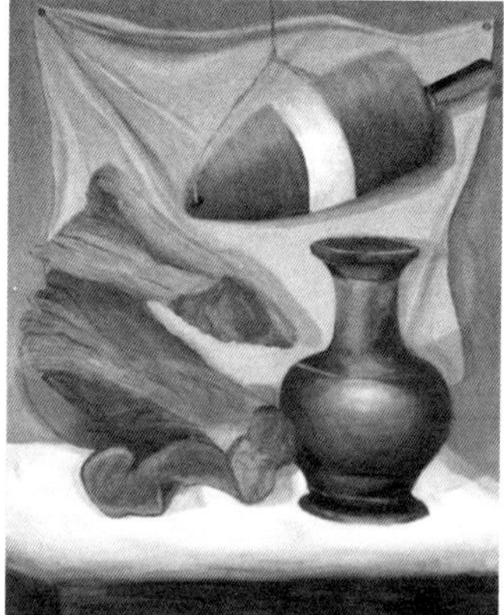

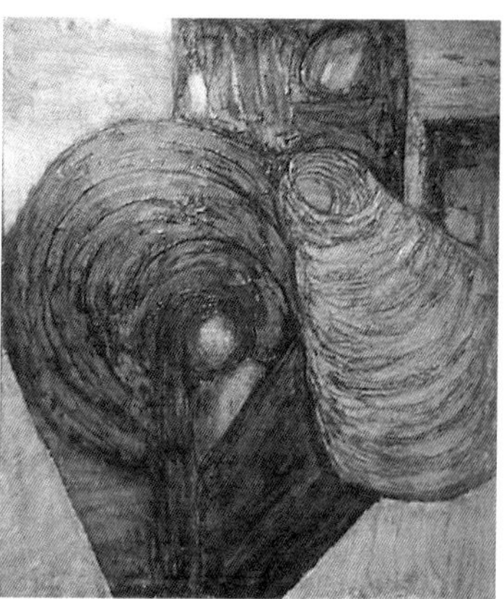

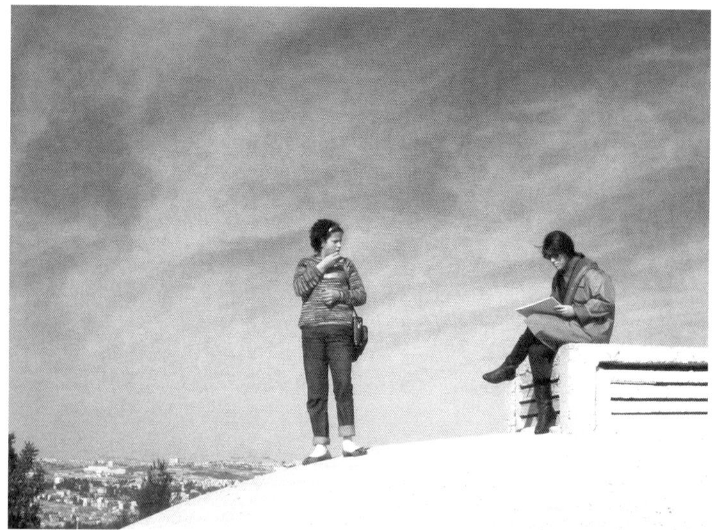

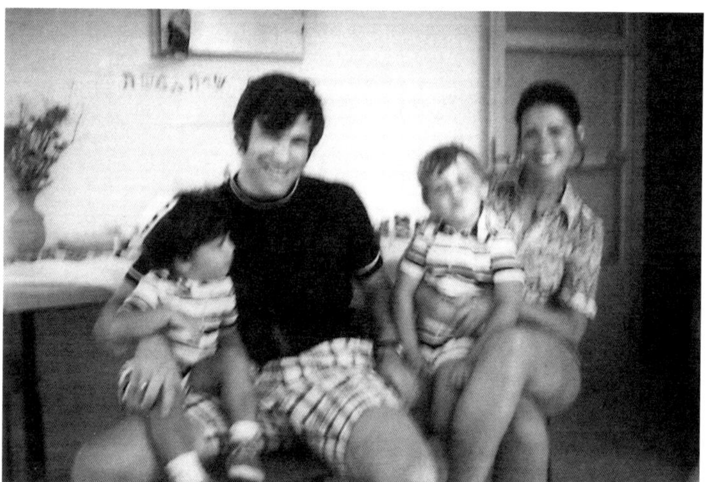

Queens College, *Still Life*, oil on canvas, 32" x 26", 1962

Closed Curves, oil on canvas, 40" x 30", 1965–66

Sketching in Jerusalem, 1966

Katz Family, Israel, 1970

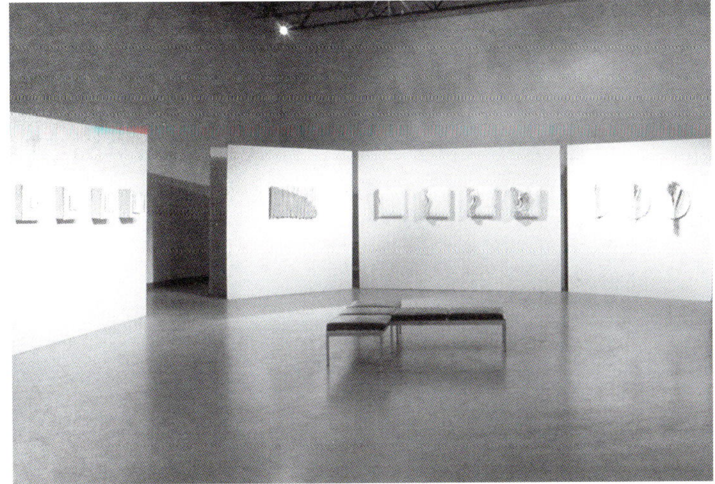

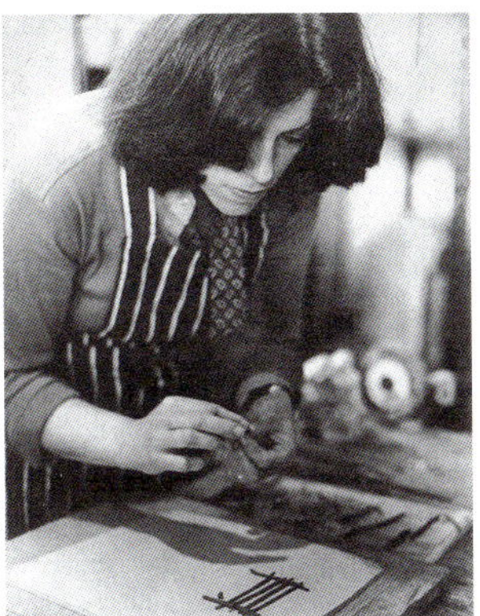

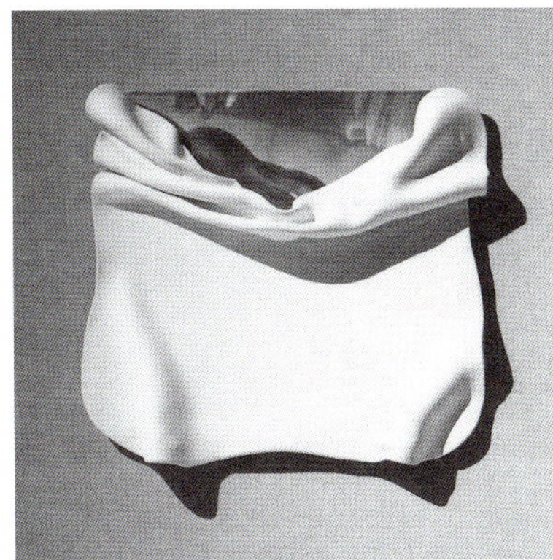

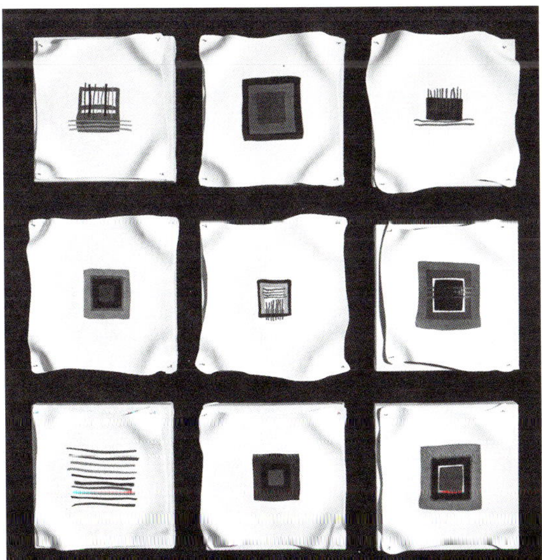

Installation, Schenectady Museum of Art, 1977

Working on *Aerialscape*, 1978

Detail, *Autumn Palette*, 1977

Aerialscape, ceramic, 36" x 36", 1978

1972–73 Family purchases first home. Dintenfass establishes private and self-contained studio in the basement.

Exhibits, The College of New Rochelle, New York, *Anniversary Juried Exhibition*.

Studio work becomes an exploration in defining a path to create art that will both occupy three-dimensional space, like architecture, but visually satisfy, like painting.

1974 Experiments with thin slabs of porcelain and white clay as a tactile, flexible medium and support for "shaped canvas" sculpture and paintings. Inspired by Japanese colored-clay techniques, including Neriage, develops linear graphic compositions inked with metallic oxides to create series of kiln-fired "etchings."

1975 Exhibits, University of Pennsylvania, Philadelphia, *Women's Cultural Trust*.

Exhibits, Tweed Museum of Art, Duluth, Minnesota, *3rd Biennial International Exhibition* (exhibition catalogue).

Receives a 1975 Installation Award at the National Craft Show in Rhinebeck, New York, exhibiting white sculptural clay forms.

Katz family rents summer house in Great Barrington, Massachusetts. Dintenfass sets up a painting studio for the summer.

1976 Solo installation, wall sculpture series, Queens Museum of Art, Queens, New York.

1977 Solo exhibition: Schenectady Museum of Art, Schenectady, New York, *Marylyn Dintenfass*. The museum's vast exhibition space catalyzes Dintenfass's interest in fabricating large-scale, grid-based modular sculptures. The artist further develops multiple component wall sculptures to create "Porcelain Progressions," a series of modular painted wall sculptures considering themes of time and movement. The exhibition marks a shift toward creating monumental works for exhibition and public spaces.

Exhibits, Tyler Art Gallery, State University College at Oswego, New York, *Oswego Invitational* (exhibition catalogue).

Exhibits, Lever House, New York, *Artist Craftsmen of New York*.

Exhibits, Pratt Institute, Brooklyn, New York, *Pratt Invitational*.

Exhibits, Salmagundi Art Club, New York, *Knickerbocker Artists: 27th Annual Exhibition*.

Receives first major commission as a result of Schenectady exhibition, a site-specific modular wall sculpture, "Quadrille," for the offices of Benton & Bowles, Inc., New York City.

Panelist, Hudson River Museum, Yonkers, New York, *Is it Art?*

1978 Dintenfass locates a large affordable industrial space and, with Judith Weber, creates Media Loft Inc. Begin a partnership to design, develop, and manage artist workspaces over the next twenty years.

Solo exhibition: Bell Gallery, Greenwich, Connecticut, *Porcelain Progressions*.

Exhibits, The Bronx Museum of the Arts, New York, *Women Artists*.

Exhibits, The National Academy Galleries, New York, *National Association of Women Artists* (juried exhibition).

Exhibits, Interart Gallery, Women's Interart Center, New York, *Raku Invitational*.

Receives Judges Award for Sculpture at the Hudson River Open, Hudson River Museum, Yonkers, New York.

Lecture and demonstration, National Association of Women Artists, National Academy of Design, New York, "Modular Constructions."

Participates in an artist collaboration grant given by the National Endowment for the Arts at the Clayworks Studio Workshop, New York.

Teaches at Haystack Mountain School, Deer Isle, Maine.

1979 Solo exhibition: Robert L. Kidd Galleries, Birmingham, Michigan, *Porcelain Progressions.*

Exhibits, Herbert F. Johnson Museum of Art, Cornell University, Ithaca, New York, *Clay, Fiber, Metal.*

Exhibits, Suzanne Gross Gallery, Philadelphia, Pennsylvania, *Art Ceramic.*

Exhibits, Bridge Gallery, White Plains, New York, *Selections from the Visual Arts Affiliates of Westchester.*

The Insurance Company of North America acquires and installs a five-part sculpture in its Philadelphia, Pennsylvania, headquarters.

Teaches at Sheridan College of Art & Design, Toronto, Canada.

Guest Artist:

Birmingham Museum of Art, Birmingham, Alabama
New York Public Library, Donnell Library Center, New York
Oakland Community College, Royal Oak, Michigan
Wesleyan University, Middletown, Connecticut
Women's Interart Center, New York

1980 Solo exhibition: The Katonah Museum, Katonah, New York, *Tracks & Traces.*

Exhibits, George Washington University, Washington, DC, 11th International Sculpture Conference, *Architectural Ceramics.*

Exhibits two large-scale installation sculptures, "Kite" and "Virgula," each measuring more than 10 by 12 feet, at *New York Clay Works,* Thorpe Intermedia Gallery, Sparkill, New York, curated by Carl Rattner.

Receives Jurors Award (Henry Geldzahler, Juror), *31st New England Exhibition of Painting and Sculpture,* Silvermine, Connecticut.

Guest Artist Lecturer, Howard University, Washington, DC.

Member of the Faculty, Parsons School of Design, New York (1980–90).

Establishes with Judith Weber second Media Loft space in New Rochelle, New York.

1981 Receives major commission for IBM building in Charlotte, North Carolina. Fabricates and installs "Cubik Themes," a 9 by 21 foot, 2,000-pound site-specific sculpture.

Receives commission from Thompson, Ventulett, Stainback & Associates—architects of the IBM building in Charlotte, North Carolina—for the firm's offices in Atlanta, Georgia.

Main Hurdman purchases and installs "Virgula," a large-scale modular sculpture, for its offices at Park Avenue Plaza, New York.

Exhibits, Galerie Inge Donath, Troisdorf, West Germany, *International Works.*

Exhibits, Bowdoin College Museum of Art, Brunswick, Maine, *Art in Craft Media.*

Exhibits, Louis K. Meisel Gallery, New York, *Gallery Works.*

Guest Artist Lecturer, Radcliffe College, Cambridge, Massachusetts.

Receives Outstanding Achievement Award at *Women in Design International Exhibition,* San Francisco, California.

Serves on Awards Panel for the State of Massachusetts Artist Fellowship Program, Cambridge, Massachusetts.

Daniel Clark Foundation and the National Endowment for the Arts co-publish *Apprenticeship,* edited by Gerry Williams, with contributions by artists such as Warren MacKenzie, John Glick, Sam Maloof, Wendell Castle, and Marylyn Dintenfass.

Teaches at Haystack Mountain School, Deer Isle, Maine.

1982 Receives second commission from Main Hurdman. Creates sculpture installation, "P.O.E.T.S.," for the president's office at Park Avenue Plaza, New York.

Exhibits, Schenectady Museum of Art, New York, *Regional Works.*

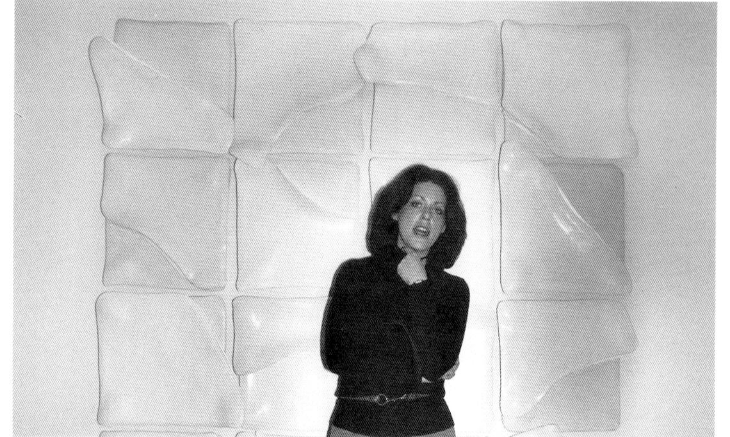

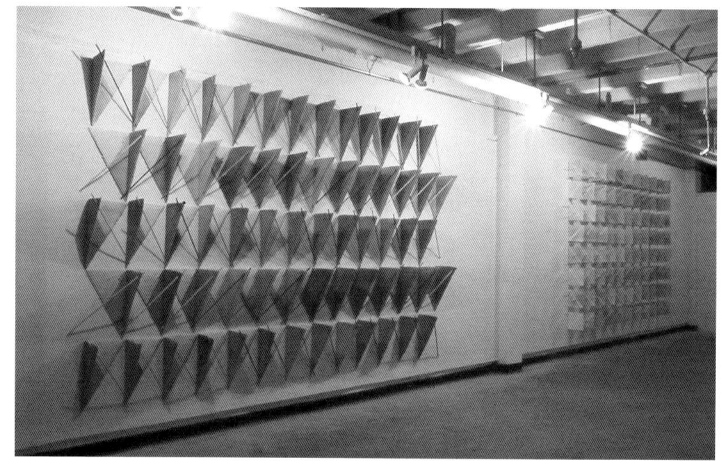

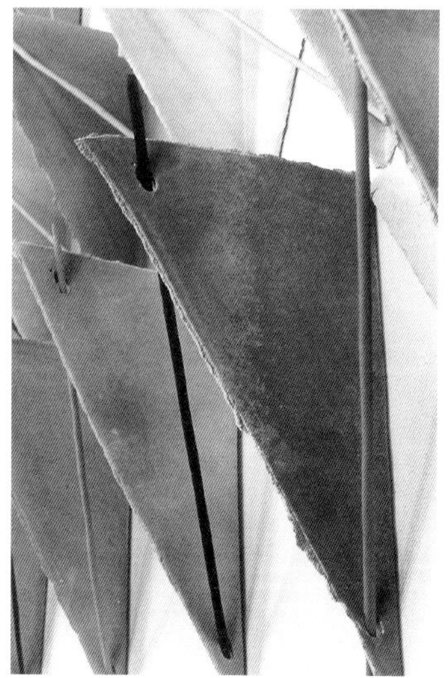

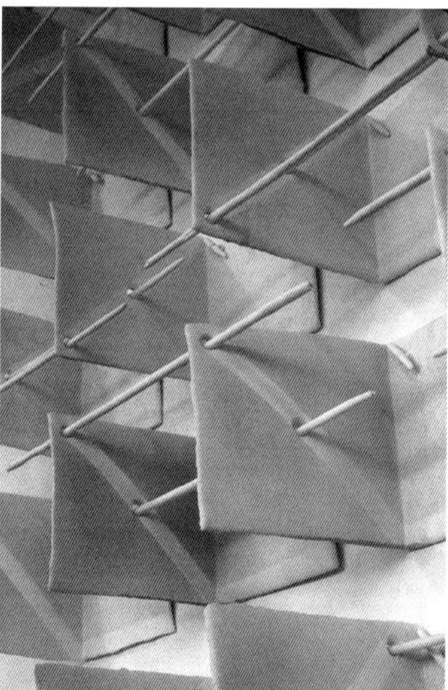

With *Quadrille,* commissioned by Benton & Bowles, NYC, 1978

Installation, *Kite* and *Virgula,* Thorpe Intermedia Gallery, Sparkill, NY, 1980

Detail, *Kite*

Detail, *Virgula*

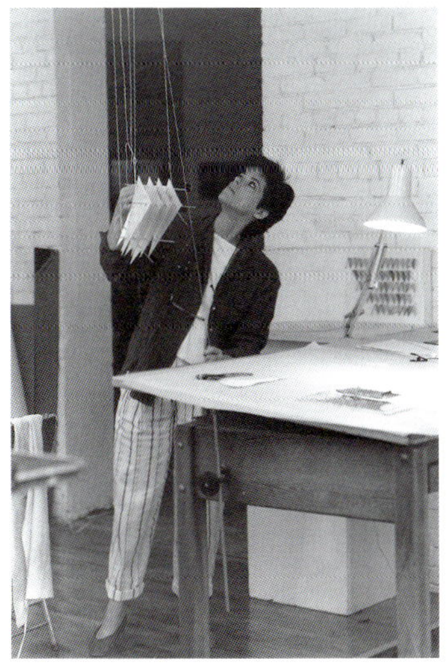

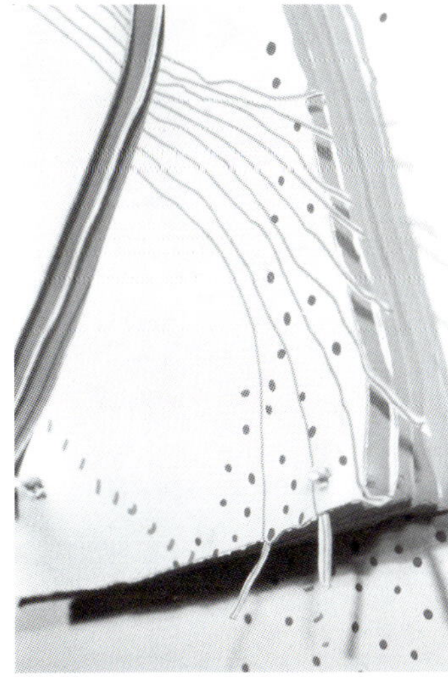

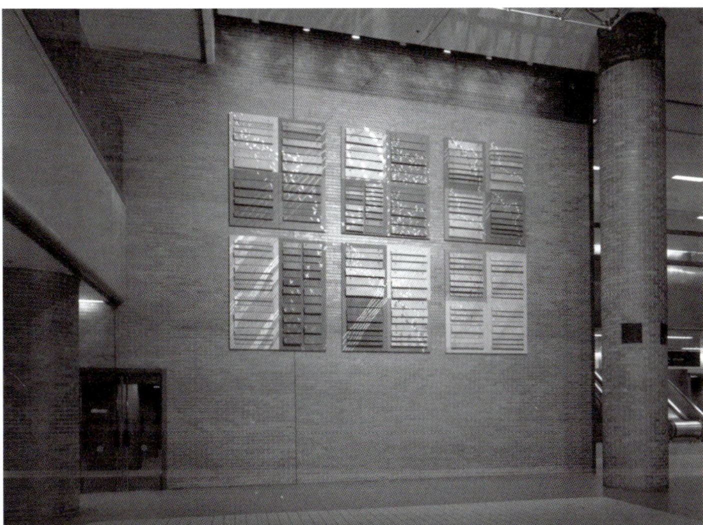

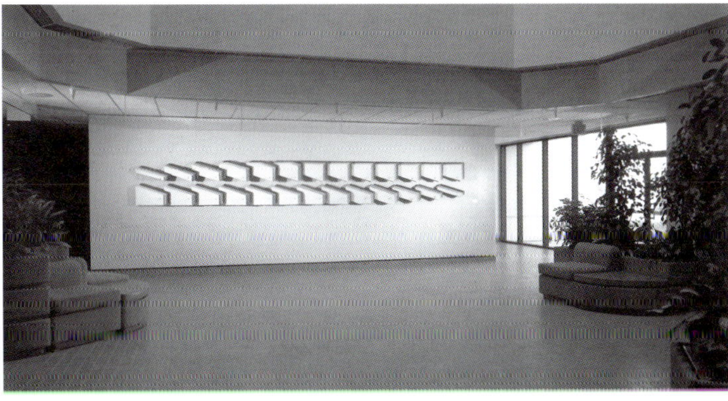

In the studio, Mamaroneck, NY

Detail, *Tracks: Rocket*, 1980

Imprint Fresco, installation, 42nd Street Terminal, Port Authority of NY/NJ, 1985

Parallax, commission for IBM, San Jose, CA, 1983

Organizes *Architectural Ceramics* at Women's Interart Center, New York, with Maxine Feldman. The ten-day symposium, funded by the National Endowment for the Arts, is dedicated to expanding innovative collaboration between artists working with ceramic media and architects.

1983 Receives second major commission from IBM. Travels to San Jose, California, for initial site visit and returns to oversee installation of "Parallax," a 3 by 22 foot sculpture, for IBM's Research Center in San Jose.

Exhibits, The Gallery at Hastings-on-Hudson, New York, *The Evolution of Seven Artists*.

Teaches at Brookhaven College, Dallas, Texas.

Guest Artist Lecturer, Montclair State College, Montclair, New Jersey.

"Profile: Marylyn Dintenfass," by April Kingsley, appears in *American Ceramics*.

Travels to Italy. Visits mosaics in Padua, Verona, and Ravenna, and attends production of *Aida* in Arena di Verona, an ancient Roman amphitheater, reinforcing her interest in the intersection between classic art, classical architecture, and contemporary experience.

1984 Receives major commission for Baltimore Federal Financial Building in Baltimore, Maryland. Creates a 3 by 12 foot wall-hung sculpture.

Receives major commission from Kaiser Permanente in Dallas, Texas. Creates "Diagonal Curve."

Two-person faculty exhibition with Barbara Nechis, Parsons School of Design, New York, *Glazing in Watercolor and Porcelain*.

Exhibits, Smithsonian Institution, National Museum of American Art (now Smithsonian American Art Museum), Renwick Gallery, Washington, DC, *Clay for Walls*, curated by Raylene Decatur (exhibition catalogue).

Exhibits, Liberty Gallery, Louisville, Kentucky, *National Invitational 1984* (exhibition catalogue).

Guest Lecturer, National Museum of American Art, Washington, DC.

Serves on Artist Commission Awards Panel for the State of Connecticut Commission on the Arts, Hartford, Connecticut.

With investor partners, Dintenfass and Weber expand Media Loft through purchase of the historic Knickerbocker Press building in New Rochelle, New York, for conversion into artist studios.

Travels to Italy. Visits with architect friend Lorenzo Berni in Milan. Visits Villa Panza, art collector Giuseppe Panza's personal minimalist collection, in Varese. Tours the house and gardens and views LeWitt wall drawings installed on the seventeenth-century walls. Sees installations by Dan Flavin, Carl Andre, Donald Judd, Bruce Nauman, James Turell, and Robert Irwin, among others.

1985 Receives third commission from IBM. Creates "Fourth Progression," a sculpture installation for its main training facility in Atlanta, Georgia.

Exhibits, Timothy Burns Gallery, St. Louis, Missouri, *Clay Murals and Tiles*.

Exhibits, Lever House, New York, *Art and the Environment*, in affiliation with A.R.E.A. (Artists Representing Environmental Arts). Creates scale model of a design that integrates art into the structure of a high-rise commercial building.

A.R.E.A. successfully submits proposal for Dintenfass to create a site-specific installation at the Port Authority of New York and New Jersey, 42nd Street Terminal, New York. The artist creates "Imprint Fresco," an 18 by 34 foot modular, grid-based installation made from wood, resins, epoxy, steel, porcelain, and paint that references both Italian Renaissance frescoes and the modular nature of contemporary architecture.

One of five featured speakers, including Michael Graves, James Wines, Robert Jensen, and Wayne Higby, National Council on Education for the Ceramic Arts Annual Conference, St. Louis, Missouri. Also moderates panel on "Art in Architecture."

Presenter, *Architectural Clay/Clay in Architecture*, Greenwich House, New York, sponsored by the New York State Council on the Arts.

Guest Artist, State University of New York, New Paltz.

Teaches at Hunter College, City University of New York.

Co-founder, CERF (Craft Emergency Relief Fund), with Josh Simpson and Carol Sedestrom. CERF provides financial assistance to artists in need and acts as a clearinghouse for career-related health and safety issues.

1986 Awarded commission, State of Connecticut, State Superior Courthouse, Enfield, Connecticut, Department of Administrative Services and the Connecticut Commission on the Arts. Creates "Diagonal Frieze," a modular 33-foot wall-sculpture installation that references classical architectural friezes yet is fabricated and installed modularly, like contemporary architecture.

Awarded Silver Medal at the First International Ceramic Exhibition in Mino, Japan, for "Wing," a 10 by 10 foot modular sculpture. Travels to Japan to accept award.

Receives commission from ADT Corporation, Waltham, Massachusetts.

Exhibits, Robert L. Kidd Galleries, Birmingham, Michigan, *Major Concepts* (exhibition catalogue).

Receives invitation from the Port Authority of New York and New Jersey to submit proposal for PATH train station mural. Arranges with Japanese tile manufacturer to fabricate work in the company's factory. One of two finalists.

Guest Artist Lecturer, Nassau Community College, Garden City, New York.

Guest Artist Workshop, Mendocino Art Center, Mendocino, California.

Authors "Working Large Scale: Portfolio" for May issue of *Ceramics Monthly*.

1987 Receives Individual Artist Fellowship from the New York Foundation for the Arts.

Awarded Ravenna Prize at the 45° Concorso Internazionale della Ceramica d'Arte in Faenza, Italy, for "Transom," a 10 by 10 foot sculpture installation. Travels to Italy to accept the award.

Receives commission for Crystal City Complex, Arlington, Virginia. Installs "Trapezoid Frieze," a 3 by 22 foot sculpture.

Exhibits, National Archives Gallery, Montreal, Canada, *New York/Montreal: Grand Prix des Métiers D'Art—Banque d'Épargne*.

Exhibits, Syracuse University School of Architecture, Syracuse, New York, *Drawings, Sketches and Models: Ceramics in Architecture*.

Exhibits, Le Moyne College Gallery, Syracuse, New York, *Empire State Selections*.

Exhibits, Fashion Institute of Technology Gallery, New York, *Artists in Space*.

Exhibits, The Gallery at Hastings-on-Hudson, New York, *Crossovers: Sculptured Painting/Painted Sculpture*.

Lectures at Bezalel Academy of Art and Design, Jerusalem, Israel.

Panel Moderator (two panels), National Sculpture Conference: Works by Women, Cincinnati, Ohio, "Working Spaces: Women Artists" and "Large Scale Work: Installation/Presentation."

Appointed to the Board of Governors, New York Foundation for the Arts. Serves until 1991.

1988 Receives MacDowell Colony Fellowship, Peterborough, New Hampshire.

Exhibits, Tower Fine Arts Gallery, SUNY College at Brockport, *Public Art: Making a Better Place to Live*.

Guest Artist, Skidmore College, Saratoga Springs, New York.

Elected Member, The International Academy of Ceramics, Geneva, Switzerland.

Serves on Artist Fellowship Selection Panel for the State of Massachusetts Artist Fellowship Program, Boston.

Travels to Sicily and Italy. Visits Positano and the Roman architectural sites of Paestum and Pompeii, reinforcing ideas for the integration of modular architectural painting and sculpture.

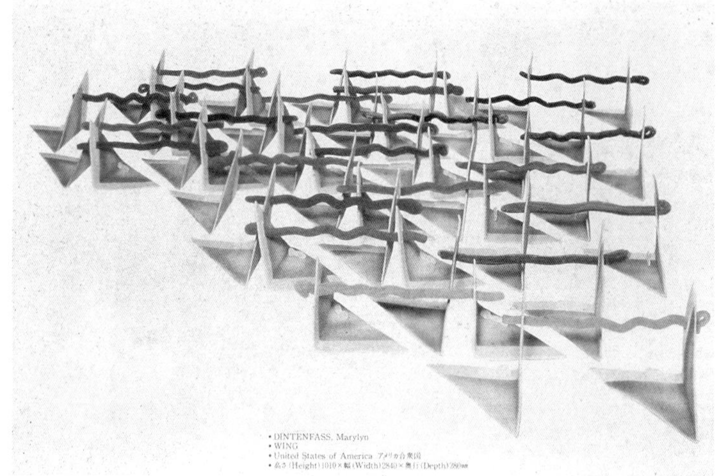

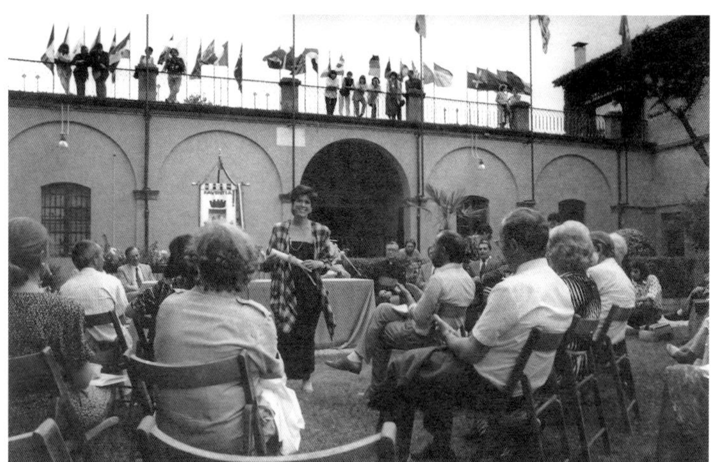

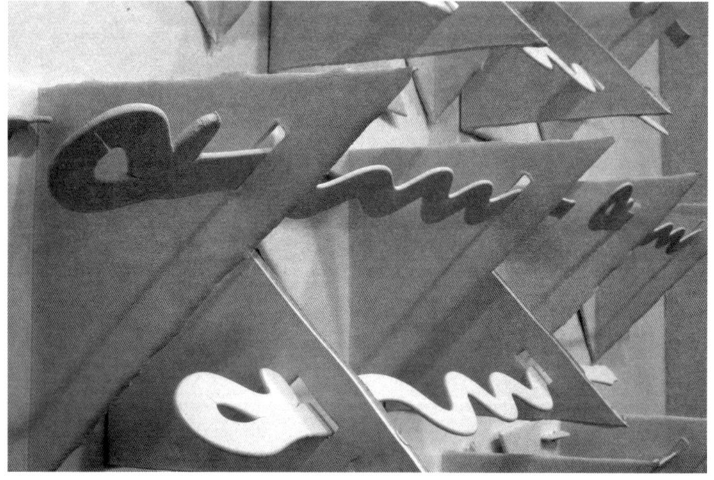

Wing, installation, Mino, Japan, 1986

Receiving Ravenna Prize for *Transom*, Faenza, Italy, 1987

Detail, *Transom*

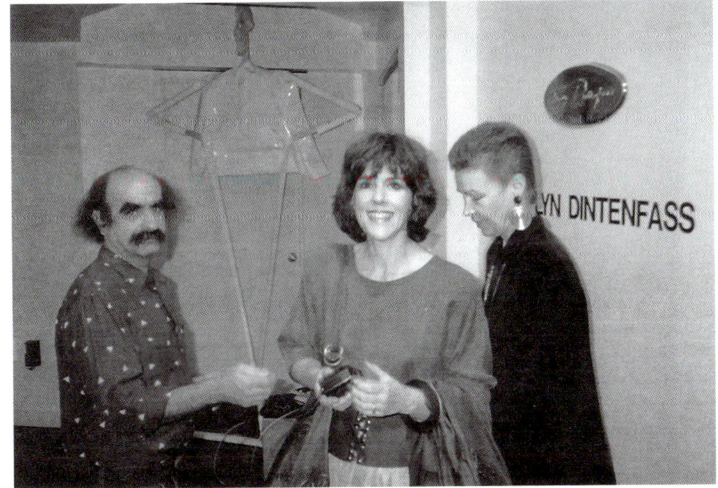

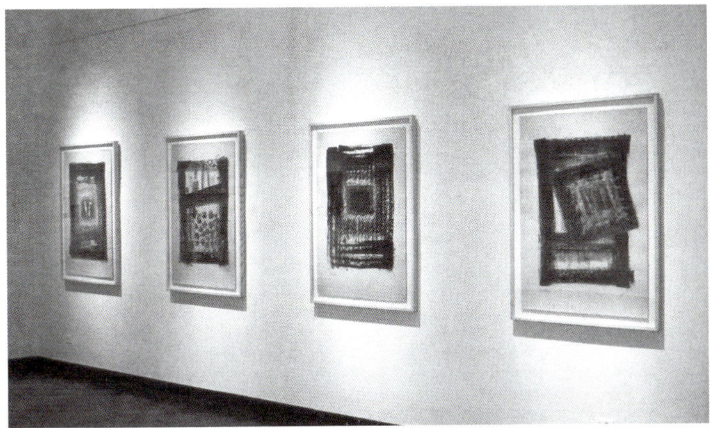

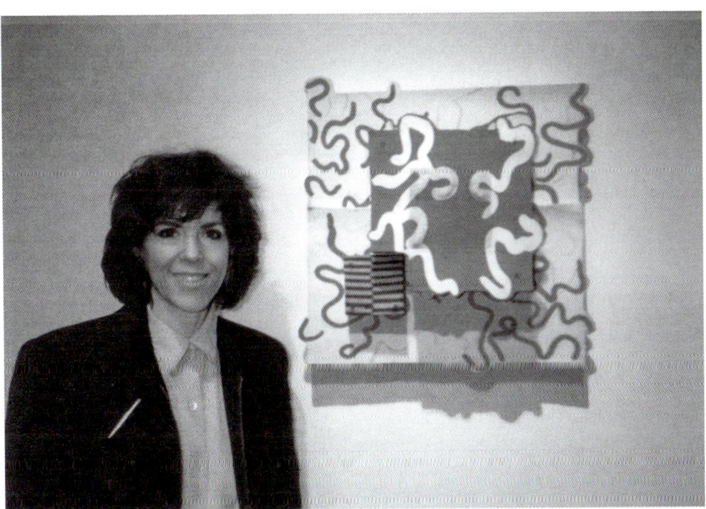

Opening, solo exhibition, Terry Dintenfass Gallery, NYC, 1991, with Zigi Ben-Haim and Harriet Bart

Solo exhibition, Terry Dintenfass Gallery, 1991

With *Paradigm: Rouge*, exhibition, Roden, The Netherlands, 1991

1989 Receives commission from American International Group, New York.

Receives commission from Ahavath Achim Synagogue, Atlanta, Georgia.

Exhibits, The Katonah Museum, Katonah, New York, *New Sculpture*.

Exhibits, Nevada Museum of Art, Reno, *Visiting Artists*.

Teaches at Sierra Nevada College, Incline Village, Nevada.

1990 Receives second MacDowell Colony Fellowship, Peterborough, New Hampshire.

Receives commission from Aetna Life Insurance Company, Headquarters, Hartford, Connecticut.

Guest Faculty, Bezalel Academy of Art and Design, Jerusalem, Israel.

WBAC Television in Boston, Massachusetts, features Dintenfass and other artists—including Zigi Ben-Haim and George Tsontakis—in the documentary film *Artists at the MacDowell Colony*, which airs on national television.

Invited, International Artists Residency, Tommerup, Odense, Denmark. Works in a brick factory with ten American artists, ten Scandinavian artists, and local art student assistants. Creates two large modular grid installation sculptures and a series of incised *Painted Tablet* paintings.

Exhibits, Kunsthallen Brandts Klaedefabric Museum, Odense, Denmark, *Clay Today*.

Panelist, PS 1, Long Island City, New York. Represents MacDowell Colony on panel presenting artist colonies.

Marriage to Gary Katz ends.

1991 Solo exhibition: Terry Dintenfass Gallery, New York, *Paradigm Series*. Exhibits sculptures and paintings. As Terry and Marylyn share the same surname, Terry at first considers, then abandons, the idea of calling the exhibition *No Relation*.

Exhibits, Mensinghe Museum, Roden, The Netherlands, *Internationale Keramiektentoonstelling*.

Guest Faculty, National College of Art and Design, Bergen/Oslo, Norway.

Guest Artist, Academie Minerva, Groningen, The Netherlands.

Prints monotypes with Kathy Caraccio in New York City. Creates *Tommerup* series of works on paper using imagery from the *Painted Tablet* series produced in Tommerup, Denmark.

1992 Receives commission for "Time Square," an 8 by 8 foot wall sculpture, from law firm Edwards & Angell in New York.

Exhibits, Triplex Gallery, Borough of Manhattan Community College, City University of New York, *Selections from the BMCC Permanent Collection*.

Exhibits, Paramount Center for the Arts, Peekskill, New York, *Art in Architecture*.

Guest Faculty, National College of Art and Design, Bergen/Oslo, Norway, second appointment.

Creates *Sticks & Stones*, a series of large-scale oil on paper monoprints, and begins continuing association with Lisa Mackie Print Studios, New York.

"The Clay Paintings of Marylyn Dintenfass," by Frederick Ted Castle, appears in *Ceramics: Art and Perception*.

Serves, Awards Panel, State of Ohio Arts Council, Individual Artist Fellowship Review, Columbus, Ohio.

1993 Exhibits, Associated American Artists Gallery, New York, *Monotypes/Monoprints* (exhibition catalogue).

Exhibits, Elsa Mott Gallery, New York, *Transcending Boundaries*.

Receives invitation to participate in the International Art Biennale, Be'er Sheva, Israel, with an artist residency at Negev Ceramica, a large ceramic tile factory in Yeroham, Israel. Produces three large-scale pieces, one of which, "Negev Carpet," is installed at

Ben Gurion University, Be'er Sheva. A second piece, "Negev Sadot" (Desert Fields), a 40 by 118 inch modular painting on square clay tiles, is installed at the City of Be'er Sheva Municipal Hall.

Exhibits, Turkish Station Gallery, Be'er Sheva, Israel, *From the Factory.*

Exhibits, Avraham Baron Art Gallery, Ben Gurion University, Be'er Sheva, Israel, *Installations.*

Guest Artist Presentation at the Embassy of the United States of America, Tel Aviv, Israel.

Videographer and director Michael Jaffe proposes filming Dintenfass working in the Negev factory. Dintenfass and Jaffe collaborate.

Body of work acquired by Mineral Technologies, Inc., for its offices in the Chrysler Building, New York.

Returns from Israel to New York via Denmark. In Denmark, visits sculptor Nina Hole. Hole and Dintenfass travel to The Netherlands.

1994 Solo exhibition: Hamline University, Saint Paul, Minnesota, *Marylyn Dintenfass, Clay InPrint.*

Exhibits, Silo Gallery, New Milford, Connecticut, *High on Tile.*

Exhibits, Shirley Fiterman Gallery, Borough of Manhattan Community College, City University of New York, *Selections from the Permanent Collection.*

Panel Moderator, National Sculpture Conference, San Francisco, California.

Panel Moderator, National Council for Education in the Ceramic Arts Conference, New Orleans, Louisiana.

Works with Michael Jaffe in a post-production facility in New York City to edit and score the video *Dintenfass in the Negev Factory.*

1995 Exhibits, Center for Book Arts, New York, *The International Library,* curated by Helmut Löhr. Exhibition travels to Europe and is now on long-term loan to the Frederick R. Weisman Art Museum, University of Minnesota, Minneapolis.

Exhibits monotypes, Click 3X, New York, *Anniversary Exhibition.*

Exhibits, Rogaland Kunstnersenter, Stavanger, Norway, *New York, New York: Clay,* curated by Judith Schwartz. Exhibition travels to Hordland Kunstnersenter, Bergen; Nordenfjeldske Kunstindustrimuseum, Trondheim; Ostfold Kunstnersenter, Fredrikstad.

Boston Consulting Group, New York, acquires collection of work for installation in its New York Headquarters, including four constructions installed in its conference room and a large modular-grid tile painting, "Negev Imprint."

Investigating options for experimenting with a new art medium, Dintenfass accompanies entrepreneur Terri Lonier to a Macworld Conference in Boston and attends a presentation entitled "Artists Make CD-ROMs." Begins developing and producing a series of digital vignettes on how artists make art.

Partners with Arthur Williams, president of the Tape House post-production facility in New York City and an art collector, to create joint venture to develop Dintenfass's HandsOn Interactive Media for the Arts digital projects.

Mayfield Publishing Company publishes third edition of *Hands in Clay: An Introduction to Ceramics,* by Charlotte F. Speight. Images of "Negev Sadot" appear on the front and back cover, and Dintenfass's work is featured in the book.

1996 Exhibits, Jane Voorhees Zimmerli Art Museum, Rutgers University, New Brunswick, New Jersey, *Unique Impressions: Contemporary Monotypes and Monoprints.*

Organizes a team of digital artists, studio artists, and camera, sound, and light technicians to produce HandsOn Interactive series.

Presents HandsOn at the MIT Enterprise Forum, New York.

Creative-directs, with HandsOn Interactive team, two new product projects for Sony Corporation and new opening sequence for the Ovation Channel.

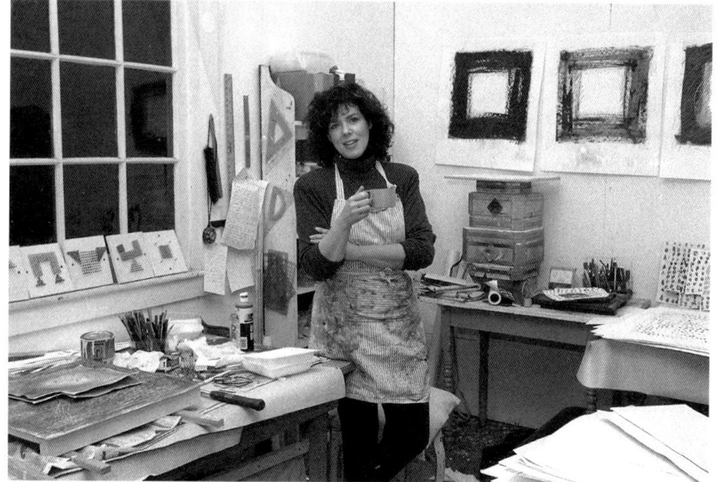

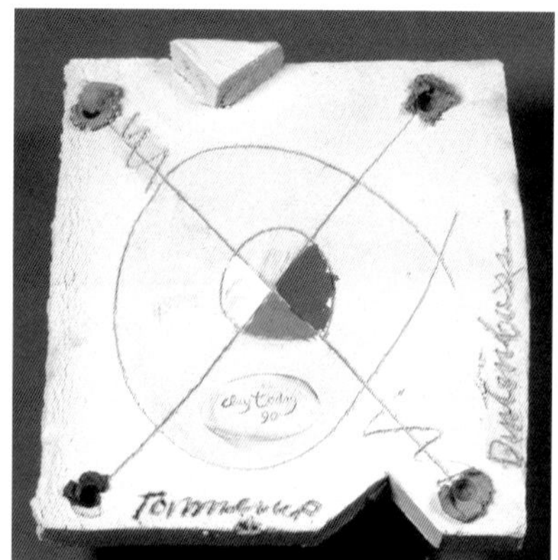

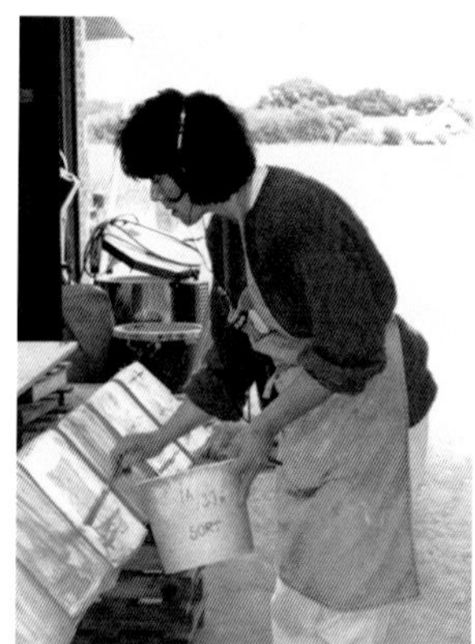

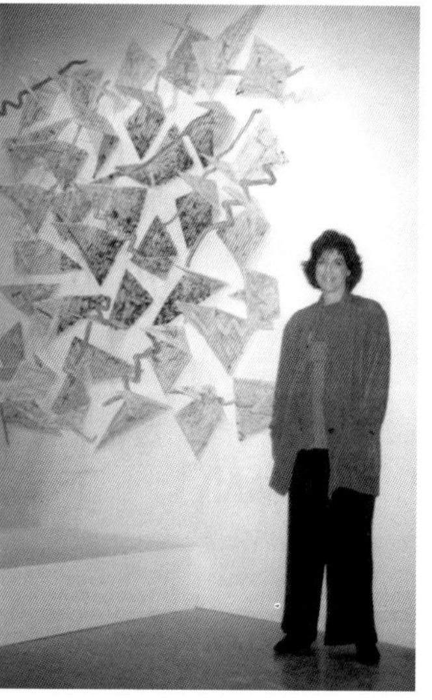

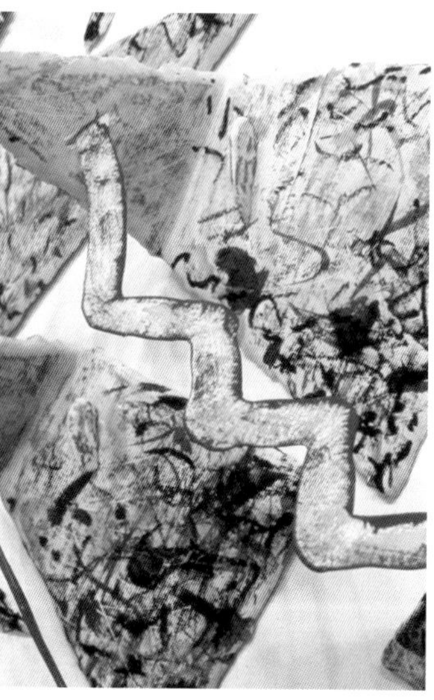

At the MacDowell Colony, Peterborough, NH, 1990

Tommerup Tablet, 1990

Painting in Tommerup, Denmark, 1990

With *Time Frame,* exhibition, Peekskill, NY, 1992

Detail, *Time Frame*

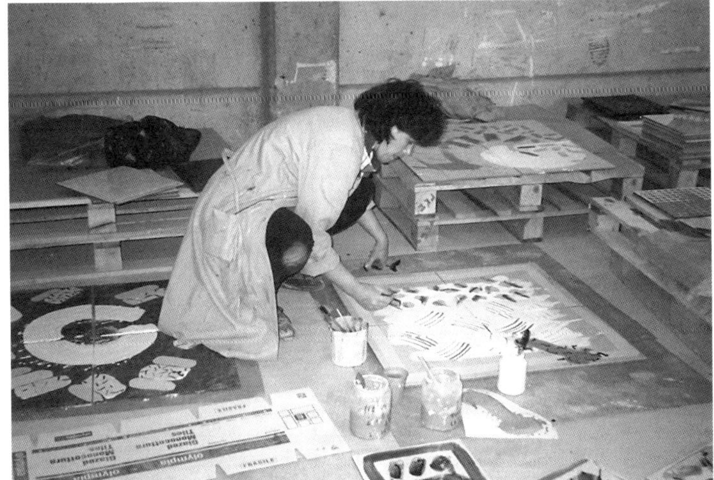

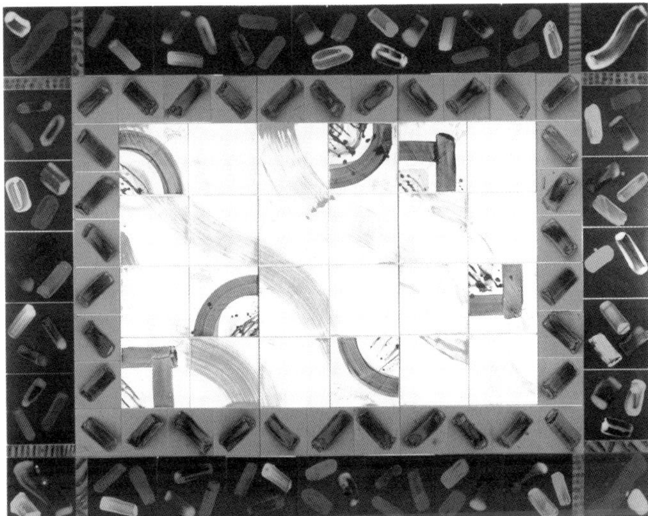

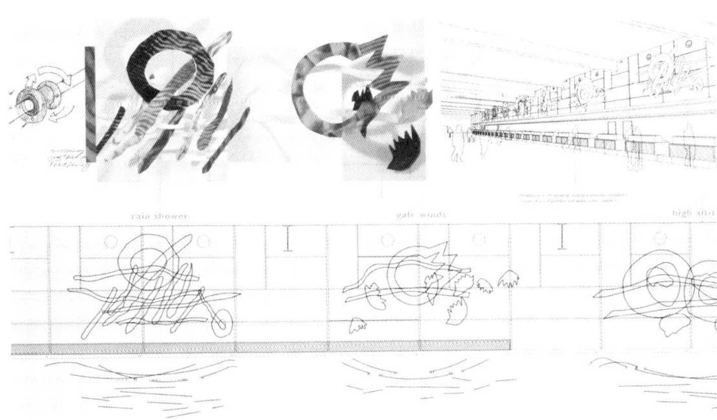

Painting in Negev tile factory, Yeroham, Israel, 1993

Negev Carpet, Ben Gurion University, Israel, 1993

Detail, Proposal for Bradley International Airport, Hartford, CT, 2001

Presents HandsOn at Consumer Electronics Show, Las Vegas, Nevada.

Presents at Macworld Conference, San Francisco, California. This is the first of eleven Macworld speaking engagements between 1996 and 2001.

1997 Presents HandsOn at the Queens Library Gallery, Queens, New York, in conjunction with *Forms & Transformations: Current Expressions in Ceramics, from Art to Industry*, curated by Judith S. Schwartz (exhibition catalogue).

Directs multi-screen presentation for Jaguar Corporation. Produces choreographed image montage with original musical score.

Chinese-language Taiwanese magazine, *Ceramic Art*, publishes "Marylyn Dintenfass: Evocative Architectural Sculpture," an eight-page full-color portfolio and feature article by Ling Pei Chin about Dintenfass's sculpture installations.

HandsOn Interactive is featured in "Molding Multimedia: One Artist's Approach to Teaching Kids Art," by Erica Rex, in *Mac Home Journal*.

Co-guest speaker at TEKNOCHIX, "Interface. . .Not in Your Face: An Evening with Artists Toni Dove and Marylyn Dintenfass," Puck Building, New York, sponsored by Bell Technologies/Blue Streak Digital.

1998 Presenter, The Metropolitan Museum of Art, New York, "Interactive Art."

Panelist, International Radio & Television Society, New York, "Interface Design."

Appointed a creative director at Viant, an international Internet consultancy known for hiring accomplished artists for creative consulting on client projects.

Travels to Utah and hikes in Zion National Park. Develops *Boulder* series of monotypes.

Moves to New York City. Relocates studio from New Rochelle, New York, to temporary space on Greene Street in Soho.

1999 Pfizer, Inc., acquires selection of works for installation in its New York offices.

Freddie Mac Headquarters acquires selection of works for installation in its offices in McLean, Virginia.

Presenter, New York University, Interactive Telecommunications Program.

Speaker, Visual Design Presentation Series, Parsons School of Design, New York.

Establishes new studio, Hudson Street in the West Village, New York. Begins producing *Hudson* and *Greenwich* series of monotypes.

Attends party hosted by Arthur Williams. Meets John Driscoll, an art dealer and collector, who had previously begun to assemble a collection of Dintenfass's work.

2000 Exhibits, Grimmerhus Keramikmuseum, Middlefart, Denmark, *Recent Acquisitions*.

Latham & Watkins, New York, acquires works on paper for its collection.

Astrolink, Bethesda, Maryland, acquires works on paper for its collection.

2001 Bayerische Landesbank acquires suite of monotypes for installation in its New York headquarters.

Receives invitation to submit proposal for key commission at the Bradley International Airport, Hartford, Connecticut. Designs comprehensive proposal for 300 foot wall installation and is named a finalist.

Begins personal relationship with John Driscoll. The couple travels to Italy and London, England.

2002 Exhibits, Babcock Galleries, New York, *Past and Present*.

Revisits *Sticks & Stones* series (1992) and produces new body of work that reinterprets themes of original series.

Begins *Uffizi* series of monoprints influenced by recent visit to Florence, Italy.

2003 Exhibits, Hunterdon Museum of Art, Clinton, New Jersey, *47th National Print Exhibition.*

Exhibits, Franklin Riehlman Fine Art, New York, *Gallery Works.*

Exhibits, Columbus College of Art and Design, Columbus, Ohio, *21st Century Ceramics*, curated by Bill Hunt (exhibition catalogue).

Panelist, Purchase College, School of Art and Design, Purchase, New York, "Careers in Art and Design."

Establishes new studio in Chelsea, New York.

2004 Exhibits, New Orleans Museum of Art, *From Another Dimension: Works on Paper by Sculptors*, curated by Daniel Piersol.

Exhibits, The Palmer Museum of Art, Pennsylvania State University, University Park, *Works on Paper: Selections from the Permanent Collection.*

Exhibits, Samuel Dorsky Museum of Art, SUNY New Paltz, New York, *Out of the Vault: Recent Acquisitions.*

Exhibits, Babcock Galleries, New York, *Close, Dintenfass, Nice, Warhol: Master Prints.*

Exhibits, The International Print Center, New York, *New Prints 2004*, curated by Barry Walker.

Freddie Mac acquires a suite of large format monotypes for its headquarters in McLean, Virginia.

Marries John Driscoll.

2005 Exhibits, Fitchburg Art Museum, Massachusetts, *Collection Directions: Acquisitions in the Twenty-first Century.*

Exhibits, Franklin Riehlman Fine Art, New York, *No Object.*

Exhibits, Babcock Galleries, New York, *Barnet, Close, Dintenfass, Warhol.*

Exhibits, Arkansas Arts Center, Little Rock, *2005 Collectors Show.*

2006 Chelsea studio floods, damaging work and files. Relocates studio to 31st Street in New York City.

Solo exhibition: Greenville County Museum of Art, Greenville, South Carolina, *Marylyn Dintenfass Paintings.*

Solo exhibition: Mississippi Museum of Art, Jackson, *Work in Progress: Marylyn Dintenfass.*

Solo exhibition: Franklin Riehlman Fine Art, New York, *Marylyn Dintenfass: Recent Paintings.*

Solo exhibition: Pelter Gallery, Greenville, South Carolina, *Marylyn Dintenfass: Works on Paper.*

Exhibits, Mississippi Museum of Art, Jackson, *Art Adored: Icons from the Permanent Collection.*

Exhibits, Paul Kasmin Gallery, New York, *Not Gay Art Now*, curated by Jack Pierson.

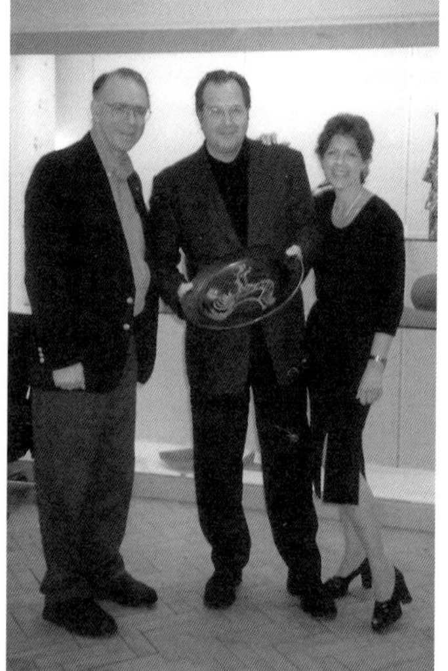

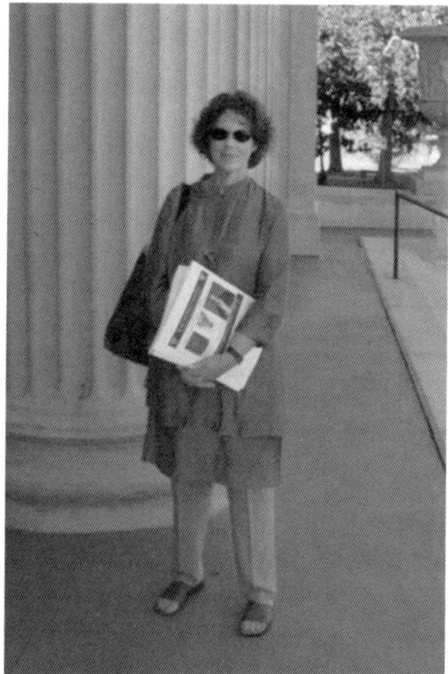

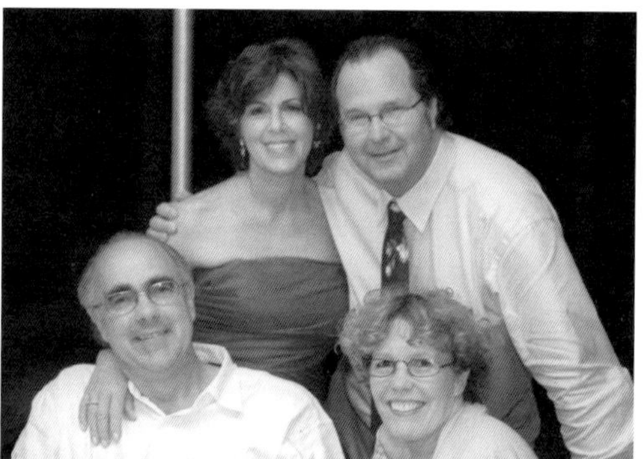

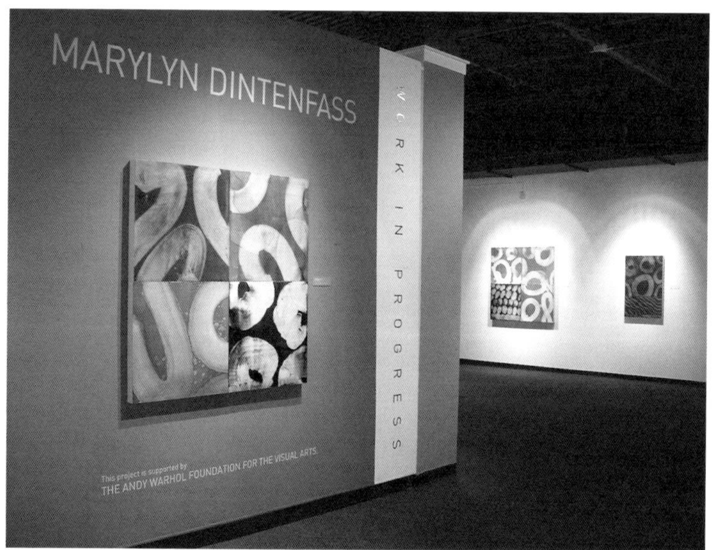

With collector Dexter Stevens and John Driscoll, London, 2001

New Orleans Museum of Art, 2004

Wedding to John Driscoll, celebrating with Lisa Mackie and John Stookey, 2004

Installation, solo exhibition, Mississippi Museum of Art, Jackson, 2006

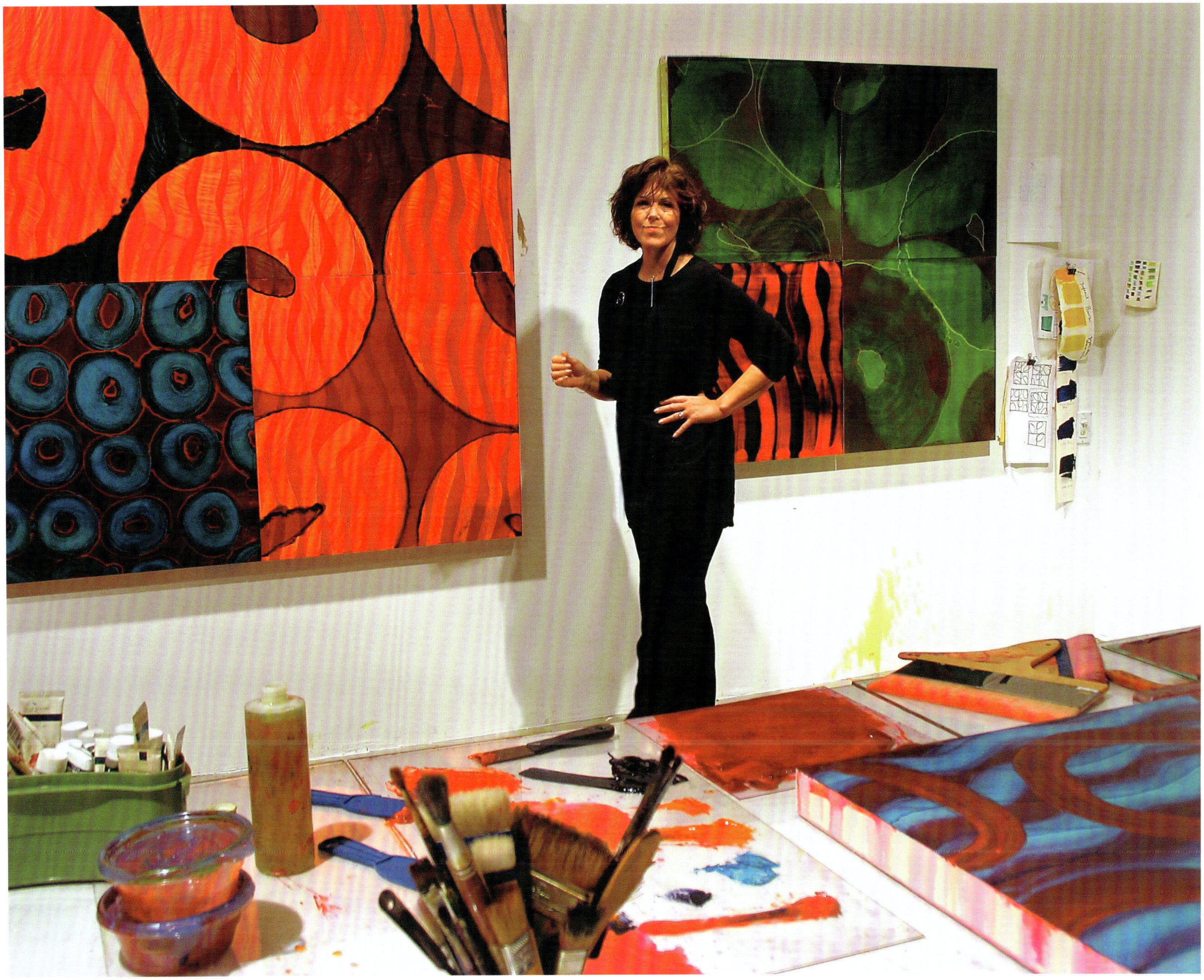

SELECTED PUBLIC COLLECTIONS

Ackland Art Museum, Chapel Hill, North Carolina
Ben Gurion University of the Negev, Be'er Sheva, Israel
Borough of Manhattan Community College, City University of New York, New York
The Butler Institute of American Art, Youngstown, Ohio
Cheekwood Museum of Art, Nashville, Tennessee
The Cleveland Museum of Art, Cleveland, Ohio
Columbus Museum of Art, Columbus, Ohio
The Detroit Institute of Arts, Detroit, Michigan
Samuel Dorsky Museum of Art, SUNY New Paltz, New York
Everson Museum of Art, Syracuse, New York
Fitchburg Art Museum, Fitchburg, Massachusetts
Flint Institute of Art, Flint, Michigan
Greenville County Museum of Art, Greenville, South Carolina
Grimmerhus Keramikmuseum, Middlefart, Denmark
Kresge Art Museum, Michigan State University, East Lansing, Michigan
The Metropolitan Museum of Art, New York
Minneapolis Institute of Arts, Minneapolis, Minnesota
Mississippi Museum of Art, Jackson, Mississippi
Municipal City Hall of Be'er Sheva, Be'er Sheva, Israel
Museo Internazionale delle Ceramiche, Faenza, Italy
Museum of Fine Arts, Houston, Texas
New Orleans Museum of Art, New Orleans, Louisiana
Palmer Museum of Art, Penn State University, University Park, Pennsylvania
Smithsonian American Art Museum, Washington, DC
South Texas Institute for the Arts, Corpus Christi, Texas
State of Connecticut Superior Court Complex, Enfield, Connecticut
Tajimi Middle School, Tajimi City, Gifu, Japan
Worcester Art Museum, Worcester, Massachusetts
Jane Voorhees Zimmerli Art Museum, Rutgers University, New Brunswick, New Jersey

SELECTED COMMISSIONS

1992 Edwards & Angell, New York
1990 Aetna Life Insurance Company, Hartford, Connecticut
1989 American International Group, New York
1989 Ahavath Achim Synagogue, Atlanta, Georgia
1987 Crystal City Complex, Arlington, Virginia
1986 ADT Corporation, Waltham, Massachusetts
1986 State of Connecticut, State Superior Courthouse, Enfield, Connecticut
1985 Olympia & York, New York
1985 IBM, Atlanta, Georgia
1984 Kaiser Permanente, Dallas, Texas
1984 Baltimore Federal Financial Building, Baltimore, Maryland
1983 IBM, San Jose, California
1982 Main Hurdman, Park Avenue Plaza, New York
1981 Main Hurdman, Park Avenue Plaza, New York
1981 IBM, Charlotte, North Carolina
1981 Thompson, Ventulett, Stainback & Associates, Atlanta, Georgia
1978 Benton & Bowles, Inc., New York

SELECTED CORPORATE COLLECTIONS

Astrolink, Bethesda, Maryland
Bayerische Landesbank, New York
Boston Consulting Group, New York
Charles E. Smith Company, Los Angeles, California
Freddie Mac Headquarters, McLean, Virginia
The Insurance Company of North America, Philadelphia, Pennsylvania
J.P. Morgan, Los Angeles, California
Latham & Watkins, New York
Mineral Technologies Inc., The Chrysler Building, New York
National Reinsurance Corporation, Stamford, Connecticut
Pfizer, Inc., New York

SELECTED SOLO EXHIBITIONS

2006 Greenville County Museum of Art, Greenville, South Carolina, *Marylyn Dintenfass Paintings*

2006 Mississippi Museum of Art, Jackson, *Work in Progress: Marylyn Dintenfass*

2006 Franklin Riehlman Fine Art, New York, *Marylyn Dintenfass: Recent Paintings*

2006 Pelter Gallery, Greenville, South Carolina, *Marylyn Dintenfass: Works on Paper*

1994 Hamline University, Saint Paul, Minnesota, *Marylyn Dintenfass, Clay InPrint*

1991 Terry Dintenfass Gallery, New York, *Paradigm Series*

1985 Port Authority of New York and New Jersey, 42nd Street Terminal, A.R.E.A. Project Site Installation

1980 The Katonah Museum, Katonah, New York, *Tracks & Traces*

1979 Robert L. Kidd Galleries, Birmingham, Michigan, *Porcelain Progressions*

1978 Bell Gallery, Greenwich, Connecticut, *Porcelain Progressions*

1977 Schenectady Museum of Art, Schenectady, New York, *Marylyn Dintenfass*

1976 Queens Museum of Art, Queens, New York, Installation

SELECTED GROUP EXHIBITIONS

2006 Mississippi Museum of Art, Jackson, *Art Adored: Icons from the Permanent Collection*

Paul Kasmin Gallery, New York, *Not Gay Art Now*. Curated by Jack Pierson

Chelsea Art Museum, New York, *City Arts* (benefit)

2005 Fitchburg Art Museum, Massachusetts, *Collection Directions: Acquisitions in the Twenty-first Century*

Franklin Riehlman Fine Art, New York, *No Object*

Babcock Galleries, New York, *Barnet, Close, Dintenfass, Warhol*

Franklin Riehlman booth, Park Avenue Armory, New York, *Art of the Twentieth Century*

Arkansas Arts Center, Little Rock, *2005 Collectors Show*

The Americas Society, New York, *City Arts* (benefit)

2004 New Orleans Museum of Art, Louisiana, *From Another Dimension: Works on Paper by Sculptors*. Curated by Daniel Piersol

The Palmer Museum of Art, Pennsylvania State University, University Park, *Works on Paper: Selections from the Permanent Collection*

Samuel Dorsky Museum of Art, SUNY New Paltz, New York, *Out of the Vault: Recent Acquisitions*

2004 The International Print Center, New York, *New Prints 2004*. Curated by Barry Walker

Babcock Galleries, New York, *Close, Dintenfass, Nice, Warhol: Master Prints*

2003 Hunterdon Museum of Art, Clinton, New Jersey, *47th National Print Exhibition*

Columbus College of Art and Design, Columbus, Ohio, *21st Century Ceramics*. Curated by Bill Hunt (exhibition catalogue)

Franklin Riehlman Fine Art, New York, *Gallery Works*

Franklin Riehlman booth, The Pennsylvania Academy of the Fine Arts, Philadelphia, *USArtists*

2002 Babcock Galleries, New York, *Past and Present*

2000 Grimmerhus Keramikmuseum, Middlefart, Denmark, *Recent Acquisitions*

1997 Queens Library Gallery, New York, *Forms & Transformations: Current Expressions in Ceramics, from Art to Industry.* Curated by Judith S. Schwartz (exhibition catalogue)

1996 Jane Voorhees Zimmerli Art Museum, Rutgers University, New Brunswick, New Jersey, *Unique Impressions: Contemporary Monotypes and Monoprints*

1995–96 Rogaland Kunstnersenter, Stavanger, Norway, *New York, New York: Clay.* Curated by Judith Schwartz. Exhibition travels to Hordland Kunstnersenter, Bergen; Nordenfjeldske Kunstindustrimuseum, Trondheim; Ostfold Kunstnersenter, Fredrikstad

1995 Click 3X, New York, *Anniversary Exhibition*

Center for Book Arts, New York, *The International Library.* Curated by Helmut Löhr

1994 Shirley Fiterman Gallery, Borough of Manhattan Community College, City University of New York, *Selections from the Permanent Collection*

Silo Gallery, New Milford, Connecticut, *High on Tile*

1993 International Art Biennale, Be'er Sheva, Israel (exhibition catalogue)

Turkish Station Gallery, *From the Factory*

Avraham Baron Art Gallery, Ben Gurion University, *Installations*

Associated American Artists Gallery, New York, *Monotypes/Monoprints* (exhibition catalogue)

Elsa Mott Gallery, New York, *Transcending Boundaries*

1992 Triplex Gallery, Borough of Manhattan Community College, City University of New York, *Selections from the BMCC Permanent Collection*

Paramount Center for the Arts, Peekskill, New York, *Art in Architecture*

1991 Mensinghe Museum, Roden, The Netherlands, *Internationale Keramiektentoonstelling*

1990 Kunsthallen Brandts Klaedefabric Museum, Odense, Denmark, *Clay Today*

1989 The Katonah Museum, Katonah, New York, *New Sculpture*

Nevada Museum of Art, Reno, *Visiting Artists*

1988 Tower Fine Arts Gallery, SUNY College at Brockport, *Public Art: Making a Better Place to Live*

1987 45° Concorso Internazionale della Ceramica d'Arte, Faenza, Italy (exhibition catalogue)

National Archives Gallery, Montreal, Canada, *New York/Montreal: Grand Prix des Métiers D'Art—Banque d'Épargne*

Syracuse University School of Architecture, Syracuse, New York, *Drawings, Sketches and Models: Ceramics in Architecture*

Le Moyne College Gallery, Syracuse, New York, *Empire State Selections*

Fashion Institute of Technology Gallery, New York, *Artists in Space*

The Gallery at Hastings-on-Hudson, New York, *Crossovers: Sculptured Painting/Painted Sculpture*

1986 First International Ceramic Exhibition, Mino, Japan (exhibition catalogue)

Robert L. Kidd Galleries, Birmingham, Michigan, *Major Concepts* (exhibition catalogue)

1985 Lever House, New York, *Art and the Environment*

Timothy Burns Gallery, St. Louis, Missouri, *Clay Murals and Tiles*

1984 Smithsonian Institution, National Museum of American Art (now Smithsonian American Art Museum), Renwick Gallery, Washington, DC, *Clay for Walls.* Curated by Raylene Decatur (exhibition catalogue)

	Liberty Gallery, Louisville, Kentucky, *National Invitational 1984* (exhibition catalogue)
	Two-person faculty exhibition with Barbara Nechis, Parsons School of Design, New York, *Glazing in Watercolor and Porcelain*
1983	The Gallery at Hastings-on-Hudson, New York, *The Evolution of Seven Artists*
1982	Schenectady Museum of Art, Schenectady, New York, *Regional Works*
	Women's Interart Center, New York, *Architectural Ceramics*
	The Craftsman's Gallery, Scarsdale, New York, *The Art of Clay*
1981	Galerie Inge Donath, Troisdorf, West Germany, *International Works*
	Bowdoin College Museum of Art, Brunswick, Maine, *Art in Craft Media*
	Louis K. Meisel Gallery, New York, *Gallery Works*
	Women in Design International Exhibition, San Francisco, California
1980	George Washington University, Washington, DC, 11th International Sculpture Conference, *Architectural Ceramics*
	Thorpe Intermedia Gallery, Sparkill, New York, *New York Clay Works.* Curated by Carl Rattner
	31st New England Exhibition of Painting and Sculpture, Silvermine, Connecticut
1979	Herbert F. Johnson Museum of Art, Cornell University, Ithaca, New York, *Clay, Fiber, Metal*
	Suzanne Gross Gallery, Philadelphia, Pennsylvania, *Art Ceramic*
	Bridge Gallery, White Plains, New York, *Selections from the Visual Arts Affiliates of Westchester*
1978	The Bronx Museum of the Arts, New York, *Women Artists*
	The National Academy Galleries, New York, *National Association of Women Artists*
	Hudson River Museum, Yonkers, New York, Hudson River Open
	Interart Gallery, Women's Interart Center, New York, *Raku Invitational*
1977	Pratt Institute, Brooklyn, New York, *Pratt Invitational*
	Tyler Art Gallery, State University College at Oswego, New York, *Oswego Invitational* (exhibition catalogue)
	Salmagundi Art Club, New York, *Knickerbocker Artists: 27th Annual Exhibition*
	Lever House, New York, *Artist Craftsmen of New York*
1976	The Craftsman's Gallery, Scarsdale, New York, *Invitational 1976*
1975	University of Pennsylvania, Philadelphia, *Women's Cultural Trust*
	Tweed Museum of Art, Duluth, Minnesota, *3rd Biennial International Exhibition* (exhibition catalogue)
	National Craft Show, Rhinebeck, New York
1972	The College of New Rochelle, New York, *Anniversary Juried Exhibition*
1971	Mamaroneck Artist's Guild, Mamaroneck, New York, *1971 Open Juried Show*

BIBLIOGRAPHY

Abott, Corine. "Psyching the Medium." *Detroit Birmingham Edition,* April 12, 1979.

Asfour, Hani, and Marylyn Dintenfass. "Building Vocal Space: Expressing Identity in the Radically Collaborative Workplace: Interview with Hani Asfour and Marylyn Dintenfass." By Kate Ehrlich and Austin Henderson. *Interactions* 8 (January/February 2001): 23–29.

Barnes, Gordon A. Judge's Statement in *3rd Biennial International Exhibition.* Duluth, MN: Tweed Museum of Art, 1975. (Exhibition catalogue)

Bergér, Sandra Christine Q., et al. *Women in Design International Compendium.* Vol. 1. Tiburon, CA: Women in Design International, 1982. (Exhibition catalogue for Women in Design International Exhibition, San Francisco, CA)

Boscherini, Giorgio, et al. *45° Concorso Internazionale della Ceramica d'Arte.* Faenza, Italy, 1987. (Exhibition catalogue)

Caldwell, John. Review of *New York Clay Works,* Thorpe Intermedia Gallery, Sparkill, NY. *New York Times,* October 19, 1980.

Castle, Frederick Ted. "The Clay Paintings of Marylyn Dintenfass." *Ceramics: Art and Perception,* no. 8 (1992): 7–9.

———. *Marylyn Dintenfass: Paradigm Series.* New York: Terry Dintenfass Gallery, 1991. (Exhibition catalogue)

Colby, Joy. "Progressions: Works in Porcelain." *Detroit News,* April 12, 1979.

Dantzic, Cynthia Maris. *100 New York Painters.* Atglen, PA: Schiffer, 2006.

Decatur, Raylene. *Clay for Walls.* Washington, DC: Smithsonian Institution, National Museum of American Art, Renwick Gallery, 1984. (Exhibition catalogue)

Dintenfass, Marylyn. "Kite" (cover image). *Poet Lore* 79, no. 1 (1984).

———. "Working Large Scale: Portfolio." *Ceramics Monthly* 34, no. 5 (1986): 33–43.

Falk, Bill. "When Art Goes Aloft." *Suburbia Today,* May 1, 1983, 16–17, 20.

Finkelstein, Haim, ed. *Ceramics Biennale: Be'er-Sheva 1993.* Be'er-Sheva, Israel: Avraham Baron Art Gallery, Ben Gurion University of the Negev, 1993. (Exhibition catalogue)

Fiore, Linda, ed. *Artist-Craftsman of New York Newsletter,* April 1983.

Flad, Mary, ed. *Architectural Craftworks: Conference Report.* Poughkeepsie, NY: Empire State Crafts Alliance, 1984.

Foighel, Hanne. "From the Desert to International Ceramics." *Berlingske Times* (Copenhagen), April 17, 1993.

Freedman, Diana. "From Literal Subject to Poetic Self." *Artspeak* 5, no. 12 (1984)

Friedman, Ann. *Oswego Invitational.* Oswego, NY: Tyler Art Gallery, State University College at Oswego, 1977. (Exhibition catalogue)

Geibel, Victoria. "The Act of Engagement." *Metropolis,* July/August 1986, 32–36, 43, 46–47.

Hagani, Lisa R. *Monotypes/Monoprints.* New York: Associated American Artists Gallery, 1993. (Exhibition catalogue)

Hall, Barbara. "Open House at Artists' Workplace." *New York Times,* November 5, 1995.

Hefetz, Magdalena, and Yoheved Marx. "First International Ceramics Biennale, Be'er Sheva, Israel, 1993." Höhr-Grenzhausen, Germany: *New Ceramics,* January 1994, 46–47.

Hirsch, Linda. "State Superior Court Building." *Hartford Courant,* October 24, 1986.

Hunt, Bill, ed. *21st Century Ceramics in the United States and Canada.* Westerville, OH: The American Ceramics Society, 2003. (Exhibition catalogue for Columbus College of Art and Design exhibition, Columbus, OH)

Kato, Naoki, et al. "Brilliant Awarded Works in the First International Ceramics Competition '86 Mino." *Tono Shimpoh* (Tajimi City, Japan), October 31, 1986.

———. *First International Ceramic Exhibition '86, Mino Japan.* Tajimi City, Japan: Organizing Committee, International Ceramics Festival '86, Mino, Japan, 1986. (Exhibition catalogue)

Katz, Ruth J. "Architectural Ceramics Show." *New York Times,* January 20, 1983.

———. "Ceramics Fires Artist's Eloquence." *New York Times,* August 2, 1981.

———. "Growth of Seven Artists Examined." *New York Times,* April 17, 1983.

Keller, Martha. "Reviews: Marylyn Dintenfass." *New Art Examiner,* June 1979.

Kidd, Robert. *Major Concepts.* Birmingham, MI: Robert L. Kidd Galleries, 1986. (Exhibition catalogue)

Kingsley, April. "Marylyn Dintenfass." *American Ceramics* 2, no. 2 (1983): 16–21.

Laperrière, Rachel, et al. *1987 Grand Prix Des Métiers D'Art—Banque d'Épargne.* Montreal, Canada, 1987. (Exhibition catalogue for *New York/Montreal: Grand Prix des Métiers D'Art—Banque d'Épargne*)

Levine, Angela. "Biennale of Clay." *Jerusalem Post Magazine* (Jerusalem, Israel), April 23, 1993.

Lincoln, Joan. "Surprise! Your Hypothetical Wall Is for Real!!" *The Crafts Report: The Newsletter of Marketing, Management and Money for Crafts People* 8, no. 84 (1982).

Ling, Pei Chin. "Marylyn Dintenfass: Evocative Architectural Sculpture." *Ceramic Art* (Taipei, Taiwan), no. 16 (1997).

Nechis, Barbara. *Watercolor from the Heart.* New York: Watson-Guptill Publications, 1993.

———. *Watercolor: The Creative Experience.* Westport, CT: North Light Publishers, 1979.

Nielsen, Teresa. "Symposium on Clay's Possibilities." *Danish Arts and Handicrafts* 3, no. 90 (1990): 14–20.

Parsley, Jacque, et al. *Porcelain 1984.* Louisville, KY: Liberty Gallery, 1984. (Exhibition catalogue for *National Invitational 1984*)

Peterson, Susan. *Contemporary Ceramics.* New York: Watson-Guptill Publications, 2000.

———. *The Craft and Art of Clay.* 3rd ed. Woodstock, NY: Overlook Press, 2000.

———. *Working with Clay: An Introduction.* Woodstock, NY: Overlook Press, 1998.

Pettus, Gini L., et al. Introduction to collection catalogue. IBM Contemporary Craft Art Collection, Field Engineering Education Center, Atlanta, Georgia, 1984.

Piersol, Daniel. "From Another Dimension: Works on Paper by Sculptors." *Arts Quarterly* (a publication of the New Orleans Museum of Art), April/May/June 2004.

Preston, Malcolm. "A Diverse Exhibition." *Newsday,* January 19, 1982.

Rattner, Carl. *New York Clay Works.* Sparkill, NY: Thorpe Intermedia Gallery, 1980. (Exhibition catalogue)

Rex, Erica. "Molding Multimedia: One Artist's Approach to Teaching Kids Art." *Mac Home Journal* 5, no. 4 (1997): 64–65.

Riddle, Mason. *Marylyn Dintenfass: Clay in Print.* Saint Paul, MN: Hamline University, 1994. (Exhibition catalogue)

Robinson, Joyce Henri. "Marylyn Dintenfass: The Art of the Sensual Grid." (Exhibition brochure for *Work in Progress: Marylyn Dintenfass,* Mississippi Museum of Art, Jackson, MS, 2006.)

Scates, Deborah A. "Media Loft: Celebrating 10 Years of Art in the Making." *Westchester Artsnews* 15, no. 4 (1994): 2, 15.

Schlossman, Betty. "Clay, Metal, Fiber Work by Women Artists." *Art Journal,* Summer 1978.

Schwartz, Judith S. Essay in *Forms & Transformations: Current Expressions in Ceramics, from Art to Industry.* Queens, NY: Queens Library Gallery, 1997. (Exhibition catalogue)

———. Essay in *New York, New York: Clay.* Stavanger, Norway: Rogaland Kunstnersenter, 1995. (Exhibition catalogue)

———. "Marylyn Dintenfass: Terry Dintenfass Gallery." *American Ceramics* 10, no. 1 (1992).

———. "New York Clay." *Ceramics Monthly,* May 1996, 47–50.

Scott, Martha B. "Silvermine's Annual." *Sunday Post,* June 15, 1980.

Sela, Mirit. "The Way to Be'er Sheva." *Kol Ha-ir* (Jerusalem), April 2, 1993.

Simone, Linda, ed. "Big Spaces, Bright Lights: Lofty Solutions to Artists' Workspace." *Westchester Artsnews* 12, nos. 5–6 (1991): 2.

Speight, Charlotte F. *Hands in Clay: An Introduction to Ceramics.* 2nd ed. Mountain View, CA: Mayfield Publishing, 1989.

Speight, Charlotte F., and John Toki. *Hands in Clay: An Introduction to Ceramics.* 3rd ed. Mountain View, CA: Mayfield Publishing, 1995. (Front and back cover illustrations: original artwork by Marylyn Dintenfass)

Staino, Patricia A. "The Changing Face of Education." *Westchester County Weekly,* April 27, 1995.

Storr-Britz, Hildegard. *Contemporary International Ceramics.* Cologne: DuMont Buchverlag, 1980.

———. *Ornaments and Surfaces on Ceramics.* Dortmund, West Germany: Kunst + Handwerk, 1977.

Van Buren, Greg. "Art in Architecture." *Valley Artists Association Newsletter* 1, no. 7 (1992).

Van Der Meulen, Henk. "'Clay Today'—internationale kleikunst in Rodens koetshuis." *Leeuwarder Courant* (Leeuwarden, The Netherlands), May 8, 1991.

Viant, Annual Report 1999. (Cover image: original artwork by Marylyn Dintenfass)

Walker, Barry. "New Prints 2004/Spring." *International Print Center New York Newsletter,* May 2004. (Published in conjunction with the exhibition *New Prints 2004,* International Print Center, New York)

Walton, Roberta S., ed. "Saga of Symbols Is Present in Ceramic Wall Construction." *Contract,* February 1986, 118.

Watson, Katharine J., et al. *Art in Craft Media.* Brunswick, ME: Bowdoin College Museum of Art, 1981. (Exhibition catalogue; exhibition traveled to William Benton Museum of Art, University of Connecticut, Storrs, CT; Rose Art Museum, Brandeis University, Waltham, MA; Museum of Art, Rhode Island School of Design, Providence, RI; Sterling and Francine Clark Art Institute, Williamstown, MA)

WBAC. "Artists at the MacDowell Colony." *Chronicles.* WBAC Television, Boston, Massachusetts, 1990. (Documentary produced by and aired on WBAC)

Williams, Gerry. *Apprenticeship in Craft.* Goffstown, NH: Daniel Clark Books, 1981.

Yelle, Richard, et al. "Marylyn Dintenfass," *Clayworks.* New York: Clayworks Studio Workshop, 1979.

Zahorski, Carole. "She's Fired Up about Clay." *Suburban People,* April 26, 1987, 20.

Zakin, Richard. *Electric Kiln Ceramics.* 2nd ed. Radnor, PA: Chilton Book Company, 1994.

Zimmer, William. "Focus on Corporate Collectors." *New York Times,* February 20, 1983.

ACKNOWLEDGMENTS

The friendship, support, dedication, and hard work of many people, colleagues, and friends have contributed immeasurably to the realization of this book. To begin, its publication coincides with the Greenville County Museum of Art's presentation of the first major public exhibition of the new group of paintings illustrated in this book. Thomas Styron, director of the museum, has been a superb colleague, and to him and his staff—Martha Severens, Claudia Beckwith, Mary Lawson, and Mary McCarthy—go my deepest appreciation for their interest in and commitment to showing my work. Similarly, Daniel Piersol, previously with the New Orleans Museum of Art and now with the Mississippi Museum of Art, has been a wonderful friend, both to my work and to me personally. He included my work in NOMA's thought-provoking exhibition *From Another Dimension: Works on Paper by Sculptors*, and subsequently curated the Mississippi Museum of Art's *Work in Progress: Marylyn Dintenfass*—supported by the Andy Warhol Foundation for the Visual Arts—which was the first public exhibition for some of the works included here. In connection with that show, Joyce Henri Robinson, curator of the Palmer Museum of Art, contributed an enlightened and eloquent essay for the accompanying brochure.

I am especially grateful to Lilly Wei, a very talented critic, for her cogent insights and literate writing of "Painting in the Here and Now," which appears in the early pages of this book. Reading her words, I feel she has embraced my work in an articulate and sensitive way.

Lisa Mackie and Kathy Caraccio—both gifted artists, and both of whom have worked with me to produce the prints that are such an important part of my work—deserve special thanks. Over the years, Lisa has spent countless late nights, until two, three, or even four in the morning, helping me achieve on paper the images that would otherwise have been trapped in my head. Harriet Bart, another wonderful artist whom I met while on a MacDowell Fellowship, has been a consistent and supportive sounding board, often taking time away from her own work to discuss issues and ideas with me. Ken Foreman, a new friend, has been unfailing in his perceptive responses to a mountain of issues that only another artist could understand. Similarly, my longtime friend Jackie Chalkley has been an aesthetic soul mate, and has seen to it over the years that some of my work has found a good home in the nation's capital. As my dealer, Franklin Riehlman has done much to get my paintings seen—not only in his gallery but also in other galleries and important art fairs. What's more, his respect and enthusiasm for my work has been an energizing force. Each of these people has, in his or her own way, helped me immeasurably and inspired my respect and appreciation.

I have also benefited from the interest, support, and insight of many critics, scholars, and essayists. At times their critical attention has boosted my spirits and allowed me the privileged belief that someone other than me was paying attention to my work. In particular, John Caldwell and Frederick Ted Castle—both sadly no longer with us—provided astute and timely considerations of my work. April Kingsley, Martha Keller, Mason Riddle, Judith Schwartz, and Cynthia Maris Dantzic have written gracefully and with cogent insight. In addition, I wish to express my appreciation to my professional colleagues at museums throughout the United States, Europe, Israel, and Japan, who have managed the acquisition process through which my work has entered the collections delineated elsewhere in this text.

My able and steadfast studio assistants, Rebecca Sears and Nico Wheadon, both talented artists in their own right, graciously oversaw the organization and coordination of photographs, manuscripts, and a myriad of other challenging details. In the midst of preparing for this book, my sixth floor studio on 27th Street in New York was flooded, resulting in much destruction and total disruption of work. Daisy and Jose Quintero saved the situation by moving me out of the damaged studio and into a new one that they largely constructed, seemingly overnight. Ian Pedigo has also been a wonderful assistant in my studio on many occasions. I am additionally grateful to Arnold Skolnick of Chameleon Books for overseeing the design and production of this book, assisted by KC Scott, as well as to Jamie Thaman for her careful copyediting. To Leslie van Breen and her colleagues at Hudson Hills Press, I express my appreciation for their efforts through this book to bring my work to a broader audience.

I am very appreciative of JoAnn Sieburg-Baker, a superb artist and photographer who has documented my most important installations all over the country and continues to provide an unerring eye; and similarly Herta Kreigner, who has been a treasured and trusted collaborator on challenging creative-design projects.

Most importantly, I wish to thank John Driscoll, an ardent collector who became my friend, and then my dear husband, for his insight, support, expertise, and encouragement throughout this project. I am also grateful to him for suggesting our conversation, which he crafted in order to provide me with the opportunity to express myself through my own words.

An artist's life is often solitary. The challenge of cultivating a vital and meaningful career over many years is often fraught with difficulty. The interest, support, and goodwill of my family and the people whom I gratefully acknowledge on this page, as well as many others, have often smoothed the path, imparted confidence, and provided insight that I might continue to work, to grow, and to live the one life in which I find the most meaning. To each and to all, thank you.

Marylyn Dintenfass

Published in the United States by
Hudson Hills Press LLC,
3556 Main Street, Manchester, Vermont 05254.

Distributed in the United States,
its territories and possessions, and Canada
by National Book Network, Inc.
Distributed outside of North America by
Antique Collectors' Club, Ltd.

Executive Director: Leslie Van Breen
Founding Publisher: Paul Anbinder

ISBN 13:978-1-55595-279-2
ISBN 10:1-55595-279-8

Produced by Chameleon Books
31 Smith Rd. Chesterfield MA 01012

Design/Production: Arnold Skolnick
Design Assistant: K.C. Scott
Copy Editor: Jamie Nan Thaman

Printed in China

PHOTOGRAPHY CREDITS

Noel Allum
Gamma One
Alex Medina
Sherri Nielsen
John O'Donnell
Ian Pedigo
Nick Saraco
Rebecca Sears
JoAnn Sieburg-Baker
Nico Wheadon

Library of Congress Cataloging-in-Publication Data

Dintenfass, Marylyn.
Marylyn Dintenfass / essay by Lilly Wei ; conversation with the artist by John Driscoll.
p. cm.
ISBN-13: 978-1-55595-279-2 (alk. paper)
ISBN-10: 1-55595-279-8 (alk. paper)
1. Dintenfass, Marylyn—Themes, motives.
I. Wei, Lilly. II. Driscoll, John Paul. III. Title.
N6537.D533A4 2007
760'.092--dc22

2006033012

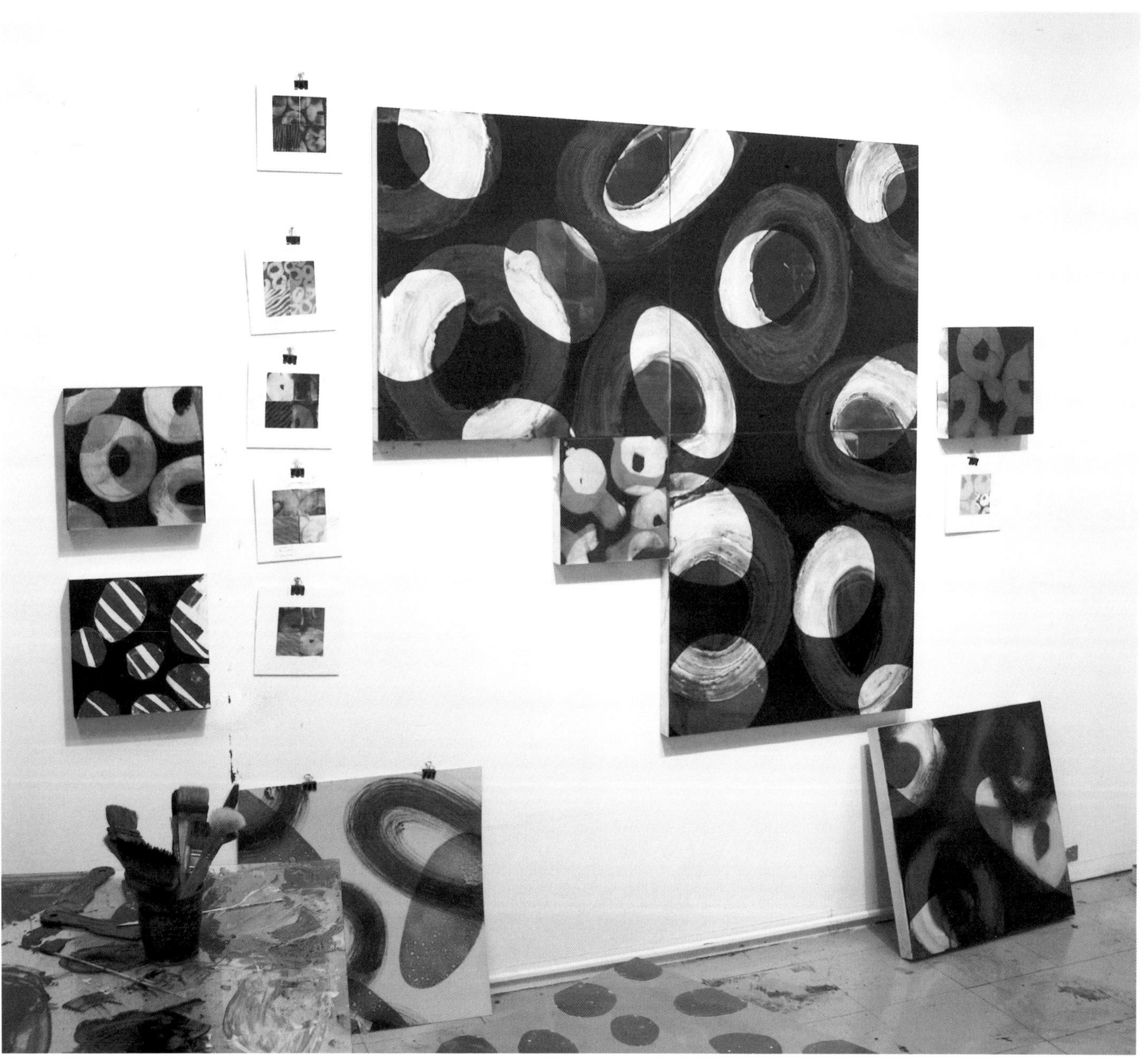

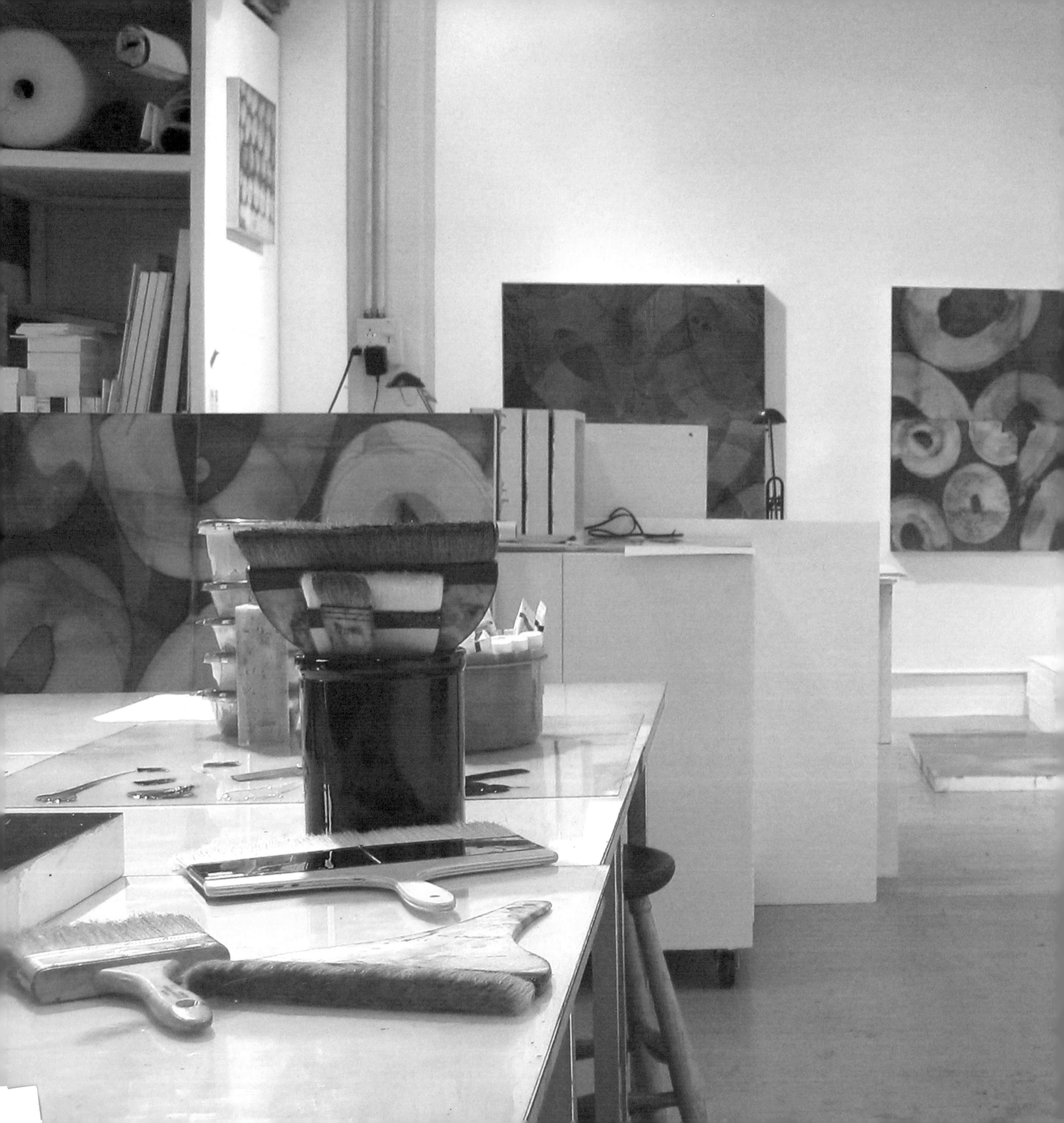